Helping You Build
Cell Churches

A comprehensive training manual for pastors, cell leaders and church planters

COMPILED BY
Brian Sauder and Larry Kreider

House To House Publications
www.dcfi.org

Helping You Build Cell Churches

compiled by Brian Sauder and Larry Kreider

A special thanks to: Jo Eberly, Paul Gustitus, LaVerne Kreider, Sarah Sauder, Ron Myer, Steve Prokopchak, Karen Ruiz and all of the others who contributed to this manual

Updated Edition © 2000, 2004
Copyright © 1998 House to House Publications
House to House Publications
Ephrata, PA USA
Telephone: 800.848.5892
Web site: www.dcfi.org

ISBN 1-886973-38-5

Unless otherwise noted, all scripture quotations are taken from the New King James (NKJV) of the Holy Bible. ©1979,1980,1972, Thomas Nelson Inc.

Blueprints by Penway Construction, Manheim, PA
Printed in the United States of America

Contents

Introduction

During the past two decades, we have experienced the Lord's grace again and again as the Lord built His church among us from house to house. During the early days of our new church plant, enthusiasm grew as we multiplied into three new cells. We expected more of the same quick multiplication, but then one of the cells died. It was a painful learning experience, but we pressed on.

Soon, the cells did multiply, and it was thrilling! As our church grew to over 2,000 people involved in cell groups, we stood amazed at what the Lord was doing. However, as pioneers in cell-based ministry, we were often destined to learn from our own many mistakes. We could have greatly benefited from a church sharing with us what they learned and encouraging us to continue on in faith. That is why the material in this training manual was written. We want to help you build as the Lord works with you to build His church.

Today, churches representing many denominations and movements throughout the nations are now transitioning to a biblical cell-based model. The church is discovering the value of New Testament Christianity. The way we apply cell-based principles varies from church to church. The Lord is giving His church wisdom to create *flexible* wineskins that will help each church to uniquely build and grow.

Leaders from throughout this nation and from around the world are continually requesting that experienced cell-based pastors and leaders from the DCFI leadership team come to their church or region to give tailor-made seminars and conferences. Others are simply requesting the material to study as a manual to give them practical scriptural insights for effective cell-based ministry.

We do not have all of the answers, but we are committed to sharing with you what the Lord has given to us. We also are expecting to learn from you at the same time, so we can pass on what you have learned to others in the body of Christ. May the Lord bless you with wisdom and revelation in the knowledge of Him today.

Your Servants in Christ,

Brian Sauder
DCFI Church Planting and Leadership School Director

Larry Kreider
DCFI International Director

Ways To Use This Manual

1 **Pastors can use this manual to train cell leaders** A pastor may use this manual as a resource to train the cell leaders in his church. The pastor teaches from this material and the cell leaders and potential cell leaders take notes in their own manual as the pastor instructs them.

2 **Use for individual study** Read this manual from beginning to end. By completing the study questions at the end of each unit, you will personalize the information for your own life and ministry.

3 **Use at a Small Group Seminar or Church Planting Clinic** Filled with notes and key biblical insights on cell-based church ministry, this manual is used for DCFI *Small Group Seminars* and *Church Planting Clinics* taught by experienced cell-based pastors and church leaders from throughout the world. There is space available for attendees to take notes as they glean further insights from the seminar instructors.

For more information about hosting a *seminar* at your church, or for information about attending one in your area, visit www.dcfi.org or call 800.848.5892.

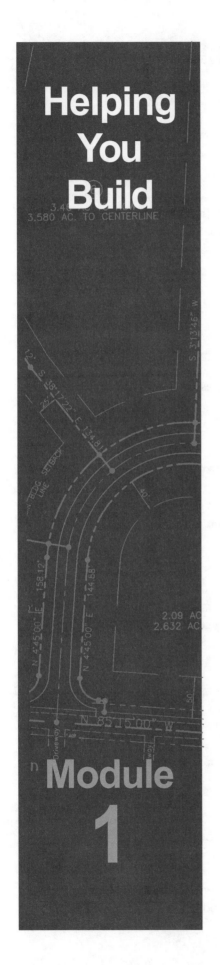

Helping You Build

Module 1

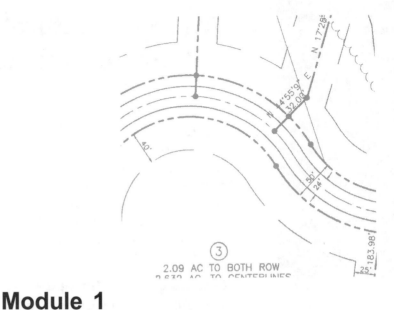

Module 1
Biblical Vision for Cells

This module gives a clear biblical overview of cell-based ministry. When we understand the scriptural values behind cell-based ministry, cell groups will become more than just another program. The importance of prayer, reaching the lost, and making disciples are all taught from a clear biblical base.

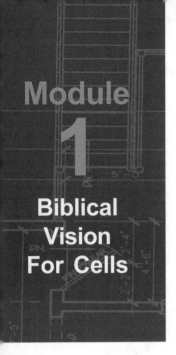

A. Twelve Scriptural Values for the Cell Group Church

Core values

The core values in our lives determine what we really believe. Unless these values are based in the scriptures, we find ourselves just trying another good idea. These twelve scriptural values give us a foundation for the cell-based church. Our vision comes from our values, and our values come from the Word of God.

Note: In this manual, the terms "cell churches" and "cell-based churches" are used interchangeably.

1. Preparing for the harvest

The Lord promises to pour out His Spirit in the last days. A harvest is coming when the Lord will draw multitudes into His kingdom. What does a farmer do in the winter? He prepares for the harvest!

God is calling His church to prepare **new wineskins** to contain the new wine of His harvest.

> Matthew 9:37; Matthew 9:17; John 4:35

2. Teaching people to know Jesus (prayer)

Many people know about the Lord, but He wants us to know Him intimately and then help others to know Him (John 17:3). Cell group ministry provides a proper spiritual atmosphere for believers to know Him.

3. Reaching the lost (evangelism)

Jesus came to seek and save those who are lost (Mark 1:17). The primary purpose of the cell group is to reach out beyond ourselves (Matthew 9:38; II Timothy 4:5). Cells that focus only inward become stagnant. Focusing outward brings life.

4. The Great Commission (discipleship)

The mandate from our Master is to make disciples, not just converts (Matthew 28:19-20). Cell groups provide the opportunity for every believer to be actively involved in making disciples. Evangelism alone will not fulfill the Great Commission.

Built in leadership training occurs in cell groups. As assistant leaders are trained, their spiritual gifts are developed and they start to train others.

5. Seeing the church as people, not a building

We must resist the "holy building myth." The church is people (called-out ones). Every person is important and chosen by the Lord. Jesus told us He will build His church. He was not talking about a physical building but a company of people. The church meets both from house to house and publicly (in the temple).

> Matthew 16:18; Acts 20:20

6. Called to do the work of ministry

We must also resist the "holy man myth." Thinking that the "holy man" (leader of a church) should do all the work of ministry is a myth. God has given each of His children gifts, talents and ministries to be used to build His church. Many of these gifts and ministries can only be effectively nurtured in a small group setting.

Believers need to be released to train others When all members are functioning properly in their gifts and ministries, the church will grow and prosper. The pastors and elders will no longer be held up as holy men on pedestals doing all the ministry. Instead, they will be released to train each believer to be a minister.
>Ephesians 4:11-12

7. Building trust and relationships

The New Testament church is built on trust and relationships, not on meetings and programs. First and foremost, we need to trust in God. Then we need to trust others with whom we serve. Cell groups become a greenhouse to encourage and strengthen trust and relationships among God's people. A greenhouse is a place made conducive to growth, blooming and bearing fruit!

When "underground" relationships are strong in cell groups, they will be strong in the entire church It is like a tree that is nourished and held up by the underground root system. God builds living stones together through the mortar of healthy relationships.
>I Peter 2:5; Ephesians 4:16

We all need three types of relationships:
- Paul relationships–those who oversee us
- Barnabas relationships–our peers in ministry and leadership
- Timothy relationships–those we are training for future leadership

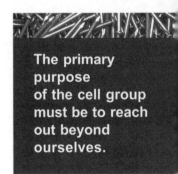

The primary purpose of the cell group must be to reach out beyond ourselves.

8. Expecting spiritual multiplication

We are commanded to be fruitful and multiply and replenish the earth. Everything with life will multiply. Believers who lead others to Christ multiply. Cell groups multiply. Churches multiply. A key to experiencing spiritual multiplication is to expect it to happen. Without faith it is impossible to please God.
>Genesis 1:28; Acts 6:1,7; 9:31

Train as many assistant leaders as possible as you prepare now for future cell group multiplication.

9. Encouraging flexibility and creativity

God values flexibility and creativity, and we need to do the same. No two snowflakes are alike, and no two biological cells are the same. We all use the same biblical principles, but the way they work out varies from culture to culture, church to church, and cell group to cell group. Expect the Lord to give you wisdom to stay creative. Sameness produces boredom. Creativity releases life! The same biblical values can be expressed differently through different people.

II Corinthians 3:17-18

10. Empowering God's people

Jesus promised His disciples they would do greater works than He did, and we are included in that promise. He has empowered us to do the works of God in our generation. Wise church leaders empower cell leaders as ministers of our Lord Jesus Christ, and wise cell leaders empower cell members.

John 14:12; II Timothy 2:2

Work yourself out of a job As a leader, do nothing someone else can do. Allow others to serve. Enjoy seeing the Lord using others to minister by His Spirit as you coach and mentor them. If you work yourself out of a job, you will have plenty to do!

11. God is building teams in His church today

Teamwork is modeled and learned in a healthy cell group. We have been created to be interdependent (to need one another). Independence is a trap. Cell groups are an excellent place to encourage each other as we work together.

II Thessalonians 1:1; I Corinthians 12:28; Amos 3:3

The four components of a healthy team
• Common vision
• Common values
• Common procedures
• God-given healthy relationships

12. Raising up spiritual parents

There are thousands of teachers today, but few spiritual fathers and mothers to nurture young Christians. Cell groups are spiritual families. Just like natural families, healthy spiritual families expect their children to eventually become parents themselves.

I Corinthians 4:15-17; I John 2:12-14

Discussion and Study Questions

1. What are values and why are they important?
2. Why must our values come from the Word of God?
3. Do new wineskins lessen the value of existing wineskins?
4. Why do you think the "holy man myth" and the "holy building myth" have been believed for so long?
5. The idea of "working yourself out of a job" makes some people feel insecure. How do you suggest helping people over this hurdle?

And releasing them!
We must not only raise up spiritual fathers and mothers, we must release them, encourage them and equip them to start their own cell groups and churches. To not release them would make us dysfunctional spiritual parents.

The cell-based church is a "wineskin" for these twelve scriptural values to be encouraged and experienced!

Module 1: Biblical Vision for Cells

B. Prayer, Evangelism and Discipleship-Relationships

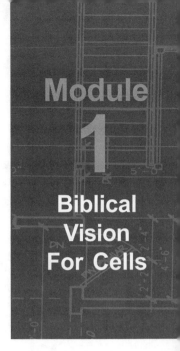

There are three basic relational values that every believer and every church should have: prayer, evangelism and discipleship (Matthew 28:16-20).

Prayer is our relationship with our God. **Evangelism** is our relationship with the unsaved. **Discipleship** is our relationship with other believers. It all starts with knowing God more intimately. Psalm 103:7 tells us, "The Lord revealed His ways to Moses and His deeds (acts) to the children of Israel."

God is looking for those who know Him (John 17:3), so He can reveal His ways to them. Moses knew God's ways; he knew that the Lord would come through. The early disciples worshiped Him. The heart of the gospel is that we know God through Jesus Christ.

A three-stranded cord cannot be easily broken (Ecclesiastes 4:12). The three-stranded cord of prayer, evangelism and discipleship is essential for us to experience healthy cell-based church life.

1.   Prayer

Spend time with Him There is no way to know God except by spending time with Him. Leaders start to struggle when they get caught up in their work and do not spend time with God and get to know Him. We need to have a daily appointment with God. There is no short cut. God is a God of relationship. When we are spending time with God and getting to know Him, we can impart grace to others. If you're struggling with having daily prayer and time in God's Word, be accountable to someone.

Pray how Jesus prayed Luke 11:1-4 shows us that Jesus was an example to the disciples in prayer. Jesus' prayer life is an example to us. Let's learn to pray the way Jesus prayed.

There is significance in each part of the Lord's prayer
- Our Father in heaven, hallowed be Your name—worship.
- Your kingdom come. Your will be done on earth as it is in heaven—surrender.
- Give us day by day our daily bread—provision.
- Forgive our sins, we also forgive those who are indebted to us—forgiveness.
- Do not lead us into temptation, but deliver us from the evil one—freedom.
- For Yours is the kingdom and the power and the glory forever—worship.

Receive a fresh infilling of the Holy Spirit daily As leaders, we often become drained. We need to be filled by reading His Word daily and receiving a constant, fresh infilling of the Holy Spirit.
       Matthew 4:4; Ephesians 5:18

Fast. If you're spiritually dry, take time to fast. Fasting brings our hearts to a place where we can hear from God in a special way. Matthew 6:16-18 teaches us about regular fasting. These verses say, *"when* you fast," not *"if* you fast." Regular fasting should be a normal part of our Christian lives.

2. Evangelism—reaching the lost

The purpose of God for every person, cell group and church is to reach people with the gospel of Jesus Christ. I John 3:8 tells us Jesus came to destroy the works of the devil. Jesus Himself said He came to seek and save that which was lost. Luke 19:10

Keep your focus on those who are unsaved In II Timothy 4:5, Paul tells Timothy to "do the work of an evangelist: fulfill your ministry." The Lord wants us to do the same. Share your testimony every chance you get! See people through the eyes of Jesus.

New Christians bring life to the cell groups Cell groups and churches will eventually stagnate and die if they are not reaching out. New Christians bring life into our cells and churches. Evangelism in our cells and churches should be seen as a life-style.

3. Discipleship—training new believers and emerging leaders

Unless we understand clearly that making disciples is near the top of God's priority list, cell group ministry will be just another religious program. Jesus commands us in Matthew 28:19 to "make disciples of all the nations..." Mark 3:14 says that "He appointed twelve, that they might be with Him and that He might send them out to preach." Jesus chose those twelve men "to be with Him."

A disciple is a learner, an apprentice Paul, the apostle, took young Timothy with Him as a disciple (Acts 16). Later, Timothy was sent out to do the same–to take the truths that he learned from Paul and impart them to others (II Timothy 2:2). In this way, Paul reached about four generations!

Mentors train leaders Moses trained Joshua as his disciple for forty years, mentoring and preparing him for leadership. Elijah became Elisha's mentor. The Lord is restoring the truth of loving discipleship to His church today.

Systematically study basic truths from the Bible If you are discipling new believers, sit down with them weekly and use a systematic study of the basic principles of the Christian life while you share from your life's experiences. DCFI's twelve book *Biblical Foundation Series* and *Foundations For Life Video Series* are tools that can be used.

Module 1: Biblical Vision for Cells

There are at least four levels of discipleship (some short term and some long term):

- Discipling new believers
- Discipling in areas of ministry (for example: music ministry, counseling, ministry of helps, hospitality, etc.)
- Discipling in areas of leadership (cell leadership, eldership, apostolic leadership, fivefold ministry, etc.)
- Practical discipleship (in areas of finances, marriage, devotions, an area of character, etc.)

Be up front about expectations! Set a time to evaluate! Jesus spent three and a half years with His disciples, and then He left them, trusting that the Holy Spirit would continue to lead them.

Everyone is to be involved Christianity is not just sitting in a pew each Sunday morning looking at the back of someone's head. Christianity is knowing Jesus, reaching out to the lost, and making disciples. The church has often been like an athletic contest with a few players on the field as thousands of spectators watch. God wants everyone to be on the field—everyone in the game! It's time for action!

Discussion and Study Questions

1. What can you do if you are struggling with having time for prayer and time in God's Word?
2. Why is evangelism such an important part of a cell group?
3. When is the last time you led someone to faith in Jesus?
4. Who has discipled you?
5. Who are the people that you have been discipling?

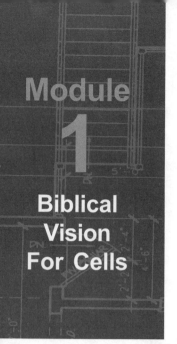

Module

1

Biblical Vision For Cells

C. A Biblical Basis for Cell Ministry

It is important for people to understand that cell ministry is strongly founded in the scriptures.

1. A God of relationship

God said, "Let us make man in our image." The Father, Son, and Holy Spirit have always experienced relationship. Should not we experience the same in the church? God created Adam with the need for relationship. He said it was not good for him to be alone. Adam saw his need for relationship.

> Genesis 1:26; 2:18

2. Noah and his family's relationships

Noah and his family persevered in the midst of a perverse generation. Their relationships with one another were critical to escaping the judgment of God through the flood.

> Genesis 6-10/Genesis 7:1

3. Moses and small groups

In Exodus 18:13-26, Moses receives advice from Jethro to release God's people into accountability groups to empower others to minister. He indicated there should be groups of 1,000's, 100's, 50's, and 10's. From the very beginning, God had a plan to keep his leaders from burning out.

4. Tribes, clans and families

In a time of crisis, this structure was essential. Achan was found in his sin by the process of going through each of these groupings of God's family. Gideon, in trying to excuse the Lord's call, also spoke of these same groupings of the Lord's family.

> Joshua 7:16-18; Judges 6:14-15

5. The Jesus model

Jesus spent most of His time with His twelve disciples. He ministered to many, but trained a few. We need to follow this example of discipleship-relationships. Jesus called His twelve disciples *to be with Him.*

> Mark 3:14

6. The early church

The early church followed Jesus' pattern of discipleship and spiritual family life. They broke bread from house to house and had larger corporate meetings. Verse 47 indicates the key to keeping all cell groups healthy—outreach! People were added to the early church daily.

> Acts 2:41-47

7. Peter at Cornelius' house

Peter met at Cornelius' house with his family and friends. There was a very natural flow of the kingdom of God from Peter to Cornelius and then on to the people with whom he had relationship.

> Acts 10:22-48

8. Mary's house

Some of the early church met in the house of Mary, John Mark's mother, and experienced cell life as they prayed together. What a wonderful demonstration of the house to house vision of the early church!

> Acts 12:12

9. The churches in Philippi

The Philippian jailor and his entire family found the Lord as Paul ministered to them in their home. This pattern of household salvation is duplicated many times in the New Testament. The believers in Philippi met in homes like Lydia's.

> Acts 16:30-34; Acts 16:15, 40

10. 20/20 vision

The early church met both publicly and from house to house. We sometimes call this the "20/20 vision." We need to see the importance of both "temple ministry" and "house to house" ministry.

> Acts 20:20

We need to see the importance of both "temple ministry" and "house to house" ministry.

11. Paul's house

Paul used his house as a ministry center near the end of his life. In his rented house, he welcomed all and taught without hindrance. The book of Acts is a history book. It opens and closes in a home.

> Acts 28:30-31

12. Churches in homes

The book of Romans gives various examples of churches meeting in the homes of individuals.

> Romans 16:3-15; I Corinthians 16:19

13. Spiritual families

The Lord sees us as a spiritual family, and in spiritual families we are equipped to minister to each other and to the world around us. Most immediate families spend time with their extended families. The same principle applies to God's kingdom. Cells meet together with other cells to form a congregation.

> II Corinthians 6:17-18; Ephesians 3:14; Ephesians 4:11-12

14. More churches in homes

The church in Colosse met in Nymphas' home (Colossians 4:15).
Paul greets the church meeting in Philemon's home (Philemon 2).

15. Church history

Moravians

Count Nicolaus Ludwig von Zinzendorf (1700-1760) allowed the settlement in 1722 of religious refugees from Moravia and Bohemia on his lands in Saxony. A religious community developed with strong small group structures. Over many decades of the eighteenth century, the Moravian system of small groups worked well; spiritual life was fostered, communal support was provided and many were released into the world missionary thrust, as well as local ministry and leadership.[1]

Methodists

The Methodist church movement in the 1700's had cell groups at the core of its divine strategy for evangelism and discipleship. John Wesley (1703-1791) was the founder of the Methodist movement which began in Great Britain. As many came to faith in Christ, Wesley and his co-leaders established a vast and interlocking network of cell groups to turn these raw converts into mature disciples and many into leaders.[1]

[1] For more on cell groups in church history, read Peter Bunton's book, *Cell Groups and House Churches, What History Teaches Us.*

16. Modern day examples

The modern pioneer of the cell ministry is Dr. Cho in Seoul, Korea. He was the first leader to take these biblical principles and build a large church. His method is based on the **Jethro model** of multiplication (some refer to his model as the 5x5 method). A cell group grows and multiplies into two groups and relationships change.

A significant variation of Cho's model has been developed by Cesar Castellanos in Bogota, Columbia. It is called the **groups of twelve** (G12) method. In the G12 method, each member of the cell is expected to start their own cell—either separately or with one or two others he has brought along. When a cell member becomes a leader, he continues to meet with his original cell leader in a separate (leaders only) G12 discipleship group. **It is important to note** that both Dr. Cho and Cesar Castellanos emphasized prayer much more than their respective cell models as the key to their success.

DCFI combines the strengths of both models in what we call *spiritual families.* Each spiritual family is unique and different, so it will apply the values of cell ministry differently. There is not one cookie-cutter model that fits every family. For example, leadership cells can be handled in many different ways. Some leadership cells may meet weekly, while others may meet every other week.

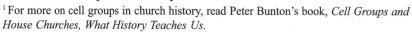

Discussion and Study Questions

1. How can cell ministry keep leaders and pastors from burning out?

2. Why is it important to have the scriptural basis for cell ministry well established in your heart?

3. What steps can we take to help people see their home as a ministry center?

4. What is 20/20 vision?

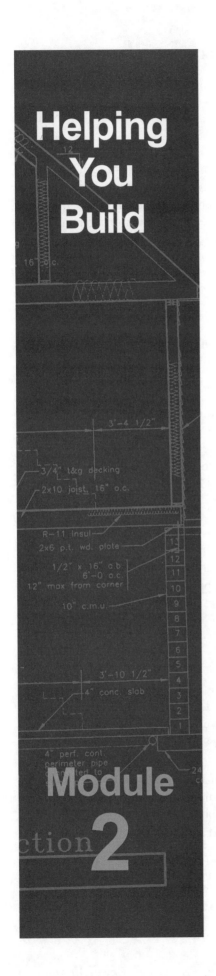

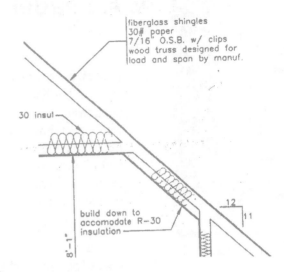

Module 2

Prayer: The Key to All Ministry

This module focuses on our need as Christian leaders and cell leaders to live a life of intimacy with God. We also learn from the scriptures the importance of having a healthy understanding of the fear of the Lord. There is no substitute for our regular and constant communion with God.

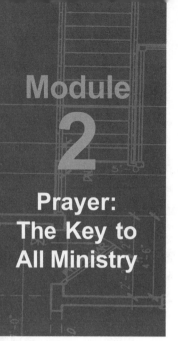

A. A Leader's Prayer Life

1. Priority: ministering to the Lord

Our number one priority as a leader is to spend time with the Father. Out of our relationship with Christ comes everything else in life and ministry. Call it what you want: quiet time, devotions, morning watch or individual worship. It is imperative for us to spend daily quality time with God. There are no substitutes for time alone with God. It is the golden thread that ties every great man or woman of God together—from Moses, to David Livingstone, to King David, to Billy Graham—the list goes on and on.

2. Developing a daily quiet time

Tomorrow when the alarm rings, we have an appointment with the Lord. Psalm 5:3 says, "My voice you shall hear in the morning, O Lord; in the morning will I direct it (my prayer) to You, and I will look up."

This is not a law, but a guideline of freedom to start you on your journey. Start somewhere, and watch your prayer life grow. Although we should pray without ceasing and learn to practice His presence twenty-four hours a day, the Lord honors our time each day set apart just for Him. As leaders, we must take time for Him to speak with us. One word from God can make all of the difference in the world.

3. The starting point: prayer for guidance

Thank the Lord for a good night's sleep and opportunities of a new day. Ask the Lord to speak to you and expect Him to speak.
   Psalm 143:8-11

4. Reading the Bible

Our greatest need is to hear a Word from the Lord every day. We need to meet with the Author! His Word is full of living power.
   Psalm 119:18,105; Matthew 4:4; Matthew 6:11; I Peter 2:2; Hebrews 4:12

Learn to enjoy the Word! Start with one of the gospels and read it verse by verse, chapter after chapter. Enjoy! Avoid stopping to do a word study at this time. Read twenty verses or a few chapters for the pure joy of reading and allow God to speak to you. Sometimes it is helpful to read aloud.
   Psalm 119:16

A spiritual washing and cleansing We are washed by the Word (Ephesians 5:26). We need a daily spiritual refreshing bath as we are refreshed by His Word!

5. Four types of prayer

Prayer is simply communication with God. But this communication can be enhanced by understanding four of the various types of prayer: adoration, confession, thanksgiving, and supplication.

Adoration

This is the purest kind of prayer It is totally for God. You don't just barge into the presence of royalty. Tell Him you love Him! Reflect on His greatness.

> I Chronicles 29:11; Psalm 8:1-9

Confession

Confession means "to agree together with" When we confess our sins and confess the Word of God, we are agreeing together with God. Sin takes on many forms. That which we call a slight exaggeration, God calls a lie. We may call it sharing a concern about someone in the church, but God calls it gossip. We may call it needing to see all the facts; God calls it unbelief. Psalm 66:18 says, "If I regard iniquity in my heart, the Lord will not hear me."

> I John 1:9; Romans 10:9

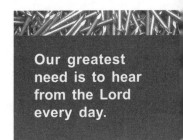

Our greatest need is to hear from the Lord every day.

Thanksgiving

Give thanks always for all things to God the Father in the name of our Lord Jesus Christ (Ephesians 5:20). Express your gratitude to the Lord; be specific. Thank Him for your family, job, business, church, ministry responsibilities, opportunities, and even hardships.

> I Thessalonians 5:18

Supplication

A definition of supplication is "to ask for, earnestly and humbly" Ask for yourself and then for others. If you are drowning, you need help before you can help others. We need to pray for our spiritual leaders every day and for other leaders the Lord has placed in our lives. Pray for missionaries, for the unsaved, for family members, for our spiritual leaders, for people in our cell group, for our leaders in our nation, for revival, etc.

In Daniel 10:12 Daniel began praying and the angel Gabriel was sent to help him because of his supplication. Even when the prince of the kingdom of Persia withstood him for 21 days, Daniel refused to quit praying!

> Matthew 7:7; I Timothy 2:1-2

There are two ministries before God's throne The ministry of intercession, which is Jesus' ministry, and the ministry of the accuser of the brethren, which is Satan's. May we be involved in the Lord's ministry.

As we are obedient to the Lord in our time alone with Him, our time alone with God will grow!

6. Affecting others

Remember the person who told you about Christ and how his life affected yours? No one is an island; our lives send ripples that influence others. Nothing is more important than daily fellowship with the Lord and reaching others for Christ. Everything else is wood, hay, and stubble according to I Corinthians 3:12.

Elijah trained others as he learned to hear God's voice. While Elijah was depressed and living in a cave, he found that God was not in the wind, the earthquake, or the fire, but spoke through a still, small voice. The Lord told him to anoint Elisha, a prophet, in his place (I Kings 19:16). For the remainder of his life, Elijah trained Elisha and other young prophets by becoming a spiritual father to them. It all came out of his own walk with the Lord as he learned to hear God's voice. Like Elijah, God has granted us the priceless privilege of fellowship with Himself as we train others.

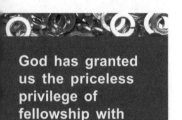

God has granted us the priceless privilege of fellowship with Himself!

7. Poisons that can paralyze and eventually destroy Christian leadership

- unbelief
- discouragement
- apathy
- taking offense

Taking quality time with the Lord each day will cause our spiritual resistance to be strong against these spiritual poisons.

8. Becoming "offense proof"

Matthew 13:57 describes how the people in Jesus' home town were offended because of Him. Jesus said in Matthew 18:7 that offenses must come. In Luke 7:23 Jesus said, "Blessed is he who is not offended because of Me." In John 16:1, Jesus declared, "These things I have spoken to you that you should not be made to stumble (be offended)." One of the greatest struggles in leadership is in the area of offenses.

The Websters Dictionary definition of "offend" is *to arouse resentment, anger, or vexation in*. In other words—to commit a sin.

Offenses come from unmet expectations. When we expect a spouse, cell leader, fellow Christian or leader, pastor, etc. to fulfill a certain expectation and it is not met, the devil gives us an open door to take up an offense.

A biblical study relates the word "offense" to *bait* used to catch animals. Monkeys are trapped by placing bait in a cage. When the monkeys reach into the cage to take the bait, they can escape only by releasing the bait and running away. If they insist on keeping the bait, they are trapped and taken into bondage. "Intelligent" monkeys (and intelligent people) often choose to hold on when they could just let go and be free!

Module 2: Prayer: The Key to All Ministry

When we forgive and release those who have offended us, we can go free. It is up to us! At various times in the scriptures, prayer and forgiveness is coupled together (Matthew 6:9-15; Mark 11:24-26). Forgiving others is crucial to maintaining a healthy, intimate relationship with Jesus.

Leaders will all face the test! There are many disillusioned leaders who have experienced unmet expectations and fallen short of the grace of God (Hebrews 12:15). In Matthew 20:1-16, Jesus told the story of a vinedresser and his workers. Those who worked all day without receiving a greater payment than those who worked part of the day were offended because their expectations were not met. Leaders must say, along with Jesus, "Father forgive them, for they know not what they do" (Luke 23:34). Romans 12:18 tells us, "If it is possible, as much as lies within you (depends on you), live peaceably with all men."

What if people continue to be offended and lie about us? Sometimes we are given a cup to drink that does not taste very good. We need to drink the cup. The Lord will vindicate us (Numbers 5:11-31). We should pray a blessing on those who have spoken against us. Ask the Lord to bless them (Matthew 5:44).

9. Learning to practice His presence

The Lord calls us to acknowledge Him in all of our ways, and then promises to direct our steps (Proverbs 3:6). We are exhorted in I Thessalonians 5:17 to pray continually (without ceasing). Jesus only did what He saw the Father doing (John 5:19). Christian leaders are called to follow His example. We can learn to practice the presence of the Lord in our lives.

Discussion and Study Questions

1. What is your greatest struggle in getting time with God? Be honest.

2. What are symptoms in your life that alert you to the fact that you are not getting sufficient time with God?

3. Give an example of an offense that you had to overcome.

4. Give an example of an unrealistic expectation you had of someone.

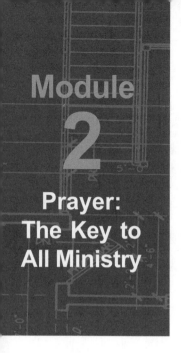

B. Intimacy with God

1. God's heart on intimacy

God wants a relationship with us! In Jeremiah 2:11-l3, we see that God's intense reaction was not because the people had forsaken *serving* Him, but they had forsaken a *relationship* with Him.

Express your love to Him If children give trinkets to parents but never express their love, parents may be disheartened. In the same way, our good deeds without intimacy are like trinkets to God.

The word *betrothal* in Hosea 2:19 speaks of *intimacy.* The word *loving-kindness* is used 250 times in the Old Testament and stresses the idea of the "belonging together" of those involved in a love relationship.

2. No shortcuts to intimacy with God

We can go no further into the holy place of intimate communion than our hearts will lead us in response to the Spirit of God. Bible study alone will not automatically bring intimacy.

We need to hunger and thirst and develop a relationship with Jesus as we study. Hebrews 11:6 says the Lord is the rewarder of those who diligently seek Him or crave after Him.

We can know Him John 17:3 says that we may intimately know the only true God, the King of Kings! Intimacy with God, however, is not a "buddy" relationship. We need to reverence and fear His Name.

3. Our model

John 5: 17 tells us that Jesus saw His Father at work, and Jesus only did what He saw His Father doing.

4. Three questions to ask yourself

- Do I take time for a love relationship—practicing His Presence all day long?
- Do I seek Him only when I need direction?
- Do I study the scriptures only when I need to have a message for others?

5. Examples of intimacy with God in the Old Testament

God pursued Moses in Exodus 24:l2: "Come up to me on the mountain."
David was a man after God's own heart:
- He was a worshiper—encouraging himself in the Lord (I Samuel 30:6).
- He was honest (Psalm 6:6).
- He had a simple faith (Psalm 131:1-2).
- He knew how to repent (Psalm 51:4).

6. God's revelation of Himself

The scriptures are a record of God's revelation of Himself to mankind. For example, Exodus 17:15 reveals God as *Jehovah Nissi*—our Banner. Genesis 22:14 reveals God as *Jehovah Jireh*—our Provider.

Learn to know God's character If we are not developing an intimate walk with the Father and do not know His character, when hard times come, we will feel like He is teasing us. We will doubt His trustworthiness and feel like He is out to get us. Learn to know His character. He is trustworthy!

More names displaying the character of God:

Jehovah Shalom—He is our peace.

Jehovah Shammah—He is there.

Jehovah Rophe—He heals.

Jehovah Rohi—He is our shepherd.

Jehovah M'Kaddesh—He sanctifies.

Jehova Tsidkenu—He is our righteousness.

Satan lies against the character of God In the Garden of Eden, Satan implied that if Adam and Eve ate from the tree of knowledge of good and evil, they would be like God, suggesting that God was withholding something from them. Adam and Eve believed the lie.

God will never express His love toward us except through the expression of His perfect love He does not give second best. We are His treasured possession (Deuteronomy 14:2).

7. Costly illusions

Leaders will have costly illusions if ministry is not an overflow of their intimacy with Him. **They become preoccupied with themselves** as public people. Others will put them on a pedestal. Leaders need to remember that the Lord is at work for *His* pleasure! (Philippians 2:13).

They will feel they need to fix everything to make everyone happy.

They will feel they can never make mistakes

They will feel guilty if they are not always busy When they do take time to retreat alone, they will feel they are not being useful.

They will have unrealistic expectations of themselves

8. Fruitful ministry comes from intimacy with God

Jesus went alone to pray (Mark 6:31). We must spend time alone with Him.

God is in control We can relax because God is in control. The "sabbath rest" is Jesus (Hebrews 4:9-10). It is a relaxed attitude that God is in control and working all things together for our good (Romans 8:28).

Surrender As we surrender, we focus on Him. In our posture of surrender, the expectations—some real, some imagined—are quieted.

Fulfillment in Him We are either motivated by fear or love. In our intimacy and quietness, we do not need to do something to feel significant or fulfilled. We are fulfilled completely in Him.

Motivated by love In our intimacy with Him, our motivations become evident. It is so easy in ministry to deviate from the pure motive (I Timothy 1:5). Galatians 5:13 says, "through love, serve one another." Without intimacy with Jesus, we can become more devoted to principle, method, vision, etc. rather than the pure motive of love.

9. Communion with God

We are better able to discern what God is saying when we commune with Him. In Jeremiah 23:18, God asks which of the prophets spends enough time with Him to hear Him.

We will remember that Jesus is with us, offering His shoulder to carry the load. Matthew 11:28 tells us His yoke is easy. We are co-laborers with Christ.

He will give us a vision Habakkuk 2:1-3 tells us to stand watch to see what He will say to us. We will know it is His vision for us—not our own ideas.

We will have communion with the Holy Spirit (II Corinthians 13:14). The fellowship of the Holy Spirit is available to us all.

He will help us to surrender day by day, moment by moment. This will develop intimacy with Him as we enjoy His presence in our lives (Psalms 46:10). We will believe what the Word of God says about us instead of what we feel.

10. Relationship vs. law

Are we hearing from God through a life-giving relationship with Him? In Exodus 20:18-20, the children of Israel wanted Moses to hear from God for them. The result: Law upon law.

Do we depend on others to hear from God for us? Hebrews 12:25 warns us not to refuse "Him who speaks." If we forsake a relationship with God, we will return to just following religious rules and allow others to hear from God for us.

Discussion and Study Questions

1. How will knowing God's character protect us from disillusionment?

2. How can ministry be an overflow of that which is in our hearts?

3. How can this "overflow ministry" guard us from costly illusions?

4. How does communion with God change us?

5. Why does it seem safer for people to depend on others to hear from God for them?

C. The Fear of the Lord

Some of this teaching is taken from *Intimate Friendship With God Through Understanding the Fear of the Lord* by Joy Dawson.

1. Definition
To fear the Lord is to reverence and trust Him It is giving Him the place of preeminence, praise, thanksgiving, and **the honor He deserves**, not what we think He deserves. He says, "I am." We say, "You are, You are." The fear of the Lord is beautiful; it does not make us afraid or cause us to shrink away; it causes us to run to Him. When we understand the fear of the Lord, we will experience intimacy and friendship (Psalm 25:4).
The fear of the Lord is the beginning of wisdom (Proverbs 9:10).

2. Understanding the fear of the Lord
To fear God is to stand in awe of His Name (Malachi 2:5). As we revere and fear the Lord, we will stand in awe of this name. What is His Name? He is Counselor, Prince of Peace, Mighty God (Isaiah 9:6). Psalm 33:8 says, "Let all the earth fear the Lord; let all the inhabitants stand in awe of Him."

3. Obeying Him
God knew Abraham feared Him because he did not withhold his son, Isaac (Genesis 22:12). When we fear God, we will obey Him because we love Him, not just because we are afraid of the consequences of disobedience. Delayed obedience and partial obedience are disobedience. The more we learn of His character and the more He reveals Himself and His faithfulness, the more fully we will obey.

4. Holiness results
The fear of the Lord will work in us a deep respect and understanding of His holiness. Revelation 4:8 says that night and day, the living creatures at God's throne are crying, "Holy, Holy is the Lord God." II Corinthians 7:1 says, "Let us cleanse ourselves from all filthiness of the flesh and spirit, perfecting holiness in the fear of God."

Giving an account The scriptures in Romans 14:12 and II Corinthians 5:10 speak of appearing before the judgment seat of God and giving an account of ourselves to God. As His children, we need not fear hell, but knowing we will be judged in view of our works (for the purpose of rewards) causes us to walk in the fear of the Lord (Revelation 22:12).

5. Hating evil

Proverbs 8:13 clearly shows that when we fear God, we will hate evil. The fear of the Lord will cause us to have the same attitude toward sin as God has. What is His attitude? He hates sin! The fear of the Lord produces hatred for sin, because we know sin grieves His heart. The level of our repentance will depend upon the degree to which we see sin as God sees it. Proverbs 16:6 says, "And by the fear of the Lord, one departs from evil." Saul wept after David spared his life, but he didn't repent (I Samuel 24).

Pride and self-sufficiency cause us to have a poor perception of our sin
Repentance is a change of heart (Acts 26:20). Luke 7:47 tells us that a person who is forgiven little, loves little. We determine to be better people, not realizing the impossibility of freedom from our sin apart from the mercy of God. Matthew 18:21-35 gives an example of a servant who perceived he could in his self-sufficiency pay back his debt.

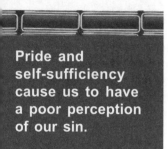

Pride and self-sufficiency cause us to have a poor perception of our sin.

6. Not fearing man

Jesus delighted in the fear of the Lord (Isaiah 11:2-3). Proverbs 29:25 tells us that the fear of man is a snare. If we are still trying to please man, we are not servants of Christ (Galatians 1: 10). The fear of man is being more impressed with other people's reaction to our actions than with God's response to us. We need to become more "God-conscious" than "self-conscious."

Quote from Thomas á Kempis "He has great tranquility who cares neither for the praises nor the fault finding of men. He will easily be content, pacified whose conscience is pure. You are not holier if you are praised, not more worthless if you are found fault with. What you are—that you are. Neither by words can you be made greater than what you are in the sight of God."

When we fear man, we hinder the purposes of God in many areas. We can't be broken and humble What would people think if they knew what we have done? Psalm 32:5 says it is important to acknowledge my sin and not hide it. Humility is a willingness to be known for who we are. This brings an openness for others to share also.

Our counseling will be tainted If we fear man, we will be a respecter of people, showing favoritism.

Our worship will be hindered Are we preoccupied with what others are thinking of us? Proverbs 23:17 tells us to continue in the fear of the Lord all day: "Teach me Your way, O Lord; I will walk in Your truth; unite my heart to fear Your name" (Psalm 86:11).

7. Controlling our words

A mark of the fear of the Lord is that our words will be free from evil (Psalm 34:11-14). The fear of the Lord produces one hundred percent honesty, one hundred percent of the time.

   James 1:26; James 3: 1-12; Proverbs 10:19; Proverbs 18:8; Proverbs 26:20

8. Free from idols

In II Kings 17:24-41, we see that the people had some fear of God, yet served their own gods. God's perception is that we fear Him only in proportion to our freedom from idols.

In the fear of the Lord, there is strong confidence and His children have refuge (Proverbs 14:26). Pray for the fear of the Lord on your children. Pray for the fear of the Lord on relationships.

"We should not be afraid of the depth of love toward one another, provided every relationship can stand the test of the light of the Holy Spirit's standard in purity in word and deed." —Joy Dawson

9. Receiving the fear of the Lord

He will put the fear of the Lord in our hearts (Jeremiah 32:40). We need to be honest and confess the lack of the fear of the Lord in our lives and cry out to Him. We need to allow Him to start working it into our hearts. Receive it in faith. Study the scriptures on the fear of the Lord.

   Hebrews 13:21

Discussion and Study Questions
1. Define the fear of the Lord in your own words.
2. Give some examples of how the fear of man can limit us.
3. How can the fear of the Lord overcome the fear of man?
4. Give an example from your life of how the fear of the Lord helped you overcome the fear of man.
5. How do we receive the fear of the Lord?

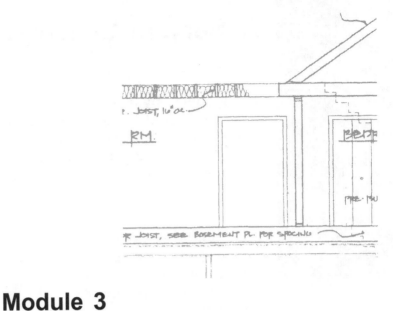

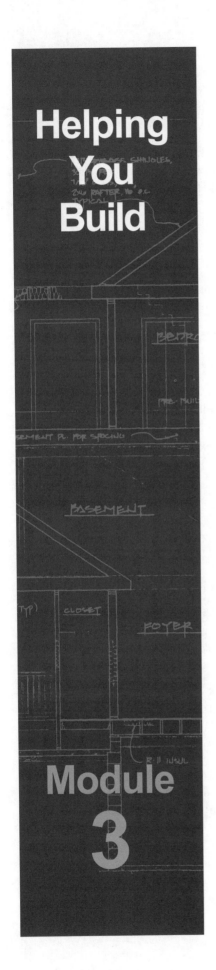

Helping You Build

Module 3

Module 3

Basic Cell Leadership

This module gives practical teaching on Jesus' example of modeling servanthood in Christian leadership. The module also covers practical biblical training on both qualifications and responsibilities for healthy cell group leaders.

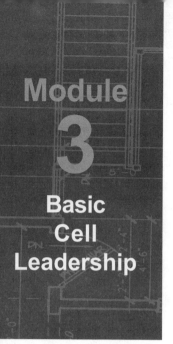

A. Servant Leadership

1. Modeled by Jesus

Philippians 2:5-7 teaches us to have the same attitude that Jesus had—the attitude of a servant. Jesus knew where He came from, why He was here, and where He was going (John 13:1-17). He was secure, and He was free to serve as a leader—a servant leader.

2. Taught by Jesus

Matthew 20:25-28 indicates that the disciples had been influenced by the leadership patterns of the Gentiles. Jesus explained to them the leadership in the kingdom of God: Servanthood!

3. Understanding "fields of ministry"

Who are you called to serve? Who is in your field of ministry (sphere of authority and responsibility)? Every leader needs to know his God-given "field of ministry." When we lead with confidence within our God-given "fields of ministry," we can be secure in who we are and lead as servants. A complete teaching on "fields of ministry" is contained in Module 14:C.

II Corinthians 10:12-16

4. Leading

We reap what we sow In II Chronicles 10:7, King Rehoboam, a new king, received advice from his father's advisors about servant leadership: "If you are kind to these people, and please them, and speak good words to them, they will be your servants forever." In other words, we reap what we sow (Galatians 6:7). Rehoboam refused their advice and paid the penalty.

Others will follow our example I Corinthians 11:1 teaches us to recognize that others follow our example as we imitate Christ.

5. Sowing seeds of truth

Servant leaders have a ministry of sowing seeds of truth into the lives of those whom they serve. Servant leaders see those they serve through "eyes of faith," expecting a harvest.

Mark 4:3-8

6. Going two by two

Servant leaders recognize the kingdom of God is built through relationships. Mark 3:14 says that Jesus called His disciples that "they might be with Him," then He sent them out two by two (Mark 6:7). I Timothy 1:5 gives us the Lord's goal—love which comes from a pure heart, a good conscience and a sincere faith. This love is modeled as we take apprentices under our wings and disciple them. I John 3:18 exhorts us to love—not with words, but with action.

7. The key to servant leadership

An attitude of serving is the key to servant leadership. In Matthew 25:40, Jesus exhorts us that whatever we do for one of the least of His brothers, we do for Him. In Matthew 9:36 we see the Lord's compassion for the crowds. His attitude was always to serve. Leadership in cell churches must have the same heart attitude to serve.

8. Taking time to know people

A true leader has a servant's heart and is willing to take the time needed to be "knit with" the people in his cell. Just like it takes several weeks for a broken bone to heal and knit together, so it takes time for relationships in the cell group to be knit together.

The church is built together through relationships "From whom the whole body, joined and knit together by what every joint supplies, according to the effective working by which every part does its share, causes growth of the body for the edifying of itself in love" (Ephesians 4:16).

9. Giving encouragement

Hebrews 3:13 tells us to encourage one another daily. This is especially true for new Christians who need regular encouragement and nurturing because they are like new plants in a greenhouse. Hebrews 5:14 tells us we grow into maturity by practicing and training ourselves to know the difference between right and wrong. Maturity does not happen overnight.

True servant leaders serve as spiritual advisors encouraging God's people in the Word as they mature in Christ. The cell is an excellent "wineskin" for regular encouragement. Cell leaders model life-styles of servanthood by encouraging cell members on a consistent basis.

Discussion and Study Questions

1. Where is the leadership style of the Gentiles still found?
2. Describe how a servant leader can still be a strong leader?
3. How does understanding your field of ministry help you be a servant leader?
4. How do servant leaders lead?
5. Why does this relational style of leadership motivate people?

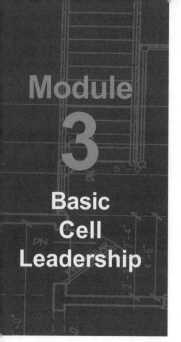

B. The Qualifications of a Cell Leader

1. True leaders are willing to serve with humility

I Peter 5:5 tells us that God resists the proud, but gives grace to the humble. Cell leaders need to have a heart to serve others. If a cell leader has been willing to serve under someone else's leadership, especially someone he hasn't always agreed with, he will probably have the grace that is needed to lead with humility. We are not looking for spiritual superstars.

2. New cell leaders need cell ministry experience

Experiencing cell life teaches new leaders how to lead; otherwise a new cell leader may have only head knowledge regarding cell leadership. "But let these also first be proved; then let them serve as deacons, being found blameless" (I Timothy 3:10). It is best for new cell leaders to have had a time of serving as an assistant leader, modeling servant leadership in a cell group setting. It can't be all theory.

3. Cell leaders should have a clear testimony

If you are called to be a cell leader, you must have a clear testimony about your salvation, water baptism and relationship with God. Areas of healing and deliverance which you have personally experienced should also be part of your testimony.

> II Timothy 1:12

Leaders should also be able to share how God is continuously working in their lives on an ongoing basis. People in the cell need to know we are real people!

4. Cell leaders should have faith

Know God has called you Cell leaders need to know God has called them. If they have been talked into it, someone else will talk them out of it (Romans 14:23). Cell leaders must be people who are full of faith and full of the Holy Spirit. Stephen was known as a man with these qualities: "And the saying pleased the whole multitude. And they chose Stephen, a man full of faith and the Holy Spirit..." (Acts 6:5).

Exercise your faith As a home cell group leader, you will need to exercise your faith by using your spiritual gifts. How can a cell leader help someone else experience spiritual gifts if he does not exercise those gifts himself? Faith is spelled RISK.

The fivefold ministry will help to equip you The fivefold ministry as described in Ephesians 4:11-12, with the gifts of apostle, prophet, evangelist, pastor and teacher are given by the Lord to build up His church. If you find yourself lacking in any of these areas, talk to your local pastor or another confidant. They can lead you to someone who has a special anointing in the area you are lacking. Romans 10:17 tells us that faith comes by hearing and hearing by the Word of God. John Wesley, the founder of the Methodist Church, had circuit riders who went from house to house equipping the saints. These circuit riders had the same job as the fivefold ministers listed in Ephesians 4. (Module 12 gives a scriptural basis for understanding the fivefold ministry in the cell-based church.)

5. Cell leaders should support the local church vision

Be convinced that the vision of your church is one you can embrace as your own All families/churches do things differently. We encourage our DCFI cell leaders to be well acquainted with our *Biblical Foundation Series* (a course on basic Christianity) and the vision of the local church so they clearly understand the mandate the Lord has given our local expression of the body of Christ.

Lack of loyalty I Corinthians 1:10 says there should be no divisions among us. A lack of loyalty to the Word of God, to the local church and to church leadership will cause great harm to God's people.

Appeal to leadership If there is any aspect of the ministry of a church that a home cell group leader cannot consent to or support in faith, he should pray and then "share his heart" with his local leadership. We need to appeal to those over us in the Lord.

Differing opinions If you are serving as a cell group leader and you find yourself having a wrong spirit toward those in spiritual leadership over you, you need to go to them. Sit down with your leaders and share your struggle. It does not mean we are rebellious or that we cannot remain loyal just because our opinions differ with another person in leadership. God wants us to pray about the differences of understanding we have and then talk about them with the appropriate leadership. Unity does not mean uniformity.

6. Cell leaders should be enthusiastic

Revelation 3:19 (Living Bible) tells us to repent and become enthusiastic about the things of God. Enthusiasm is a choice! Enthusiasm is contagious!
Colossians 3:23 says, "And whatever you do, do it heartily, as to the Lord and not to men." Do it with all your heart! An enthusiastic leader will produce enthusiastic Christians in the cell group. Remember, God's kingdom is the most exciting place to be in the world!

7. A cell leader should not be a new Christian

A new Christian should not be a cell group leader because he needs time and experience before being entrusted with taking care of others. Elisha was trained by Elijah. Timothy was trained by Paul. In each case, the training took a reasonable amount of time.

Leaders in training If new Christians want to serve in leadership, they could start out as assistant cell leaders. In this role they are essentially "leaders in training" (I Timothy 3:6). This honors their desire for leadership, but it does not put undo pressure on them by giving them premature responsibility.

Allow them to fail When an assistant cell leader is learning during this apprenticeship period, he or she must be allowed to fail. We, too, made mistakes as we progressed through the learning process. If we remember our mistakes, we will extend grace and not be tempted to adopt unreasonable expectations for assistant cell leaders.

8. Married cell leaders should be in unity with their spouse

It's important that leading a cell group does not cause disunity in a marriage. The spouse should not only confirm his or her partner's call to serve, but if possible, be actively engaged in serving the group also.

The scriptures affirm that **God uses both men and women** as home cell group leaders in the church. Priscilla and Aquila worked together as a team in the New Testament (Romans 16:3). It is possible that she was giving primary leadership to the group of people God placed within their spiritual care, while her husband supported her.

Priscilla and Aquila worked together as a team in the New Testament.

Women in leadership We have seen the Lord use women in a leadership role in the home cell group setting while their husbands play a supportive role.

Unsaved spouse When a potential cell leader has a spouse who is unsaved, it is best for the spouse to agree with his or her involvement in cell ministry.

Newly married If a couple is newly married, be aware that leading a cell group is an added responsibility. Some newlyweds may not be ready for this ministry, while others may be prepared to serve in this way.

9. Cell leaders should tithe to the local church

Malachi 3:10 states, "'Bring all the tithes into the storehouse, that there may be food in My house, and prove Me now in this,' says the Lord of Hosts, 'if I will not open for you the windows of heaven and pour out for you such blessing that there will not be room enough to receive it.'" The storehouse is the local church, the place where God's people bring their tithes and offerings. A tithe is ten percent of our income. This is a part of God's plan to supply the needs of leadership and fulfill the vision of the church.

Where is our treasure? Wherever we invest our money is where our true interests lie: "For where your treasure is, there your heart will be also" (Matthew 6:21). Our hearts need to be in our local church, including our own cell group. Whether or not we give our tithe to the local church is a clear measure of our commitment to the local church where we are placed. If cell group leaders are not tithing to their own local church, they find it very difficult to teach this biblical principle with conviction to those in their cell groups, since they are not applying it to their own lives.

Resource on tithing available The purpose of the tithe is to honor the Lord and to honor leadership. A complete teaching on the tithe is available in the booklet entitled *The Tithe, A Test in Trust* by Larry Kreider, available from *House to House Publications.*

10. Cell leaders should be accountable

Hebrews 13:17 tells us to "Obey those who rule over you, and be submissive, for they watch out for your souls, as those who must give account. Let them do so with joy and not with grief, for that would be unprofitable for you." The word *accountability* literally means *to give an account.* Personal accountability is *not* having others tell us what to do. **Personal accountability is finding out from God what He wants us to do and then asking others to "hold us accountable" to obey what God has called us to do.**

The leadership team (eldership of the local church) is ultimately responsible before the Lord for each person in the cell groups The elders in the local church "give an account" to the Lord for those under their spiritual oversight (Hebrew 13:17). The cell leader, then, is an extension of the leadership team of the local church and is accountable to the elders of the church. The elders are accountable to the senior leader (senior pastor) of the church who is accountable to apostolic overseers the Lord has placed over him.

Accountability brings protection If we are accountable to those responsible for us, we can expect those we are responsible for to be accountable to us. It is essential for the cell group leader to converse regularly and to pray both with those who give him oversight concerning his particular area of service and with those in his cell group.

11. Cell leaders should be teachable and reliable

Have the potential cell leaders been open to input? Are they teachable? Can you trust them to fulfill responsibilities given to them? Are they reliable and trustworthy? II Timothy 2:2

12. Cell leaders should feel a healthy sense of inadequacy

Having the feeling, "How could God ever use me?" is usually a qualification for cell leadership. God told Moses, "Come now, therefore, and I will send you to Pharaoh that you may bring My people, the children of Israel, out of Egypt. But Moses said to God, 'Who am I that I should go to Pharaoh, and that I should bring the children of Israel out of Egypt?' So He said, 'I will certainly be with you...'" (Exodus 3:10-12).

The Lord is with you! God told Joshua, "Have I not commanded you? Be strong and of good courage; do not be afraid, nor be dismayed, for the Lord your God is with you wherever you go" (Joshua 1:9).

Gideon's story of inadequacy Gideon said to Him, "O my lord, if the Lord is with us, why then has all this happened to us? And where are all His miracles which our fathers told us about, saying, 'Did not the Lord bring us up from Egypt?' But now the Lord has forsaken us and delivered us into the hands of the Midianites." Then the Lord turned to him and said, "Go in this might of yours, and you shall save Israel from the hand of the Midianites. Have I not sent you?" So he said to Him, 'O my Lord, how can I save Israel? Indeed my clan is the weakest in Manasseh, and I am the least in my father's house.' And the Lord said to him, 'Surely I will be with you, and you shall defeat the Midianites as one man" (Judges 6:13-16).

Jeremiah's story of inadequacy Then said I [Jeremiah]: "Ah, Lord God! Behold, I cannot speak, for I am a youth." But the Lord said to me: "Do not say, 'I am a youth,' for you shall go to whom I send you, and whatever I command you, you shall speak. Do not be afraid of their faces, for I am with you to deliver you," says the Lord (Jeremiah 1:6-8).

The type of people God uses are those who are dependent on Him! Each of these men felt a profound sense of inadequacy when the Lord called them to leadership. That is the type of person the Lord seeks to use—those who are completely dependent on Him! II Corinthians 12:9 tells us, "for my strength is made perfect in weakness."

We must be convinced that if God doesn't show up, it is all over!
If you don't think you have all the natural gifts you need, or feel you have made too many mistakes, be encouraged—you are in good company!

The very thing that people think disqualifies them, actually qualifies them.

Discussion and Study Questions

1. Why does a cell leader need cell ministry experience?

2. What are some things you could do to help a potential leader build faith in his or her life?

3. What can you do if a new Christian wants to be a cell leader?

4. Why is it important for a cell leader to tithe to his local church?

5. Feeling inadequate seems more like a disqualification than a qualification. How does this work?

6. How can you have faith and feel inadequate at the same time?

C. The Responsibilities of a Cell Leader

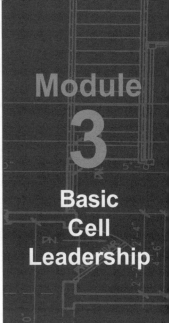

1. Cell leaders pray covering for cell members

The cell leader's main responsibility is to daily "cover" each person in his cell group in prayer. Prayer provides a spiritual protection or covering for the cell members. Some of this can be delegated to assistant cell leaders. Galatians 4:19 says, "I labor in birth again until Christ is formed in you."

Cell leaders have the authority to bind evil and loose a blessing "Assuredly, I say to you, whatever you bind on earth will be bound in heaven, and whatever you loose on earth will be loosed in heaven" (Matthew 18:18). God has given believers the authority to bind the powers of evil and to loose blessing and freedom in the name of Jesus!

Cell leaders understand hindrances from the enemy "For we do not wrestle against flesh and blood, but against principalities, against powers, against the rulers of darkness of this age, against spiritual hosts of wickedness in the heavenly places" (Ephesians 6:12). Many people don't know they are being influenced by demonic spirits; they may simply seem disinterested or unresponsive. Prayer in Jesus' name is a key for their release.

Remember, prayer is powerful! "For though we walk in the flesh, we do not war according to the flesh. For the weapons of our warfare are not carnal but mighty in God for pulling down strongholds" (II Corinthians 10:3-4).

Cell leaders can pray specific scriptures for cell members Praying the scriptures has been a helpful way for some to pray; for example: "I pray that (Bob's) love may abound more and more..." (Philippians 1:9-11). Other scriptures to pray are Colossians 1:9-12, Ephesians 1:15-21 and Ephesians 3:14-19. As a leader you must set the standard in prayer.

2. Cell leaders pray with their assistant leader(s) and their overseer on a regular basis

These prayer connections are vital! When cell leaders pray with their spiritual overseers, it sets a standard for cell members to pray with their cell leadership and with one another. Praying together helps us to know the hearts of our leaders. This fosters spiritual intimacy and strengthens relationships.

There is power in agreement "I say to you that if two of you agree on earth concerning anything that they ask, it will be done for them by My Father in heaven" (Matthew 18:19).

Remember to pray with expectancy! Through doubt and unbelief, the enemy will try to break our communication line with God. Get the prayer anointing! If your cell group seems to be lacking in the area of prayer, have someone come into your cell group who has an anointing in the area of prayer. Effective, fervent prayer is contagious.

3. Cell leaders train assistant cell leaders

Training assistant cell leaders is a key to future growth. There are two types of training: classroom training and mentoring.

II Timothy 2:2

Classroom training

- Many churches use the *House to House* book by Larry Kreider as a textbook to train cell leaders. This book tells how to lead a cell group effectively and how DOVE Christian Fellowship International became a family of cell-based churches committed to church planting worldwide.
- This *Helping You Build Cell Churches Manual* can also be used to train cell leaders.
- Monthly cell leaders' meetings for the purpose of training and encouragement are crucial.
- *The House to House Church Planting and Leadership Video Correspondence School Module 1* is also used by many churches for systematic training for cell leaders and future cell leaders.
- Cell leaders' training days should be held a few times each year, perhaps on a Saturday with various workshops and training sessions for small group leaders.
- This need can also be met by the cell leaders attending a *DCFI Cell Ministry Seminar.*

Mentoring (spiritual fathering and mothering)

The best, most effective training is one-on-one training where a potential cell leader is discipled by his cell leader or assistant cell leader. Ask a potential cell leader to go along with you when you go into the hospital to pray for the sick, or to join you when you meet with someone who is discouraged and needs someone to pray a prayer of faith with him.

Jesus set the pattern for on-the-job-training He spent most of his time training a few men, not teaching great crowds. At the start of a new cell, the cell leader should pray for at least one or more assistant leaders to serve with him.

The home cell group becomes the basic training center for all kinds of ministry. Missionaries do not suddenly and miraculously become trained overnight and leave for foreign fields. They get training and practice in their home cell groups.

Train the assistant cell leaders to pray
The assistant cell leader should look for ways to assist the cell leader by praying

for and with people, discipling, encouraging, and serving in practical ways. In the absence of the leader, he gives leadership to the cell group. The assistant cell leader should also bring to the cell leader's attention areas of concern: potential problems, needs, or "blind spots." The cell leader can then train the assistant leader(s) to cover these areas in prayer as Jesus taught His disciples to pray (Luke 11:1-13).

Train the assistant cell leaders in their responsibilities
The assistants should be trained to diligently pray for those in their cell group and help the cell leader to contact individuals regularly by phone or in person to comfort, strengthen, and encourage them. They will also serve in practical ways which may include providing rides to meetings as needed and giving cell group information to cell members. They may also be involved in giving care to new believers and helping with discipleship.

4. Recognize the three basic types of assistant leaders

- **Developmental**—those being trained for future leadership. Jesus had twelve assistants, but seemed to be training Peter as His chief assistant.
- **Perpetual**—this is someone who is not a potential leader; however, when a home cell group multiplies, this assistant leader gives a sense of stability and continuity to one of the new cells. When the cell multiplies into two, this person often becomes an assistant leader in one of these new cells. This person may not ever be called to be a cell group leader. This is how God has made him—a supportive leader.
- **Catalyst**—this is someone in church leadership, a person who has a "fivefold ministry gift," or a person who serves as staff in the church or in a ministry. This person may not be able to take an active role in cell leadership due to traveling ministry or the responsibility to other cells or ministries. However, this person will prove to be supportive to the cell leader and will be a good resource and example of Christ's love within the cell.

5. Cell leaders set the example in transparency and honesty

You can set the example by sharing your own personal needs and problems with those in your cell group. The Bible tells us in II Corinthians 12:9 that we should boast in our weaknesses so that the power of Christ may rest upon us. When we are open about areas of struggle that we've had and share how the Lord has given us grace to conquer by His Word, it causes us to be transparent. This keeps us from being placed upon a pedestal.

Show them by our lives, rather than just telling them We can minister most effectively by showing the people in our cell group the Word of God by the way we live our lives, rather than by giving them our own opinions. We earn the right to speak into people's lives.
I Corinthians 11:1

Trust takes time It takes time to build trust. True leaders will take time to build good, trusting relationships with people. If you don't have relationships with the people in your cell, it will be very difficult for them to receive advice or correction from you. We must build relationships, not only within the setting of the home cell meeting, but outside the meeting as well.

     Ephesians 4:16

6. Cell leaders are called to encourage, not to control

Hebrews 3:13 tells us to encourage one another daily. Cell leaders who are immature or insecure may seek to control God's people rather than encourage them to hear the Lord's voice for themselves. We need to help the believers in our cell learn how to receive direction from the Lord themselves.

     Jeremiah 33:3

The cell leader's leadership is limited in these ways:
- He cannot deviate in any way from scripture.
- He cannot assume the guiding role of the Holy Spirit in the life of another believer. Each believer must ultimately hear from God for himself.
- He cannot act contrary to the values and guiding principles set by the leadership team of his local church.
- He cannot misuse his role of leadership by being abusive, manipulative, or self-serving.

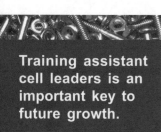

Training assistant cell leaders is an important key to future growth.

Encourage cell members to depend on the Lord, not us! We should not encourage cell members to depend on us by telling them what to do. Rather, we should encourage them to hear from the Lord themselves and depend on His Word. This includes advice on family finances, family size, child rearing styles, political differences, decisions about their living standards and so on. A cell leader can give counsel based on his understanding of the Word of God, but issues not clearly defined by scripture must ultimately be left to the conscience of each believer.

     Colossians 1:28

7. Cell leaders submit to the leadership of the local church

Cell leaders are a type of deacon in the local church (I Timothy 3:8-13 and Philippians 1:1). Cell leaders are an extension of the eldership. They are accountable to the eldership (and/or pastoral leadership), and cell leaders need to keep elders (and/or pastoral leadership) informed as to what the Lord is doing in the cell.

Elders have the final responsibility If a cell leader desires to step down from leadership, he "leads the cell group back" to the elders who have final responsibility. The elders are the ones who appointed the cell leader and gave him the authority and the responsibility to lead the cell, so the cell needs to be given back to the church leadership.

8. **Cell leaders need to communicate clearly to cell members**

I Timothy 4:12 indicates we should be an example in word and conduct. We communicate by words and actions. Different people relate to different types of communication. (They each have their own "satellite dish" set a certain way.) Some receive communication verbally, while others prefer written communication. Some are more receptive to details. Examples of communication follow: Type birthday and anniversary dates for cell members to send cards to each other; and when planning a cell retreat, check with your church leadership so it does not conflict with church events; share vision constantly!

9. **Cell leaders are responsible to make decisions**

It is important to invite input from cell members, but cell leaders (with assistant leaders) need to make the final decision. Involve the whole cell in the process. New Testament decision-making is learned in the cell group setting. Indecision on the part of the cell leader causes frustration among the people in the cell group.

10. **Wise cell leaders delegate and facilitate**

The cell leader is a facilitator. In I Corinthians 1:14, Paul delegated baptism to others. A wise cell leader will work himself out of a job. We need to be careful to delegate but not abdicate. (We still have the responsibility.) Planning outreaches, picnics, meals for shut-ins, etc. can often be delegated to others. People learn and take ownership by doing the job.

Get everyone involved! In I Corinthians 14:26, each one brings something to the cell meeting! Remember, the cell is not a miniature celebration meeting! Everyone can participate in a cell meeting! Call people before the meeting and ask them to share, pray, greet, etc. Do not do anything in the meeting that someone else can do.

The cell leader brings stability If assistant leaders or cell members do a good job in the task they were assigned, encourage them. If they make a mistake, find out what went wrong. Cell leaders want to help them succeed!

11. **The cell leader promotes cell life**

Much of cell life happens outside the meetings. Remember: relationships are the key! (Acts 2:42-47). When people pray together informally after the meeting, sometimes more is accomplished than in the "formal" meeting itself. Watching a football game on television together can be a tremendous relationship builder. Hospitality is the Lord's plan for relationship building.

12. The cell leader is responsible to oversee the cell meetings

Although cell leaders delegate as much responsibility as they can to others, they are still responsible for the protection and the spiritual health of the cell meetings. For example, some prayer requests in a cell meeting should be handled outside of the cell meeting. If someone is struggling with a life-controlling problem or in areas that need deliverance, it may be best to pray for them after the cell meeting is over or at another time.

Discussion and Study Questions

1. In your own words describe a "prayer covering."

2. Why is it important to recognize the three different kinds of assistant cell leaders?

3. What does the term "cell life" mean to you?

4. How can a cell leader practically delegate but not abdicate?

5. Who has the final responsibility for the cell group?

Helping You Build

Module 4

Module 4
Cell Groups Reaching Out

The purpose of cell groups is for reaching out. In this module, we will learn how the natural, God-given plan of oikos evangelism allows us to reach out to those right around us. We share practical tips and ideas for cell evangelism and tell how a cell can also have a world missions vision.

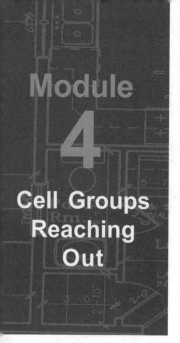

A. Oikos Evangelism

1. The biblical model of oikos evangelism

The primary focus of each home cell group should be outreach. This can take place effectively by following the New Testament pattern of *oikos* evangelism. Oikos evangelism is a natural God-given plan for practical evangelism and discipleship.

What is an oikos? *Oikos* is the Greek word for *household or house of people.* Your oikos is that group of people to whom you relate on a regular basis. Peter, in Acts chapter 10, was used by the Lord to share Christ with many of Cornelius's oikos members (Acts 10:2, 24).

2. Definition

There are five basic groups of people who make up your oikos:

- your family and relatives
- those who have common interests with you
- those who live in the same geographical location as you
- those who have a common vocation
- others with whom you have regular contact

3. Scriptural examples of oikos evangelism

Here are some scriptures that give us a picture of oikos evangelism that took place in the life of Jesus:

- Luke 5:27-32—Levi invited his oikos members to dinner with Jesus.
- Luke 8:39—Jesus told the Gadarene demonic to go home to his oikos.
- Luke 19:9—Zacchaeus invited Jesus to his home and his entire household (oikos) came to place their faith in Christ.
- John 1:40-42—Andrew asked Simon to come and get to know Jesus. Simon was a member of Andrew's oikos.
- John 1:44-45—Philip asked Nathaniel to come and get to know Jesus. Nathaniel was a member of Philip's oikos.

4. The most natural way to fulfill the Great Commission

Nearly every person has at least 20 people in his or her oikos who need to come to Christ for salvation or who have a specific need or problem in their lives. And all of those persons have 20 people in their oikos with needs. In other words, you and I have the potential of 400 persons (20x20) within our oikos. If there are 10 people in your cell group, your cell has the potential of touching 4,000 people for Christ! Amazing, isn't it! It is natural because the cell members already have established relationships with these people.

Pray for two or three people in your oikos Ask everyone in your cell group to write down 20 people in their oikos who need the Lord. Then ask them to prayerfully choose two or three to focus their prayers on. During the next months, continue to pray for these people and watch the Lord begin to use cell members to reach people with the Good News of Christ.

5. The power of our testimony (Revelation 12:11)

Paul, the apostle, set an example for us by taking advantage of many opportunities to share his testimony with others. We can examine one of these occasions in Acts 26:4-23, when Paul was speaking to King Agrippa. These verses show a clear pattern to use for our own personal testimony.

Before conversion In Acts 26:4-11, Paul described his outward sin and his inward need. Having been deeply committed to his Jewish faith, he became obsessed with a passion to defend his religion no matter how wrong his actions. His conviction ultimately drove him to persecute the Christian church and thereby resist the Spirit of God. Being under this conviction of sin (vs. 14), his great need was to admit he had been wrong.

Conversion In Acts 26:12-18, Paul described how his inward need was met. A description of how Paul met Christ is presented, including an account of where Paul was and what happened to him. God met his need by humbling him and allowing him to see who Jesus really was.

After conversion In Acts 26:19-23, Paul described how his outward life changed. We read how Paul obtained Christ's help and began to humbly carry out God's will for his life.

Our personal testimony can follow this same outline, consisting of:

* Mentioning what the inward need was in our lives, prior to our salvation, that brought us to Christ.
* Describing the circumstance of our conversion and how the inward need was met (i.e. where, when and what happened).
* Relating how our inward need has now been met after receiving Jesus and how our outward life has changed.

People should hear that we have experienced the same needs they have These needs are common to all men, though in varying degrees. Christ has met these needs in our lives. In our testimonies, we should be sure to include not only the outward sins that bound us but the inward needs that drove us.

Have everyone in your cell group write their testimony and practice sharing it!

6. Five ways people come to Christ in cell ministry

* Cell members are encouraged and trained to be witnesses for Christ.
* Invite the unsaved to the cell group.
* People who are saved at the celebration "net" are immediately invited to cell groups.
* Cell groups have outreach events tailored to reach the unsaved.
* Cells get involved in church-wide evangelistic events and bring the lost along.

Discussion and Study Questions

1. List twenty people from your oikos.
2. Take five minutes to pray over this list and determine which ones you should focus on to pray for their salvation.
3. If you have been a Christian for a while, you might have to ask the Lord to show you how you can get involved with pre-Christians. Any ideas?
4. Briefly describe your inward need before conversion. Briefly describe your conversion. Briefly describe how you changed after conversion.

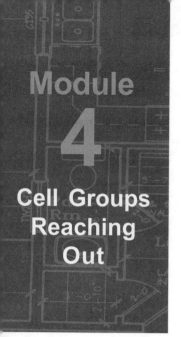

B. Practical Ideas for Cell Outreach

Cell groups should be evangelistic Cell group members should have a strategy for reaching people who live in their neighborhoods and communities. In this way, they expand their scope and vision, and the lost are brought into God's kingdom.

Don't become discouraged if you don't see immediate fruit from your outreach. There seems to be a spiritual principle here—as we reach out, growth comes. The reaching out puts something in motion in our spiritual lives and in our cell group. But the growth doesn't always come specifically from the outreach.

For example, a cell might canvas a neighborhood door to door, but instead of somebody coming to the cell from one of the houses that was visited, a cell member's relative might get saved and start to attend the cell meetings.

1. Joining the parade
A few cells join together to construct a float to participate in their community's local parade. Decorate the float with "Jesus banners" and balloons, proclaiming the Good News in an easy-to-understand way.

2. Picnic evangelism
Cell members invite unsaved friends and relatives for a day of games, snacks and entertainment at a local park. Entertainment can be provided from the talent right in the cell group—a music concert, soloist performance, a short drama with a spiritual message, etc.

3. Serving hurting people
Research which organizations in your area need volunteers to serve—teen centers, hospitals, jails, homeless shelters—and go as a cell group to help out when needed. When you begin to see life through God's eyes of compassion, it is guaranteed that He will break your heart, and keep it broken before Him.

4. Serving your community
Clean up your local playground or park. Paint swing-sets or buildings in the park. Plant flowers in the springtime. The township or park may even provide the supplies you would need. Just picking up trash is a simple way to say, "We care."

5. **Children's story hour**

   In the summertime, have a children's story hour for the neighborhood kids. Put together a flyer advertising its location and time. You could do it for a few weeks or a few months. Don't feel you need an elaborate program. Simply read a Bible story with lots of colorful pictures and offer a small snack. Jesus' love is shared!

6. **Outreach to internationals**

   After a foreign exchange student (formerly a Buddhist) living with a cell member accepted the Lord, a few people in the cell met once a week to answer this young woman's many questions. Is there a new believer in your cell who may have more questions to ask? Or maybe the new believer has friends with questions to ask about God.

7. **Prayer walks and prayer drives**

   Set aside an evening to pray for your city. Teams can be sent in cars or walking to cover certain areas. For the nightcap, everyone could meet at a public place in the community to pray. A "Jericho march" might even be a possibility.

8. **Block party**

   Hold a "food and games" night in a cell member's housing development or block. Include children and adults and simply reach out to them, making friends while providing free food and games for all ages. Free hot dogs and cotton candy will ensure the event is a success!

9. **Holiday outreach**

   An Easter egg hunt is a great way to share the gospel with the community. Buy small, inexpensive baskets before getting together as a cell group to decorate some colorful eggs and plan an egg-hunt for the children in your community (include gospel tracts in each basket).

   At Christmas time, collect nonperishable food items or toiletries each night at several cell meetings. Bless a needy person or ministry.

10. **Showing your compassion**

    As a cell group, support a needy child from another country through a reputable ministry. Take turns corresponding with the child, and pray regularly for the child at each cell meeting. When the cell multiplies, one of the new cells can continue the support.

11. Adopting a family

Find a local family in need and support them at regular intervals throughout the year. Take them festive food over the holidays, gifts at Christmas, and invite them along to the pool for a summer swim. Focusing on one family or outreach is often more effective than trying to reach out in too many different directions. Your cell will discover that blessings abound when you take time to share Christ as the center of your lives.

12. Questionnaires

Custom write a questionnaire to interview people in your cell neighborhood. This will help you get to know the people, their needs and open doors to share Christ. Have the last question lead into an opportunity to share an evangelism tool explaining the gospel to them. You could politely knock on doors or find people in public places like parks. Always ask people's permission to do the questionnaire.

13. Booth at community fair or festival

Set up a booth at a county fair or street festival where people can get "free prayer" or ask questions about God. Have a "hawker" who has the job of enticing people to come in and talk to someone in the booth. Use the *Two Question Test* booklet or another evangelistic tool to make it easy for people. Cells have even set up a whole street festival so they could have an evangelism booth there.

14. Crusades and special evangelistic outreaches

See crusades and church wide evangelistic outreaches as a cell-based outreach, rather than a program for evangelism. In other words, mobilize the entire cell to serve in the crusade or special evangelistic project sponsored by your local church or by the churches of your community. Seeing this evangelistic outreach as being cell-based can give more ownership and a sense of teamwork to cell members and provides opportunities for the cell to be involved in practical discipleship as people come to Christ.

Discussion and Study Questions

1. Creative thinking stimulates creative thinking. Come up with a new idea for a cell outreach that is not listed here.

2. When is the last time you led someone to faith in Jesus Christ?

3. Are you confident that you could explain the gospel in a nonreligious way to someone in 3-5 minutes? Try it now and time yourself.

4. What evangelism tools have you used?

5. Which one has been the most effective for you and why?

15. Love in bloom!

Flowers! Plant a few flowers in inexpensive clay pots or homemade planters to share with others. Pray over the pots together as a cell group. Send one pot home with each family to give to someone they are reaching out to.

16. Just doing it

If you don't like these ideas, come up with your own and get started!

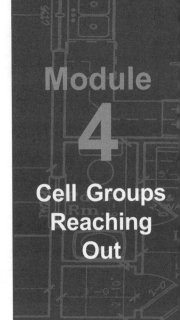

C. Cell Groups and Missions—Reaching the World

Missions vision

All cells and churches must be focused outward toward the lost. This extends beyond our neighbors to the nations of the world. Because of the small group dynamics within a cell group, it is a perfect environment to see the missions vision of each cell member expand and develop. Each member of the group, naturally, will be at a different place within his or her personal views and exposure to missions. Through teaching and discussions, you can have fun introducing your group to God's heart for the nations.

1.   Exposure

We need to continually expose our souls and spirits to this scripture:
"Go therefore and make disciples of all the nations, baptizing them in the name of the Father and of the Son and of the Holy Spirit, teaching them to observe all things that I have commanded you..." (Matthew 28:19-20).

See the big picture God shows us a big picture, bigger than our own backyards, even bigger than our own nation. We need to open our eyes to see, to become *exposed!* The reality of the Great Commission may shock people, but sometimes that is what it takes before we personally will take action and respond to what we see and hear.

Expose people to the needs By *exposing* individuals to the commands to share the gospel in other nations, they will be faced with the realities of the unevangelized peoples, the poor, the uneducated, the lack of clean water, etc. Use the internet, encyclopedias, dictionaries, statistics, maps and other resources to expose people to the need.

2.   Education

Now we know of the need; what can we do? Don't leave people overwhelmed with the task. Talk about the many church organizations with whom they can partner in reaching the unreached peoples. Encourage them that they can make a difference. Remember, Jesus ministered: body, soul and spirit. We, too, need to minister to the whole person, supplying food, clothing, love, and the gospel.

Where are the nations with the greatest need; where are the most unevangelized peoples? Look at the meaning of "mission" words. For example, the definition of "peoples" is *a body of persons that are united by a common culture, tradition or sense of kinship; they typically have the same language, institution, and beliefs.* You can use the same resources as you did to expose, but this time take a bite into it, not just a taste! Begin to pray as a cell group for a specific unevangelized people group somewhere in the world.

3. Training

Once your people are exposed about missions, you will find the need and desire for them to gain some practical training so they can do something.

Starting with evangelism–how to share your faith in a practical way Most believers are not confident in sharing their faith with others. Some have never been trained in the use of their personal salvation testimony. You can also train them to relate in foreign cultures. This can be a fun, relationship building time, as well as preparing them for contact they may have personally with people from other nations.

Give them a tool Sometimes people need a tool to hold before they will work on the job site, so train them in something practical with an international twist. One idea is to familiarize the cell members with one of the major vocations of people from a particular city in another nation. This would enable them to talk to someone from that city about their job. For example, a conversation about sugar cane with a Brazilian farmer through an interpreter could give a person confidence and the open door to share the gospel. Even if it is a non-spiritual tool, it may open the door they need to be confident to minister to the nations.

4. Practicals

Take the cell to a ministry that ministers to people different from themselves It's time to put the training into practice! This doesn't always mean an overseas trip or even an out-of-state trip! Be bold to take them to the highways and byways—the places that are crying out for the ministry of Jesus Christ. At times, cell groups do actually go on short term missions trips together. This can be a powerfully bonding and eye-opening experience.

Encourage them to be lights in a dark world Remember Matthew 5:14-16: "You are the light of the world..." Allow them the opportunity to be lights in dark places they usually wouldn't go. This may even be a place within your town! There are many forms of outreach and evangelism that are wonderful opportunities for cell groups to develop a vision and heart for people who don't know Christ. Keep in mind that your cell multiplication might be sending your assistant leaders to the mission field.

5. Embracing missions and missionaries

You will be able to challenge the cell members to make a commitment before the Lord to be a part of fulfilling the Great Commission. Not everyone may be called to go, but we are all called to fulfill the Great Commission. Have the group take on the responsibility to pray for missionaries, financially support missionaries, or go to the people who do not know Jesus. Maybe your group can "embrace" a missionary from your church or a missionary in a country for which your group has a vision.

Embracing is a close, personal touch between two individuals. We have found that, although the physical aspects of embracing cannot be done from afar, many other aspects of embracing can be accomplished. Caring, praying, sending birthday cards, etc., can be a blessing to missionaries. It can also be a way in which people who don't feel called to go, but do want to fulfill their call to missions, can affect other nations.

6. Practical "embrace a missionary" ideas for cells

One church family's strategy is to "embrace" every missionary by developing a strong support team of cell group members, families and individuals who encourage and support them. Here are some ideas for cell groups to support their church's missionaries or even college students who are studying in another area.

Birthday idea On a blank piece of paper, encourage everyone to write a cheerful note or sketch a cartoon for your missionary's upcoming birthday.

Group calls Find a speaker phone and call your missionary at a cell meeting! The missionary's ears will be buzzing, but he will have a giant smile on his face!

Fun funds Build relationships while working toward a common cause—raising funds for the missionary your cell supports. Have a car wash, sell subs, or make Christmas candy together and bless your cell's missionary with the proceeds.

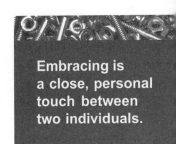

Embracing is a close, personal touch between two individuals.

Work together Periodically commit to writing a letter to your missionary. You could supply airmail envelopes. Have copies of the address handy.

Courier service Send care boxes with teams visiting your missionaries. Important: call to find out about available space before making plans.

Share what you have! Collect magazines, books, newspaper clippings and teaching tapes from cell members and mail the pack to your missionary.

Face to face Make sure you have "your" missionary speak at your cell every time he or she comes home on furlough: the personal touch does wonders!

Work project Visit a local ministry—a drug treatment program, a pregnancy center, a homeless shelter, a ministry to truckers. Tour the program and participate in any activities or work projects they have.

Children can get involved, too! Have the cell children make cards and artwork to send to your missionary.

Money box Decorate a box to be displayed at each cell meeting. Encourage cell members to place money in it when they can for the missionary you support. Send the money periodically, along with notes from each cell member.

E-mail messages After cell one evening, gather around a cell member's computer and spend time emailing some short messages from each cell member to the missionary you embrace.

Vitamin care package Each cell member wrap a small personal gift (lotion, pens, soaps, candy) along with a spiritual vitamin (scripture verse). Tell the missionaries to open one gift per day during Thanksgiving week (a holiday they would not celebrate abroad!). They will be forever grateful!

Funniest cell videos During a cell meeting, party or picnic, make a short video, complete with fun messages from each cell member. Send it to your missionary.

Photogenic cell members Compile a photo album for your missionaries with photos of each cell member and family. They'll love the personal touch!

Pray, pray, pray! Delegate a certain day for prayer each week for your missionary. Or assign cell members to pray one day a week for the missionary, thus covering all seven days of the week.

7. Embracing a people group

This takes the step of embracing a missionary a step further where a cell group or a few cell groups can embrace an entire people group. This takes place when a cell group responds to the need they see in an unreached people.

Ways to embrace a people group The cell group can pray, and it can communicate with missionaries working with that people group. A cell group could visit this people group; they could send Bibles; they could assist with children's ministry resources, worship music materials, or practical items as they arise. This can be the source of incredible blessings, not only for those within the unreached people group but also for the cell. With the end goal of evangelism and church planting in mind, a cell can be an instrument in a people group being reached with the love of Jesus Christ!

8. Helpful resources
Adults
World Mission by Johnathan Lewis, Editor, William Carey Library.
Material World—A Global Family Portrait by Peter Menzel, Sierra Club Books.
Life and Work on the Missions Field by J. Herbert Kane, Baker Book House.
Operation World by Patrick Johnstone, YWAM Publishing. Call 1-800-922-2143.
Friend Raising by Betty Barnett, YWAM Publishing.
Re-Entry by Peter Jordan, YWAM Publishing.

Children
You Can Change Your World by Jill Johnstone, Zondervan Publishing.
When I Grow Up by Terry Whalin, David C. Cook Publishing Co.

Discussion and Study Questions

1. How can a missions emphasis keep a local church healthy?

2. What responsibility does a cell group embracing a missionary family carry?

3. What happens when a cell group is embracing a missionary and the cell group multiplies?

4. Do you know where and how to get a passport? Call your local Post Office and find out.

5. Find a world map and pray over it. Are there any countries that you would like to visit with a short-term mission team?

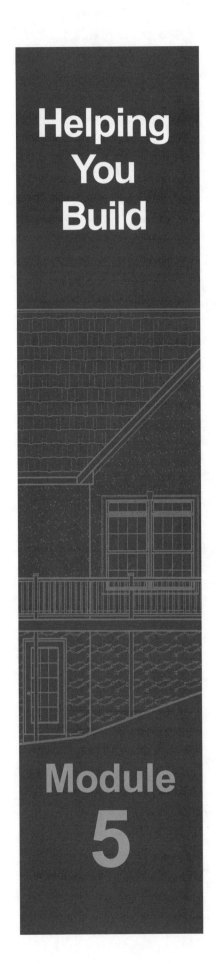

Module 5

Spiritual Parenting

The cell group is a spiritual family. This module trains cell leaders to serve their cell group as spiritual parents from both the fathering aspect and the mothering (nurturing) aspect. Practical discipleship for new believers is also taught.

Module 5

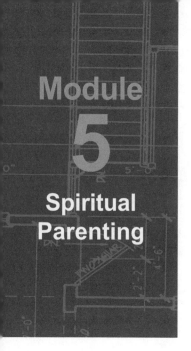

A. Spiritual Fathering

1. The restoration of spiritual fathers
The Lord is turning the hearts of fathers toward their sons and the hearts of sons toward their fathers. He is also causing a great hunger for spiritual fathers and mothers. Malachi speaks of this prophetically in Malachi 4:5-6.

2. A God of families
Ephesians 3:14-15 speaks of His whole family in heaven and earth. The church is not an institution; it is a family. In II Corinthians 6:17-18, the Lord says, "I will be a Father to you, and you will be My sons and daughters...." For a family to be healthy, there needs to be parental guidance. You can impress people from a distance, but you can only change them up close!

3. The need for spiritual fathering
According to I Corinthians 4:15-17, there are "ten thousand instructors, but not many fathers." Because of the lack of spiritual fathers, many spiritual children today are aborted (fall away). The church has often focused on meetings rather than on fathering! **Timothy was "fathered" by Paul.** Fathering takes time and effort, but it is worth it all! Stable spiritual families have spiritual parents. A cell leader is a spiritual parent.

Fathering starts in the cell group One person cannot be an effective spiritual father to a large group of people. Jesus fathered twelve men and then sent them out to be spiritual fathers. Pastors, elders and church leaders are called by God to be spiritual midwives to train/teach all of us to be spiritual fathers.

You can be a father, regardless of your experience If you never had the input of a natural father in your life, you can still become a father. The same truth applies to becoming a spiritual father. God is a Father to the fatherless.

4. Children, young men, and fathers
According to I John 2:12-14, we are either spiritual babies, spiritual young men (or women) or spiritual fathers (or mothers). In every church and in every cell group, it is important to understand the spiritual maturity level of each person. **Eventually, all of us should become spiritual parents.**

• **Spiritual children**
  Children know their sins are forgiven, and they know the Father. Every cell should have babies—brand new believers. It is exciting to see how the Lord answers children's prayers even when their prayers may not always be theologically correct. But that is okay, because they are babies!

The sad thing is that the church can be filled with children (some 50 years old) who have never grown up! Spiritual children need to be expected to eventually become spiritual young men/women. Babies are self-centered. The natural tendency of children is to be selfish. We expect children to grow up!

- **Spiritual young men and women**

Spiritual young men and women have overcome the wicked one and know the Word of God abides in them. They have learned to feed themselves.

Young men can often be arrogant and dogmatic and need to be "tempered" by fatherhood. They need to become fathers and experience its joys and disciplines. The only way to become a father is to have children (by adoption or by natural birth). Reading and memorizing scriptures from the Bible is not enough! Most young men (women) do not feel ready to have their first child, both in the natural and in the spiritual. But the Lord gives them grace for parenting!

- **Spiritual fathers and mothers**

God's will is for everyone to become a spiritual parent. Cell ministry is an ideal structure for spiritual parenting. The cell is a spiritual family. The cell leader and assistant leaders are spiritual parents.

Parents take responsibility for children and young men or women Fathers have a heart of compassion. They see the whole picture. They have experienced many seasons of life.

Start with one spiritual child (for a season) and help him grow in his relationship with Christ. The heart of every healthy father is to give a double "portion" to his son (Elijah/Elisha anointing).

> **Start with one spiritual child and help him grow in his relationship with Christ.**

5. Created to become spiritual parents

The key to being a father is to know the Father. Jesus gives us life. We must give it away or we become sluggish and bored (not living up to our full potential). Giving away what God has given to us releases joy!

It is time for the church to take up the mantle of spiritual parenting Parachurch ministries have modeled spiritual fathering very effectively for years! Jesus took 12 untrained men (Mark 3:14) and fathered them for three and one half years. He calls us to do the same.

6. The promise to Abraham

God called Abraham to be the father of many nations. In Genesis 15:4-6, God instructed Abraham to go outside at night to look at the stars. He told Abraham that he would have as many descendants as the stars. Abraham believed God, and the spiritual multiplication began. In Genesis 17:1-7, God even changed his name from Abram (meaning honored father) to Abraham meaning the "father of many nations."

7. The reward of fathering

Read I Thessalonians 2:7-8,19-20. Paul spoke about his sons being his glory or reward. Our spiritual children will bring us joy as they fulfill their destiny in Christ Jesus.

8. Are you a spiritual child or a parent?

Malachi 4:6 says God will "turn the hearts of the fathers to the children, and the hearts of the children to their fathers" in the last days (also Luke 1:17). Jeremiah 31:13 teaches us the young and old will serve together.

9. Spiritual reproduction

Paul refers to Timothy as his son (II Timothy 2:2), and exhorts him to train other sons (faithful men) who can teach others. This training should include practical Christian living—devotions, budgeting, how to love our spouses and children, being on time, etc.

Cell groups are not a program of the church, but an opportunity for spiritual moms and dads to train spiritual children who will soon have their own spiritual families as they become spiritual parents themselves.

Dysfunctional parents vs. healthy parents Only a dysfunctional parent would try to keep his son or daughter at home to help him fulfill his vision. Healthy parents desire to send out their sons and daughters to start their own homes. This is why cells multiply and this is why churches need to multiply and plant new churches. **Fathers desire to see their children grow up** and have their own homes and families.

Spiritual parenting is long overdue The Lord has been using a "megaphone"—trying to speak to His church about spiritual parenting for nearly 2000 years, but the church has been deaf. We have focused on meetings and programs rather than on spiritual fathering. **We all need fathers, and we all need to be fathers.**

10. Applying to everyone

It starts on the grassroots level and extends to all areas of leadership.

- **Cell leaders and assistant leaders** Cell leadership is all about caring for the cell members and seeing them "grow up" into mature ministers and disciplers. Cell members are the spiritual children in the cell.
- **Local church leaders (senior elders, elders, and pastors)** Local church leaders are to be spiritual fathers. Mature fathers release their children to step out and try new things. They protect them, but also allow them to make mistakes. Secure local church leaders have the glory of seeing their sons develop as leaders and succeed.

- **Overseers of local church leadership (apostolic fathers)** Apostolic fathers are experienced mature leaders who will mentor, coach, train, support, trust, and believe in local church leaders or church planters. Their fathering gives the younger leaders a great sense of protection and confidence to go for it and pursue the call of God on their lives.

11. Why the lack of spiritual parents?

Ignorance (clergy-laity understanding) Acts 17:30 says that "these times of ignorance God overlooked, but now commands men everywhere to repent." Now we know we are called to spiritual parenting.

Apathy Getting caught up in the things of the world. Revelation 3:19 (Living Bible) tells us to repent and become enthusiastic about the things of God. We must make spiritual parenting a priority in our lives.

Insecurity "How could God use me?" II Timothy 1:7 tells us God has not given us a spirit of fear. We must believe God has given us spiritual treasures to be passed on to others.

Hurts from the past "I tried and got hurt." Paul said in II Timothy 4:16-17, "...all forsook me, may it not be charged against them, but the Lord stood with me and strengthened me." We have all been mistreated and disappointed. God is looking for us to rise up in obedience, past our fear of getting hurt again. The Bible is full of people who had good reasons to quit!

Lack of modeling God is a father to the fatherless. If you never had a parent's guidance (natural or spiritual) you can make a difference in the next generation! He will teach you. Some of the best spiritual fathers have never had the input of a natural father in their lives.

When we take a step of obedience and become a spiritual parent to others, the Lord will often provide spiritual parents for us. We reap what we sow!

Mario Murillo once said, "To do anything less than what you were created to do will bore you." **You were created to be a spiritual parent!**

Discussion and Study Questions
1. Do you see yourself as a spiritual child, young person or a parent?
2. How can we be dysfunctional spiritual parents?
3. Why are Christian leaders looking for fathers?
4. How do you get a spiritual child to grow up?

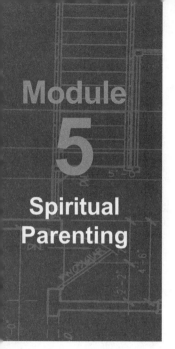

B. Spiritual Mothering

Although spiritual fathering is meant to include both genders, it is helpful to look at the role of the mother-heart of God as it relates to spiritual parenting. God created women unique from men. The differences between men and women are a blessing and bring balance to our lives. We can have a richer and fuller comprehension of the Father's love for us and learn how to relate to others with deeper compassion and intimacy.

1. Definition of spiritual mothering
"Spiritual mothering takes place when a woman possessing faith and spiritual maturity enters into a nurturing relationship with a younger woman in order to encourage and equip her to live for God's glory."
—*Spiritual Mothering* by Susan Hunt

A spiritual mother comes alongside, puts her arm around another woman and says, "You can make it!"

2. The mother-heart of God
God has a nurturing heart. One Hebrew name for God is El Shaddai. *El* comes from the root meaning *might and strength*. *Shad* is Hebrew for *breast* or *many breasted one*. It shows tenderness and the desire to nurture us and make us fruitful (Isaiah 49:15; Matthew 23:37).

3. The Titus 2 mandate (Titus 2:2-5)
Older women should teach younger women Paul was exhorting Titus what to teach, and into this context he exhorted older women to put their energies into training and teaching younger women.

Teach the virtue of maturity God desires women of reverence (who fear God), women who are free from slander, and women who are not captive to addictive behavior.

Spiritually mature women unselfishly give of themselves They submit their will to God and to His leadership. They have learned the secret of Philippians 2:3, "Do nothing from selfishness or empty conceit, but with humility of mind let each of you regard one another as more important than [herself]; do not merely look out for your own personal interests, but also for the interests of others."

4. More than relationship

Spiritual mothering is not just relational. Our focus should be one of glorifying God and yielding to His will and purpose in our lives!

Your focus must be upward Luke 1:35-56 says that when Elizabeth and Mary met, their focus was upward. It was not formed by what they needed from each other. Elizabeth encouraged Mary, who in turn, burst forth in praise to God.

   Philippians 2:3

5. Aspects of spiritual mothering

Vulnerability Spiritual mothering is not just mentoring, but a sense of vulnerability and willingness to open our lives to one another.

Encouraging and accepting As a spiritual mother shares her life openly and encourages and accepts as Christ accepts, the younger woman learns to open up also. It is the character of Christ which qualifies us to be spiritual mothers.

Age differences enrich relationships. Spiritual mothering takes on different aspects in different seasons of life. Age differences often enhance spiritual mothering dynamics.

Spiritual mothering for a specific area of need There are different areas of spiritual mothering. Some may be spiritual mothers to someone only in the areas of family relationships, finances, ministry, etc.

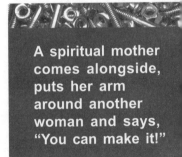

A spiritual mother comes alongside, puts her arm around another woman and says, "You can make it!"

Time frame options Spiritual mothering can take place for a predetermined period of time or be a long term relationship. It can be informal and infrequent or structured. Phone calls and formal instruction can both be effective. The relationship is vital!

6. What hinders spiritual mothering

Suffering from a poor self-image We need to care more about what God thinks of us than what people think. The pressures of life sometimes cause us to conform or act a certain way. A poor self-image makes us fearful of failing or being rejected. But when the fear of God comes on us, we ask what God thinks of us. This brings freedom.

Selfishness can be a problem
"I'm too busy."
"I've raised my children."
"I'm retired."

7. **To start**

Know you are called to do it Spiritual mothering cannot be just another thing on your "to do" list. Christian women today have enough meetings to attend and things to do. Developing a spiritual mothering relationship must be something the Lord speaks to you personally.

It must be birthed in prayer Pray for the women God is calling you to spiritually mother. Consider writing notes or making encouraging phone calls to the women. Ask a younger woman if you can help her in some way or invite her into your home for tea.

Learn to share your "uncloaked" life with someone At the Last Supper, Jesus took off His outer garment and washed the disciples' feet. Before we serve others as spiritual mothers, we must take off our "outer garments." It can get messy when we open up our lives to others, but this kind of honesty is humbling and liberating at the same time!

Discussion and Study Questions

1. What are the qualifications of a spiritual mother?

2. What should be the focus of spiritual mothering?

3. Why aren't there more spiritual mothers around?

4. Where can someone start who wants to become a spiritual mom?

5. Give another Bible example of spiritual mothering.

C. Discipling New Christians

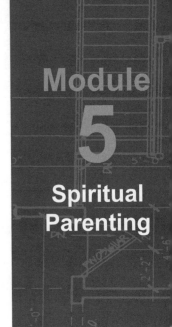

1. Let the Holy Spirit disciple them

A key to discipling new Christians is to let the Holy Spirit disciple them. In John 5:17, Jesus said, "My Father has been working until now, and I have been working." So if the Father is already working in a new Christian's heart, our approach should be to find out what the Father is doing in his or her heart and reinforce and encourage it.

For example perhaps God is speaking to a new Christian about loving his spouse and kids and putting those relationships in order. If we start strongly telling him he has to quit smoking, we could actually be working against what the Holy Spirit is divinely doing in his life at the moment. We could be working against God instead of with Him. Conviction from the Holy Spirit is always precise and specific. God generally deals with people in one area at a time. It's easier for everyone if we cooperate with what God is already doing in the new Christian's heart.

2. Restraint comes from revelation

New Christians must cultivate a relationship with God This must hold top priority. All other relationships must stem from this one. When our relationship with God is healthy and vibrant, the other areas will follow accordingly.

Revelation before restraint Proverbs 29:18 states, "Where there is no revelation, the people cast off restraint; but happy is he who keeps the law." This word *revelation* means *prophetic vision*. So without a vision from God or a revelation of God, there will be no restraint. Sometimes we look at this all wrong. We think that if we practice restraint (don't do this or that), a relationship with God will follow. However, the Bible says the exact opposite.

Vision deters sin Simply stated, the best deterrent to sin for a new believer is *vision*, not *rules*. In fact, Paul wrote to the Christians in Rome telling them the law actually stimulates sin. Romans 7:8,10 records Paul's words: "But sin, taking opportunity by the commandment, produced in me every manner of evil desire. For apart from law, sin was dead...and the commandment, which was to bring life, I found to bring death."

It is the job of the Holy Spirit to convict of sin, not ours (John 16:8). We need to trust that He is well able to do this and not try to do His job. New believers need to hear that they are God's workmanship created in Christ Jesus to do good works, which God prepared in advance for them to do (Ephesians 2:10). They need to understand that God wants to know them personally and intimately.

In I Samuel 25 when Abigail appealed to David to not punish her foolish husband Nabal, she said: "When the Lord has done for my lord according to all the good that he has promised concerning you, and has appointed you ruler over Israel, that this will be no grief to you, nor offense of heart to my lord, either that you have shed blood without cause, or that my lord has avenged himself..." (I Samuel 25:30-31). It worked! Abigail reminded David that he was called to be King of Israel. It saved him from doing something that could have short-circuited that call.

The "restraint" a new Christian needs in order to obey God's Word will come from his relationship with God and an awareness of God's call on his life. If there is no revelation from God, there will be no restraint.

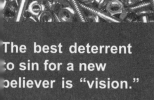

The best deterrent to sin for a new believer is "vision."

3. The Word sanctifies them

John 17:15-17 says, "I do not pray that You should take them out of the world, but that You should keep them from the evil one. They are not of the world, just as I am not of the world. Sanctify them by Your truth. Your word is truth." Jesus said that the truth will sanctify us and that the Word is the truth. If we can keep new Christians reading the Word of God, the sanctification process will be happening.

4. Encourage them

Joseph was a Levite from Cyprus who was such an encourager that the apostles actually changed his name to Barnabas, literally translated as "son of encouragement." He came alongside people and believed in them when no one else thought they were qualified.

He reached out to Saul when he was such a "hot" item that no one else would touch him because they didn't trust him with his history of persecuting Christians. "When he came to Jerusalem, he tried to join the disciples, but they were all afraid of him, not believing that he really was a disciple. But Barnabas took him and brought him to the apostles. He told them how Saul on his journey had seen the Lord and that the Lord had spoken to him, and how in Damascus he had preached fearlessly in the Name of Jesus" (Acts 9:26-27).

Barnabas was an encourager. **New Christians need continual encouragement.**

Module 5: Spiritual Parenting

5. Spiritual freedom

It is absolutely essential for new Christians to experience deliverance from demonic spirits or demonic influences on their lives. Past involvement in things like sexual immorality, pornography, occult practices or false religions can leave demonic strongholds in the lives of new believers. Sometimes a whole weekend retreat (Freedom Weekend) is set aside to identify and renounce these influences. Our experience has been that addressing spiritual strongholds in this way accelerates the growth of new Christians.

6. Developing their gifts

Find out the new Christian's spiritual gifts and look for a place to release them. This will give them a greater feeling of truly belonging to the cell group or church.

Barnabas recognized Saul's gift Barnabas saw a great need for the new Christians at Antioch to be taught, so he recruited Saul to go along with him to teach: "Then Barnabas went to Tarsus to look for Saul, and when he found him, he brought him to Antioch. So for a whole year Barnabas and Saul met with the church and taught great numbers of people" (Acts 11:25-26). He saw Saul's gift of teaching and found a place where teaching was needed.

Barnabas later stood with John Mark and encouraged him Paul was convinced John Mark was a failure: "Barnabas wanted to take John, also called Mark, with them, but Paul did not think it wise to take him, because he had deserted them in Pamphylia and had not continued with them in the work. They had such a sharp disagreement that they parted company. Barnabas took Mark and sailed for Cyprus, but Paul chose Silas and left, commended by the brothers to the grace of the Lord" (Acts 15:37-40). Barnabas's encouragement later paid off as Mark proved himself to Paul and wrote the second gospel. **Spiritual gifts need to be identified and released.**

7. Expecting the best, but accepting the worst

New Christians can be messy, but if new Christians are not allowed to make mistakes and learn, they will not gain spiritual strength. Proverbs 14:4 says, "Where no oxen are, the trough is clean; but much increase comes by the strength of an ox." Even Lazarus came out of the grave with some graveclothes still hanging on.

Love and accept them. Perhaps the best philosophy in handling new Christians is to try to always expect the best, but accept the worst. The general atmosphere of love and acceptance in a cell is a safe place for individuals to step out and try new things. Expect new Christians to do great things, but **be there for them if they crash and burn**. This support is very important.

8. Teaching new believers basic foundational biblical truths

In the same way that children start in kindergarten and progress year by year to graduate from high school, new believers need systematic discipleship. This is usually done most effectively either one-on-one or in a small group setting. DCFI's twelve book *Biblical Foundation Series* and the *Foundation for Life Video Series* are both excellent tools to use for systematic discipleship. If we take a shortcut in the systematic teaching of Bible basics, we will hamper the growth of the new Christians.

Discussion and Study Questions

1. How can we let the Holy Spirit disciple new Christians?

2. How can we recognize what the Holy Spirit is doing in a new Christian's life?

3. How can the gifts of a new believer be recognized?

4. How can we practically help new believers learn the basic biblical foundational truths from God's Word?

5. What are some ways to help a new Christian feel a part of a cell group? A local church?

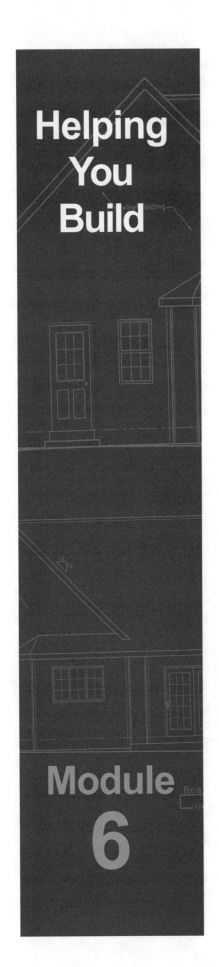

Helping
You
Build

Module
6

Module 6

Mistakes to Avoid in Cell-Based Ministry

During the past 20 years of cell-based ministry, we have made many mistakes and have often had to stop and make course corrections. Why should you make the same mistakes? In this module, you will learn how to avoid three dozen of the major mistakes we have made as we share candidly from our experiences in cell-based ministry.

A. A Dozen Mistakes to Avoid

Our hope is that you will learn from the mistakes we have made. The scriptures encourage us to learn from the mistakes of others. "Now all these things happened to them as examples, and they were written for our admonition, on whom the ends of the ages have come" (I Corinthians 10:11).

1. Lack of clear leadership (Numbers 27:16)

Judges 5:2 tells us that when leaders lead, the people freely volunteer. If God's appointed leaders do not blow a clear trumpet sound, someone else will!

There are three basic principles of leadership:
- God speaks through a leader.
- God speaks through a team.
- God speaks through His people.

Proper leadership will honor each of these principles Every cell and every church needs a leader called by God, a team to serve with him, and a heart that is open to listen to God's people.

2. Lack of clear training for cell leaders and assistant leaders

Paul gave Timothy clear training and encouraged him to train others (II Timothy 2:2). Cell leaders should **meet together for training once each month.** Whenever church leaders stop regular on-going training for cell leaders, effective cell ministry begins to decline!

Training is also **on-the-job-training** as cell leaders mentor assistant cell leaders for future leadership. **A cell-based church needs to have a 4-12 week training track for future cell leaders and assistant leaders.**

 The book *House to House* by Larry Kreider can be used as a training manual to train cell leaders. The *Teacher Training Course* is a practical hands-on tool for mentoring-style cell leadership training. Using video tapes, demonstration and self-evaluation on video, new leaders are trained to teach in cell groups.

3. Compromising the God-given vision

Galatians 1:10 tells us that if we are a slave to men (seeking to please men), we cannot be a servant of Christ. Beware of the migratory flock that migrates from church to church. These people will pressure you to return to old ways of doing things. It is easy to go back to a "meeting mentality." Cell ministry takes a lot of hard work! Vision must be spoken and communicated publicly at least 20 times per year. Habakkuk 2:2 tells us to write the vision down.

4. Forgetting the purpose of the cell is outreach

Allowing cells to lose vision for outreach and evangelism and only concentrating on their needs is a major mistake! The Dead Sea is stagnant because all the rivers run into it and none flow out. Ingrown toenails cause pain to the body because they focus inward.

Remember, the church is not a hospital but an army Armies have medical units for people to get healed, but they are then sent back out to battle. We are called to be fishers of men (Mark 1:17). In the book of Acts, each day those being saved were added to the church (Acts 2:47).

5. Exalting a cell vision above Jesus

Keep yourselves from idols (I John 5:21). Jesus shares His glory with none other, not even a good cell vision. This was the biggest mistake we ever made! We repented to the entire church for exalting the cell vision above Jesus. The test is this: What do we think mostly about—Jesus or cells? What you live for is what you worship.

6. Lack of flexibility

Romans 8:14 says that those who are led by the Spirit are the sons of God. For a season we had only family cells, with no homogeneous groups. This was a mistake. Today we have youth cells, businessmen's cells, family cells, single cells, etc., whatever wineskin is needed for the new wine to give freedom for growth and maturity. Beware of having a "cookie cutter" mentality.

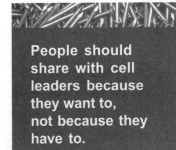

People should share with cell leaders because they want to, not because they have to.

7. Unhealthy control

• **Requiring cell members to always share needs with cell leaders first was unhealthy** Where the Spirit of the Lord is, there is liberty (II Corinthians 3:17). For a while, we told cell members they should share their needs with a cell leader first before sharing with a pastor or other person. This was a mistake! Sometimes people are uncomfortable sharing deep problems with cell leaders, especially those new to the cell. It takes time to build trust. People should share with cell leaders because they want to, not because they have to. If cell members do not confide in their cell leader, the leader should remain secure, knowing that the members will come around when they have established a relationship of trust with them.

• **Telling new people which cell to attend was unhealthy** In the beginning of our cell adventure, we encouraged people to attend the closest cell to their house, mostly because it made practical sense. But we discovered that people want to attend a cell where they have relationships, and this will not always be the cell in closest proximity to their house. The kingdom of God is not built by geography, but by relationship! Cells must be built by relationship.

- **Not allowing cell members to change cells if they didn't fit in was unhealthy** We used to take the stance that if people had relationship problems in a cell, they had to work it out within the cell group. But this creates a lot of unnecessary problems. We learned that it is best to allow cell members to go to a cell where they feel called of the Lord to attend. People are like pieces to a puzzle. They need to find where they fit. Cell leaders, too, must have a sense of faith that the pieces of the puzzle fit.

8. Teaching methods rather than the Word of God

If we only teach new methods, believers will trust in the wisdom of man rather than in the Word of God (II Timothy 3:16-17). For example, if we teach cell multiplication from our vision rather than from the Word, it becomes a program with no life.

Some churches become cell program-based churches! Beware of using cell group buzz words. Explain what you are doing at congregational meetings by using the Word of God. Explain the cell as a spiritual family whose desire is to release its children to start their own families (I John 2:12-14); otherwise cell ministry becomes a fad or the latest church program.

Different times, we have picked up methods from others without understanding the values behind the methods. Each time this has caused a problem. If we understand the values being taught, the methods will follow.

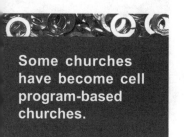

Some churches have become cell program-based churches.

9. Lack of pastoral care and regular contact with cell leaders

Who pastors the cell leaders? It should be pastors and elders with the assistance of section leaders. A section leader is a cell leader who has a fathering relationship with a few other cell leaders. The relationship between pastors and/or elders and cell leadership is crucial. I Thessalonians 5:12 tells us to "recognize" (respect) those who labor among us and are over us in the Lord. Cell leaders cannot be taken for granted. They need regular encouragement and prayer support. Cell leaders must be pastored.

10. Too much emphasis on the cell meeting and not enough emphasis on the relationships

In Acts 2:42-47, The New Testament church was filled with life and fellowship, not just cell meetings. The key is not so much what happens in cell meetings, but what happens after the meeting and during the week.

Build relationships with people outside of the meetings Cell leaders who say, "People don't come to our cell meetings," usually are not building relationships with the people outside the cell group meetings.

- Keep the meetings short (between an hour and an hour and a half).
- What happens after meetings is sometimes the most important. After the meeting, people often share intimately and pray for each other informally as they relate one-to-one.

Module 6: Mistakes to Avoid in Cell-Based Ministry

- Cell retreats are excellent times of building relationships in a casual atmosphere away from life's distractions.
- Cell members should visit each other and be welcomed into each other's homes.
- And remember, the cell meeting should not be a miniature Sunday morning celebration meeting!

Remember, the meeting itself is not the end, it is a means to the end. The end is spiritual fathering!

11. Expecting every assistant leader to be a future cell leader

I Corinthians 12:11 indicates that God "distributes gifts as He wills." It is important to have as many assistant cell leaders as possible so we can train them to be future leaders. Assistant leaders receive from God a healthy stewardship for the cell; however, not every assistant leader will become a cell leader. Some assistant leaders have a supportive gift.

12. Lack of training for new believers and church leadership

New believers need a systematic biblical foundation in their lives, like a first grade through twelfth grade education. Attending a cell group and celebration alone will not give new believers proper training. They need to systematically study the Bible. Also, just because people are cell leaders does not automatically mean they are prepared for church eldership. They need more training.

II Timothy 2:15; Matthew 28:19-20

Resource for training new believers We use the twelve *Biblical Foundation Series* books by Larry Kreider to teach the basic doctrines and truths of the Christian life to a new believer. (They can be used for new believers one-on-one or in a classroom setting.) We also have produced a video series to help train new believers in basic Christianity entitled *Foundations for Life.*

Resource for training cell-based church leadership and church planters For extensive leadership training, the *House to House Church Planting and Leadership School* provides three modules of 45 class hours each on video tape or DVD. Each of the three video modules has a notebook complete with home-work assignments to complete after viewing classes.

Discussion and Study Questions

1. Why is it so important for leaders to sound a clear trumpet call for the church?
2. Which of these mistakes have you personally made?
3. How is it possible for cell ministry to become an idol?
4. At the end of this manual is a brief history of DOVE Christian Fellowship International. Read it now to help you put these mistakes in context.

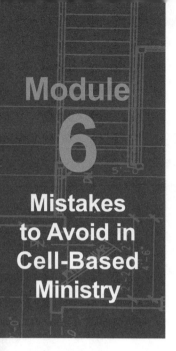

B. Another Dozen Mistakes to Avoid

1. Too highly-structured cell meetings
According to I Corinthians 12:4-6, there are different ministries and different gifts. If everyone expects the cell to be the same each week, boredom quickly sets in.

The cell should not be a miniature Sunday morning meeting The purpose of the cell is completely different! Each cell meeting should be different! We must be open to changing our plans! Stay creative. For creative ideas for cell meetings, see Module 7, B.

2. Lack of preparation for cell meetings (a lack of structure)
Romans 12:11 tells us to not be "lagging in diligence." Without preparation, the cell becomes a social club. We honor people by preparing, and then being open to change as the Holy Spirit leads. A complete lack of structure will eventually frustrate people! Sometimes we say we are obeying the Holy Spirit, but in reality, it is laziness.

3. Telling people which cell to be involved with, rather than allowing the Holy Spirit to show them where to serve
We are not to "lord over those entrusted to us," but we need to be examples to the flock (I Peter 5:2-3). For example, a family once wanted to change cells due to conflict with a cell leader. We told them to stay, and they left the church. Years later, we saw our mistake and asked their forgiveness.

Although there may be crisis cases that are an exception to this guideline, it is best to **allow cell members to go to a cell where they feel they are called.** Cell leaders must have faith and peace about those who are in their cell group. Of course, if there is a deep problem, the church leadership may need to get involved.

4. Setting unattainable, fleshly-motivated goals
In the early days of our church we set multiplication goals for cell groups based more on mathematical calculations rather than on Holy Spirit-led guidance. This was a big mistake.

God is concerned about our motivations We can build our lives on "gold, silver and precious stones, or on wood, hay and stubble," according to I Corinthians 3:11-14, but one day everyone's work will go through fire to reveal if it accomplished anything. We must build only by the Holy Spirit's direction. Because we believe goals are important, we encourage a healthy cell to have a goal to multiply approximately once each year. This is not a bondage but a freedom. If we aim at nothing we hit nothing, but goals must be birthed in prayer and set by the Holy Spirit's direction.

5. Building by geography, rather than by relationship

At one point, we required everyone to go to a cell in their neighborhood. It became a bondage to the people and was unhealthy control. Later we repented to them and encouraged them to listen to the Holy Spirit.

The church is built by relationships, not geography! Sometimes people will bypass two or three cell group meetings on the way to a cell group where they have relationships. Eventually as cells multiply, most people get involved in a cell locally because it makes practical sense. But they will do it because they have faith in their hearts, not because church leadership told them to.

> Ephesians 4:16; I Corinthians 12:18

6. Copying methods from other churches without understanding their values

I Samuel 16:7 says, "Man looks at the outward appearance, but the Lord looks at the heart."

Are we doing what Jesus has really called us to do? Or are we copying a good idea from others? The first time we went to visit the world's largest church in Korea, we learned that the Korean believers were multiplying their cells every six months. We asked our cell leaders to do the same, and we burned out the cell leaders. Glean ideas from others, then lay it all before the Lord and ask Him what to do. Understand why they do what they do! Every culture is different! The same principles and values apply everywhere, but it works out differently in each culture.

7. A lack of accountable connection to the body of Christ

In the early days of our church, a team of church leaders gave us oversight. We later didn't have people outside of ourselves to help us because we thought we could handle things ourselves. Pride had crept in. We had no outside court of appeal.

Connect with others you trust—those who will encourage the vision the Lord has given to you and will speak the truth in love to you.

Where has He connected you? In the Old Testament there were twelve tribes and yet they were all the children of Israel. God has raised up many families of churches (tribes) today. Cells need to be connected to other cells in a local church and churches need to be connected to other churches for accountability and protection.

> II Corinthians 10:13

8. An overemphasis on charts and forms (red tape)

We used to have cell leaders fill out detailed cell reports describing what happened at every cell meeting. We've come to realize that the cell leader's *relationship* with church leadership is much more important than highly detailed cell reports. Although a simple cell report may be advantageous at times, cell leaders need to be honored as people, not just scribes who spend their time filling out a mountain of paperwork. Cell leaders need a relationship with pastors and elders in the church.

9. Not expecting cells to multiply

When we stop believing our cell will eventually multiply, our cell begins to stagnate. Speak about cell multiplication. Pray about cell multiplication. Consult with your cell overseer about multiplication. Expect it to happen!

10. Multiplying cells prematurely without trained leadership

Premature cell multiplication hurts God's people in cell groups. It took years for some of these leaders to recover and lead another cell when we multiplied cells before proper leadership was trained. You are better off having a large cell for a season, rather than starting a new cell without prepared leadership just because the cell is too large. Romans 14:23 says, "Whatever is not from faith is sin."

11. Quickly forcing people into a new cell when a cell dissolves

We are to shepherd the flock over which the Holy Spirit has made us overseers (Acts 20:28). When a cell dissolves, we encourage pastors to have a transition cell led by a pastor or elder for these people to help them eventually find their place in another cell. Give people time to discern where the Lord is placing them. Are we concerned about people or about having a nice cell structure? People are the Lord's priority.

12. Emphasizing house to house and excluding "the temple"

Both celebration (temple ministry) and cell (house to house ministry) are important! There may be times to place more emphasis on house to house ministry, and other times to place more emphasis on temple ministry. At times we get off balance, but that is okay. Every time you take a step, you are off balance. But if you never take a step, you never go anywhere. Acts 2:46; Acts 20:20

Discussion and Study Questions

1. Why must relationships be emphasized over structure?

2. Why is it important to understand the values behind a vision before duplicating the vision at your church?

3. Why is it important to build the cells by relationship instead of geographically?

4. Why must a local church have an accountable connection to the body of Christ?

5. Someone once said that a mistake isn't a mistake unless you don't learn from it. Your comments please.

Module 6: Mistakes to Avoid in Cell-Based Ministry

C. More Mistakes, More Expensive by the Dozen!

1. A lack of prayer

Acknowledge Jesus in the midst of your cell meetings. Healthy cells will focus on prayer! "For where two or three are gathered together in My Name, I am there in the midst of them" (Matthew 18:20).

When there is a fervency in prayer, personally, as a cell, or as a church, God will cover many of our mistakes But when there is a lack of prayer, small problems become mountains. Cells are prayer centers. Cells also provide a natural prayer chain for the local church.

2. A lack of clear communication

Habakkuk 2:1-3 tells us to write the vision down so we can run.

If communication is not clear, people will speculate and draw their own conclusions. People receive information in different ways. Some read their church bulletins while others do not. Some need verbal communication. Use every method of communication possible.

Communication from church leadership should be given to cell leaders first, before it is given to everyone. This honors the cell leaders.

3. A lack of training for pastors and elders

Priscilla and Aquila explained the way of God more accurately to Apollos (Acts 18:24-28). He was being trained. We closed four congregations in 15 years due to a lack of training for pastors and elders of cell-based churches. When we recognized our lack of training for leaders of cell-based churches, we started a *Church Planting and Leadership School* that is now also offered as a video correspondence school and used throughout the body of Christ. This is another level of leadership training.

4. Under-emphasizing the need for leadership

Any truth taken to extreme can become unhealthy. For a season, we overemphasized *relationships* without the need for leadership. Because of this imbalance of teaching, seeds were sown that caused some people to become uninvolved in any church, staying home without spiritual oversight.

Hebrews 13:17

Characteristics that determine a local church
- People in relationship with God
- People in relationship with others
- People who share common vision
- People who have clear leadership established among them

5. Forgetting that all new wineskins eventually get old

Luke 5:37-39 tells us that people often say, "the old is better." After 10 years of cell-based ministry, we found that some youth did not fit in some of our cells and congregations. Several of our wineskins had become old. We must continue to create new cells and congregations to be constantly prepared for the harvest the Lord is bringing in.

6. Not realizing the cell-based church is only one of the ways the Lord builds His church

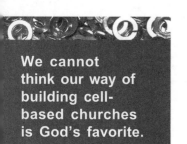

> We cannot think our way of building cell-based churches is God's favorite.

"Therefore let him who thinks he stands take heed lest he fall" (I Corinthians 10:12). We cannot think our way of building cell-based churches is God's favorite. There are three types of churches: cell-based, program-based and program-based with cells. God uses all three kinds of churches! Each church leader must be convinced in his heart as to how the Lord has called him to build the church he oversees.

7. Valuing and focusing more on human relationships than on Jesus and His Great Commission

Human relationships can become idolatry and sometimes dysfunctional. Beware of this "tower of Babel" mind-set when it comes to relationships. Relationships must not become an end in themselves. As we go and make disciples of all nations, Jesus promises us, "Lo, I am with you always" (Matthew 28:19-20).

8. Thinking a good leader must be good at everything

Good leaders find others to resource their weaknesses (I Corinthians 12:18-24). Even Michael Jordan, the famous U.S.A. basketball player, is not good at every sport. He tried to be a professional baseball player and quit.

9. Calling cell leaders "pastors"

A pastor is a gift given to the body of Christ to equip the saints to minister (Ephesians 4:11). Most cell leaders do not have the gift of a pastor. They have a pastor's heart (a shepherd's heart) but are not pastors. When we called cell leaders "pastors," either it was overwhelming to them or they wanted to be ordained.

The role of a deacon is the closest scriptural job description for a cell leader found in the New Testament (I Timothy 3:8-13).

10. Not recognizing the components of a spiritual team

Acts 13:13 speaks of Paul and his party (team) being involved in church planting. Just being friends is not enough. We need to understand spiritual gifts, role preferences, and differences in personalities.

Components needed for a team to be effective
• shared vision
• shared values
• shared procedure
• healthy God-given relationships
If any of these components are missing, the team will not be effective.

11. Not providing a proper connection for missionaries

In Acts 13-14, Paul and Barnabas were sent out of the church at Antioch and later reported back to the church at Antioch. Every missionary from a local church should be "embraced" by a cell group. The cell group writes to them, prays for them, encourages them and serves the missionary practically when on furlough. This causes the cell group to be practically involved in world missions.

12. Forgetting the Lord's mandate to plant new churches

God is a God of missions. He loved the world so much He gave His best–His only Son. If we want the Lord's blessing, He requires obedience: a commitment to missions and church planting.

Healthy churches reproduce and multiply Everything with life reproduces and multiplies. Healthy cells plant new cells, and healthy churches plant new churches.
> Mark 16:15

Discussion and Study Questions
1. Which of these mistakes surprised you and why?
2. Mistakes teach us lessons we will not forget. Share a mistake that you made that you will never repeat again.
3. How can missionaries get lost in a cell-based church?
4. Why is church planting so important?
5. Why is it important to be honest and share our mistakes?

C. More Mistakes, More Expensive by the Dozen!

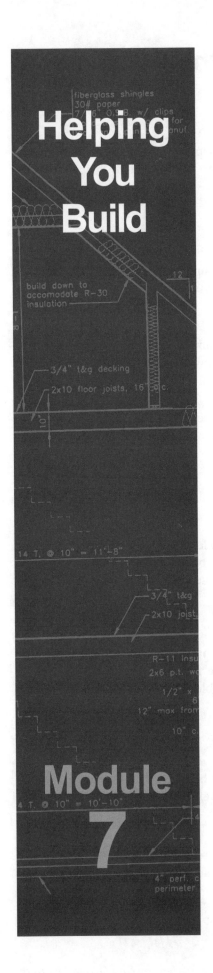

Helping You Build

Module 7

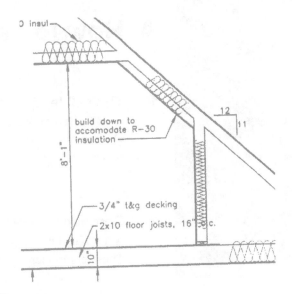

Module 7

Healthy Cell Group Meetings

I n this module, we will learn practical spiritual insights for healthy cell group meetings. Cell life will be examined along with options regarding children receiving ministry in a cell group setting.

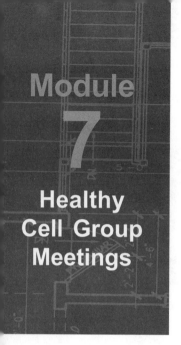

A. How to Lead a Healthy Cell Meeting

1. The cell leader acts as a facilitator

As a facilitator, we coach and give each person the opportunity to participate (I Corinthians 14:26). The cell meeting is not to be a miniature Sunday morning service; everyone should be involved.

2. Components of a cell meeting

A lot of cell meetings will have four major components.

These components are sometimes called the 4W's:

- **Welcome**

  The idea here is to make everyone feel comfortable. For example, start the meeting with an icebreaker, testimony, or prayer.

- **Worship**

  Worship in cell groups can vary greatly. Some cells are blessed with a guitar or piano playing worship leader and others are not. Worship can be facilitated through a CD, by singing accapella, by reading a Psalm or even a few minutes of silent meditation.

  Psalm 150

- **Word**

  Teaching in the cell structure should be on a level with those who are attending the cell. It should be short (10-15 minutes or so), include lots of interaction (involve the children and teens if they are present), and have practical life application.

  I Timothy 4:11

  Although longer periods of Bible teaching are needed in the cell-based church, the cell is not the proper place for this. This need can be met through a church-sponsored school of the Bible or other special times of biblical teaching.

- **Works—prayer and evangelism**

  Prayer in the cell meeting should involve everyone. If the cell leader does all the praying, no one else will learn to become bold in prayer. Cell leaders should be free to share about their own needs as well.

  I Timothy 2:1-4

  Evangelism gives the cell an outward focus. If evangelism is not regularly practiced by cell members, there will be no growth. New believers bring positive change to cells.

  II Timothy 4:5

3. The length of the actual cell meeting

The time before and after the cell meeting is a vital part of cell church life. It is essential to keep the actual meeting fairly short (one hour to one and a half hours). Relationships develop as people are given time to communicate with one another and perhaps pray one-on-one for each other. It is a time for cell members to plan times together outside of the cell meeting. Be sure the cell meeting does not last too long: allow plenty of time for relational interaction. The "meeting after the meeting" is often more important than the actual cell meeting.

4. Food

Food served at the cell meeting can be fun, entertaining and promote relationships. It usually adds an element of warm hospitality. However, food can also become competitive between members or an extra expense for the hosts. Don't allow food to become the focus. If snacks are regularly served at the cell meeting, keep them simple and allow cell members to share the responsibility to bring them.

> Acts 2:42-47

> **Relationships develop as people are given time to communicate and pray with one another.**

5. Spiritual gifts

The cell meeting in the home is an excellent place to teach, practice and exercise spiritual gifts. Cell leaders need to nurture the spiritual gifts evident in the cell members' lives. Give grace when there are mistakes and explain to members the purpose of the spiritual gifts. Regularly ask gifted fivefold ministers to come to your cell to teach, train and mentor cell members.

> I Thessalonians 5:19-21

6. Children

Children in the cell meetings are a blessing to the cell. Inter-generational cells add differing perspectives that keep the cell from becoming one-dimensional. Children can understand the concept of cell. Children age eight and older can be in for the entire meeting. Younger children can be in their own cell or participate for part of the cell meeting in a special children's time. Many creative options for children in cells are presented later on in this Module.

> Matthew 18:2-6

7. Choosing a home

Choosing the right home in which to meet is an important decision. The home should be clean, comfortable, large enough for everyone to meet in one room, and well lit. The home should have owners who can deal with damage and disorder without becoming angry and possessive. The cell should not meet in the cell leaders' home if at all possible. It adds extra responsibility for the cell leader. Allow this to be another cell member's ministry to the cell. Frequently, cell groups will rotate the meeting location between various cell members' homes.

> Matthew 10:11-13

8. Maintaining order

Facilitating the cell means maintaining proper order and structure to the cell. If a cell becomes too loose, very little can be accomplished. However, too much structure will not allow for the freedom necessary to encourage everyone to participate. It is important to not allow someone to take control of the meeting by insisting on a lengthy discussion. Remember, cell leaders are an extension of the leadership of the church. Church leaders can give counsel on problems that may arise. Everything that happens in the cell meeting needs to edify and build up the others in the cell group.

> I Corinthians 14:33; I Corinthians 14:26

9. Preparation

Be prepared for the cell meeting. Lack of preparation and prayer is presumption and laziness. When someone new and unsaved attends the cell, be flexible to change the format and ask for salvation testimonies from cell members.

> Joshua 1:10-11

10. Flexibility

Cells should not become predictable, but flexible. Always be looking outwardly to see how the cell can function to serve others.

> II Corinthians 3:17

Discussion and Study Questions

1. What are some signs of a healthy cell meeting?

2. Why is it desirable for the cell not to meet in the cell leader's home?

3. A natural cell in our body is very liquid and flexible. Describe the similarities with a cell group.

4. Describe some practical ways for the leader to keep pushing the ministry away from themselves to others in the group.

5. What can elders and overseers practically do to make the cell leader's job easier?

B. Cell Life

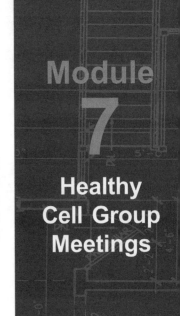

1. Our God is a creative God

In creation, the Lord created thousands of varieties and species of plants and animals; He made each one unique. Each cell and every church should also be uniquely different from every other church and cell. Cell meetings should be fresh and creative. Monotony is boring! Be prepared, yet spontaneous. Although most cell meetings include the same biblical elements, the Holy Spirit will apply these in various ways.

> Genesis 1

2. Cell life

Let's look at a typical life of a cell group over a month.

Week 1—Cell meeting featuring the 4W's.

Week 2—Cell leader meets with the assistant leaders for prayer and planning.

Week 3—Cell meeting featuring the 4W's or cell group meets and takes the whole night to pray for people in their oikos.

Week 4—Cell group has a backyard barbecue outreach with their friends and neighbors invited.

Some cells meet weekly: one week all together and the next week separately as a women's or men's meeting (meeting for breakfast, etc.).

3. Cell ideas

There are many fun and ministry oriented things a cell can do. The following are a few ideas that have been used:

- Spend an entire cell meeting in prayer or worship.
- Parties for any occasion—This is a good time to invite the unsaved.
- Work parties (painting, roof work, seeding a lawn, etc.).
- Prayer walks or drives through your community.
- Women's/men's night out.
- Surveys door-to-door to find families with whom to share the gospel.
- Go Christmas caroling.
- Provide meals to the needy.
- Watch a video or audio tape for a change of pace.
- Share personal testimonies with pictures (before and after salvation, wedding albums, photo albums, etc.). This is a lot of fun!
- Pray for healings.
- Pray for the gifts of the Holy Spirit.
- Share how you are doing in your walk with Jesus.
- Ask the question, "How are you doing with your teenagers/your family?"
- Ask the question, "To whom are you accountable in your Christian life?"
- Have a water baptism with the new believers.
- Take communion.

- Sometimes keep the older children, ages eight and up, in cell meetings. This helps to keep it simple and lively.
- Have a youth leader share about staying young.
- Answer the question, "If I had a million dollars I would..."
- In January, talk about goal setting, personally and for the cell.
- Teach "oikos" evangelism regularly.
- Talk about vision. "What is the purpose of this cell?"
- Have breakfast together Saturday or Sunday morning.
- Go on a weekend retreat together.
- Have cell members read a chapter out of the *House to House* book before the cell meeting and discuss it at the meeting.

4. Do's and don'ts

There are many "do's" and "don'ts" when it comes to leading cells:
- Do encourage input and spiritual gifts, even from the immature in Christ.
- Do meet at least once a month with assistant leaders.
- Do call the people in your cell. Ask, "How can I pray for you?"
- Do show appreciation to the host of the cell.
- Do nurture assistant cell leaders.
- Do speak frequently of multiplication.
- Do kindness outreaches. Give away a beverage, wash windows, etc.
- Don't be afraid to lead, but involve everyone.
- Don't have a "mini" celebration meeting.
- Don't become predictable in your meetings.
- Don't meet in the cell leader's home. Have someone else host the meeting. This spreads out the load.
- Don't counsel the opposite sex alone.

5. Participating in a local cell group

Acts 2:42-47 describes many benefits to participating in a local cell group. We are able to have fellowship and teaching. We can break bread and participate in prayer. We enjoy a commonality of value and beliefs together. We can help meet others' needs or have our own needs met. We can share meals together and enjoy praising God together. The result will be life. When there is life in a cell, there will be growth. People are attracted to life.

Hebrews 10:24-25

Discussion and Study Questions

1. Why should each cell group have its own personality?
2. Which of the cell ideas listed were new to you?
3. What other ideas does this list stimulate in your mind?
4. Which of the "do's" have you not done yet?
5. Which of the "don'ts" have you done?

6. More creative ideas

Available resource: *Creative Ideas For Home Cell Groups* by Karen Ruiz and Sarah Mohler. This booklet has many ideas and tips for cell groups, complete with real-life home cell group stories.

C. Children In Cells

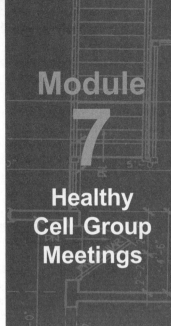

1. God's heart toward children

The Lord values children. Children should take an active role in cell life. Remember, children are the church of today! The perspectives of the parents and other adults in the home cell group will play a major role in determining how each individual home cell group integrates children.

> Psalm 22:9-10; Luke 18:16

2. Various creative options for children in cell ministry

Just as every culture is different, there are various preferences that parents and cell leaders have in ministering effectively to children in cells, and then releasing children as effective ministers in a cell setting. Here are some of the many options for you to consider.

- **Family participation plus separate children's ministry time** Probably 80% or more of the cell groups in North America prefer this option. Children join their parents for the first part of the cell meeting and meet separately for the second part. Children are incorporated into the time of worship, testimonies, and prayer. Then the children receive their own ministry in another room in the home or perhaps in a neighboring home, if it is appropriate.

    Who ministers to the children when they meet separately? Here are some ideas:
    Various cell members could take turns ministering to the children on a rotating basis. Older children can minister to younger children. Parents could take turns ministering to the children. A team can be formed using only one parent from a family so the other parent can attend the meeting. This will help keep unity and continuity in the cell.

- **Total family participation** In this option, children are with their parents for the entire cell meeting. The teaching and worship is geared to the children, and families learn together. Supplemental ministry to parents might be added by an occasional men's breakfast or ladies' outing.

- **Basic child care** Another option some parents prefer is to hire a baby-sitter for their own younger children. This gives the parents a "night out." They can receive uninterrupted ministry and learn to minister to others while their children are cared for at home. This method is more common in Europe.

- **Outside children's ministry** In some cases, a non-cell member comes in each cell night to minister to the children. An offering is taken for the baby-sitter at each cell meeting.

- **Cells serving each other** Some cells share children's resources with one another. Another option is a person with a call to children's ministry could minister to the children in another cell that meets on a different night than his or her own group.

- **Cells with no children's ministry** Some homogeneous cells of senior citizens, youth, singles or married couples without children may not have a children's ministry or focus. Couples with children should not get involved in a homogenous cell of this type.

3. Vital relationships with Jesus for children

Every child can be a mature Christian for his own age. Faith development is a process occurring alongside the other aspects of growth.

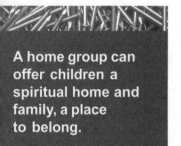

A home group can offer children a spiritual home and family, a place to belong.

4. Benefits for children

A home group can offer children a spiritual home and family—a place to belong. In the home group, children have the opportunity to express love and gratitude to God through worship and praise. Discipleship can also take place in this safe and loving environment. Seeds are sown in children's lives which will bear fruit. Cell groups can be lots of fun for children!

5. Desire of God's power

Encourage children to lay their hands on those who are sick and pray for healing. Children can demonstrate the Holy Spirit's power, just like adults. The Lord honors the prayers of our children.

> I Corinthians 2:4-5

6. Resources available for children in the home cell group

We recommend DCFI's *Biblical Foundations for Children,* complete with 48 lessons, activities and games teaching basic Christianity to children, published by *House to House Publications*.

Other resources (find at your local Christian bookstore):
Close to Jesus, Concordia
100 Series, David C. Cook

Christian children's literature (find at your local Christian bookstore):
What Would Jesus Do? Mack Thomas
Tell Me the Story, Max Lucado
What Is God Like? Mary Erickson
Object lessons, games, devotionals
Adapt Sunday School materials

7. Questions every home cell group must ask

What is our concept of ministry to children?

How can the children be part of our group vision?

How will an unchurched family fit into our structure?

How will we handle disobedient or demanding children?

8. Underestimating the power of ministry to children

Many men and women of God today were profoundly influenced for Christ as children. The Lord in this generation is turning the hearts of the fathers to children, and the hearts of the children to fathers (Malachi 4:6). May the Lord give you much wisdom as you minister to children under the power of the Holy Spirit.

9. Tips for including children in cell group meetings

Kids in charge!

Give each older child a turn at planning cell activities for the rest of the children. Supervised by an adult, the child is in charge. He or she may choose to share a scripture that means a lot to him personally, or choose to have the rest of the children do pantomimes of Bible events and then guess what it is. The child in charge may appoint scripture readers or persons to close in prayer. This gives children an opportunity to be creative and also exercise spiritual gifts.

Fresh ideas

Take some money from offerings taken at the cell to purchase materials such as teacher's guidebooks, stickers, etc., to keep fresh ideas rolling. Visit your local Christian bookstore for new children's ministry tools.

Let's dance

Supply the children with homemade instruments or noisemakers and allow them to express themselves! You could also use a Christian children's music video and dance before the Lord like David did!

Children love to worship

Gear worship time for children, and let them freely participate. Have them pray for the adults. They can later go to another part of the house for crafts and a Bible lesson of their own.

But we only have two children!

If there are only one or two children in a cell group, purchase Bible activity books and fresh crayons for the children to use during some of the adult meetings.

Working with a special needs child

Do you have a physically challenged or hyperactive child in your cell group? A helpful idea is to have a special friend just for that child. This special friend could be another adult or older child who would help this child participate along with the other children in ministry times.

A creative worship workshop for children

Encourage kids to worship the Lord by showing them how! Cell group adults prepare a teaching time for the children. Start by teaching the kids "Jesus Loves Me" in sign language. Hand out cards with the scriptural meaning of each child's name and encourage them to act out their name in front of the group. Act out some of the names of our heavenly Father: Righteous Judge, Lion of the Tribe of Judah, Light of the World and Lamb of God.

10. "Creating a Session for Kids" At Cell Group

Or, "Oh, no, I'm in charge of the children tonight!"

You can create your own exciting children's ministry plan for the children in your home group! Begin with a Bible story or story book; read through it several times. (A children's Bible will tell the story at "kid level.")

Think about:

• What is one specific principle in this story that I want to teach the children?
• How is this specific principle demonstrated in the story?
• How is this specific principle demonstrated in my life? In the lives of children?
• What objects, activities or experiences could I provide to help children understand this story?

Collect visual aids or props that will help you tell the story Build in opportunities for the children to participate. Ask questions; create body motions or sound effects they can do as you tell the story. Remember that young children think concretely, not abstractly; they learn by doing and experiencing.

Create an activity that relates to the story or main principle

• Role play the story with props.
• Make puppets from paper bags, cardboard tubes, or paper plates.
• Use play dough to create objects or scenery from the story.
• Make a collage from magazine pictures or from various types of paper (provide pre-cut shapes or paper to be cut or torn by children).
• Make puzzles. Trace a simple shape related to the story for each child; add a Bible verse; allow children to color, then to cut apart the shape to make a puzzle; children may take turns putting together each other's puzzles.
• Create a surprise bag. Place items related to the story into a bag; children take turns pulling out one item and telling about its relevance to the story.

Your ministry time can include singing, story-telling, discussion, prayer, Bible memory, activities and a snack. Keep things moving and be excited about learning together. It's contagious!

Discussion and Study Questions

1. Why is it important for children to enjoy the cell group?
2. Which of the options do you prefer?
3. How can everyone in the cell be involved in developing a vision for how to minister to the kids?
4. Do you have any tips to add to the list?
5. Use the "Creating a Session For Kids at Cell Group" guide and put together a sample session for kids.

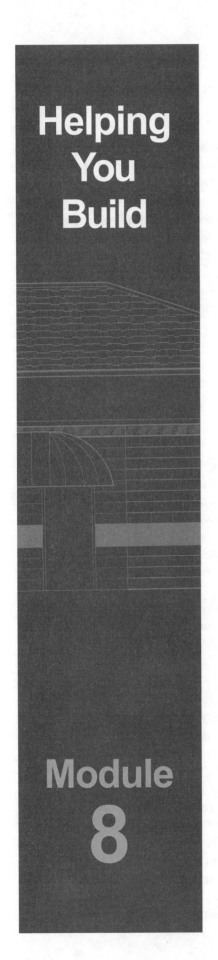

Helping You Build

Module **8**

Module 8

Practical Cell Ministry and Cell Life

In this module, we will look at keys to cell multiplication and discover the importance of Holy Spirit-led flexibility in cell ministry including hospitality and different kinds of homogenous cells that can be started. Healthy cell group growth will also be discussed.

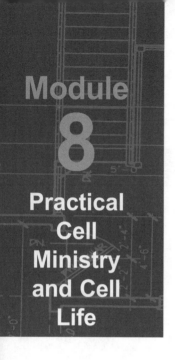

Module

8

Practical
Cell
Ministry
and Cell
Life

A. Cell Group Multiplication

1. A God of multiplication

God blessed His creation and said, "Be fruitful and multiply" (Genesis 1:28). The Lord told Noah to multiply in Genesis 8:15-17 and again in Genesis 9:7. God places a seed inside everything for the purpose of reproduction. The fruit is in the seed.

Everything that is healthy and filled with life will multiply Animals multiply, plants multiply, all of God's creation multiplies. One kernel of corn will produce 1,440,000 kernels of corn by the second generation.

In order for life to be maintained, there must be multiplication The principle of multiplication was an important part of the early church. See scriptures such as Acts 6:1-7, Acts 9:31, and Acts 12:24-25. The result of this growth is found in Acts 13:1-3 when Barnabas and Saul were multiplied out.

Addition vs. multiplication Ten *plus* eight equals 18. Ten *times* eight equals 80! That's a big difference!

2. Practical steps for healthy cell multiplication

• **Speak the vision for cell multiplication** The leaders must keep speaking about multiplication. Vision must be spoken often for people to really "hear" it. A cell leader should be clear from the very first cell meeting that the cell group's purpose is to grow and multiply. It is God's will for the cell to multiply. The cell leader's faith and expectation will set the pace for the cell members. Talk about it as a positive experience. The cell was started for a purpose. Multiplication will fulfill that purpose.

• **Use the analogy of a family** Healthy families have the expectation that their children will eventually grow up, marry and start their own families. The same truth applies to healthy cells.

• **Be open to creative models of cell multiplication** A new cell leader might remain in his existing cell to receive ministry while starting another cell. For example, Bill and his family keep attending their existing cell, even when Bill starts another cell to reach co-workers on his job.

• **Have as many assistant cell leaders as possible** When people become assistant cell leaders, they receive spiritual responsibility for those in the cell along with the cell leader. This is a part of their training.

• **Pour your time into faithful people/future leaders** (II Timothy 2:2). Although everyone is important, Paul tells Timothy to focus most of his time and energy on those who are faithful. See future leaders through eyes of faith (Hebrews 11:6). Without faith, it is impossible to please God. Believe God can prepare them to lead a cell. Jesus gave His best time to the twelve.

- **Have the assistant leaders receive regular training** in cell leadership. Don't expect them to just know what to do. Have them read books on cell ministry and take them to a cell conference or seminar. Mentor them and give them as much responsibility as they feel called to take.

- **When the timing is right,** through prayer and fasting, ask one (or more) of your assistant leaders if they feel called to **start a new cell.** Maybe the cell leaders will start the new cell and the assistant will assume leadership of the existing cell.

- **Share the vision for multiplication with the cell group** and the date the new cell will begin. Ask everyone in the cell to pray regarding which cell they are called to serve with. People will need time to pray and hear from God.

- **Have a commissioning on a cell night** while praying for one another as the new cell is birthed. Sometimes an elder or section leader can be there to help. It makes it more of an important event: "We reached our goal."

- **Celebrate the cell multiplication at the weekend celebration** meeting. This gives other cells faith that their cell can multiply also.

- **Cell multiplication can be accelerated** as church leaders publicly proclaim vision for cell multiplication from the scriptures. Faith comes by hearing and hearing by the Word of God (Romans 10:17). Examples of cells that have multiplied in the church should be noted and celebrated by church leaders.

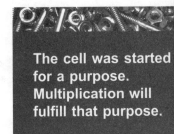

The cell was started for a purpose. Multiplication will fulfill that purpose.

3. Five key ingredients of cells that multiply

In Joel Cominsky's book, *Cell Group Explosion*, he researched cell groups around the world in different cultures, countries, etc. He identified the following five key ingredients of cells that multiply.

1. Cell leaders prayed daily for cell members.
2. There was weekly interaction among cell members.
3. There were clear goals set for multiplication.
4. There was prompt visitor follow-up.
5. Cell leaders made it a priority to prepare for cell meetings.

4. No multiplication?

Sometimes we just don't know what to do. The cell group may seem dead and there are no assistant leaders. As cell leaders and pastoral overseers rise up in faith and pray, the breakthrough usually will come. This has happened over and over again. Pray!

In all honesty, not every cell group has successfully multiplied There have been groups that have been beyond help. Sometimes there is death after multiplication. Death should not be threatening if the organism has run its life course. Even in the natural world, it is easier to birth something new than to raise the dead.

5.   The cell group that has grown too large

The largest cell in the history of DCFI was 85 people! A large cell group can generate large offerings, excellent work projects, and lots of participants in cell activities; however, the negatives far outweigh the positives. In a large cell, not everyone is able to relate to everyone. It is difficult to serve the children. An extra large home and parking area are necessary. People will lack faith to grow any larger and will not bring their friends. Potential leaders are intimidated by the size of the group, and it's overwhelming to those who are in leadership.

What to do with a large cell? An approach could be to begin smaller prayer groups within the cell group. Cell leaders could then mentor prayer group leaders into possible cell leaders or assistants. This was proven successful in the 85 person cell group.

The large cell eventually became a church! The cell leaders of the large cell wisely started five prayer groups within the cell group. Eventually, these prayer groups met in separate homes and became four cell groups. Today, this cell multiplication has birthed a new healthy cell-based church.

6.   Multiplying leaders

The one essential element of starting new cells is leadership. Literally, multiplying cells is multiplying leaders. There is no other way. Leadership training must be a priority. Invite potential cell leaders to special times of training so they can "catch" this vision for their lives.

Discussion and Study Questions

1. How can a church go from addition to multiplication?

2. What can you do with a large cell group?

3. How does "speaking vision" help people?

4. Why would you want more than one assistant cell leader?

5. Why do you have a commissioning when a cell multiplies?

7. Encouraging future leaders

Many potential leaders do not think they have what it takes to be future cell leaders or assistant leaders. They need to be encouraged. At one point in our church, we invited more than two dozen potential cell leaders to a restaurant for a meal, and then we told them about the potential we see in their lives as future cell leaders and assistant leaders. We prayed for each of them individually. One year later, nearly all of them were serving in leadership in cell ministry. Future leaders must be encouraged to take a step of faith.

B. Hospitality and Flexible Cell Ministry

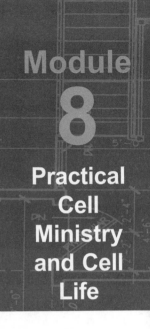

Module

8

Practical
Cell
Ministry
and Cell
Life

1. Hospitality

Definition "Cheerfully sharing food, shelter or spiritual refreshment with those the Lord brings into your life." Practicing New Testament hospitality is critical to experiencing New Testament church life. Cell ministry without hospitality becomes mundane and programmatic.

Hospitality is a wonderful gift given to us to minister to a dying society. Hospitality is something that must be practiced. Women are not the only ones who can minister in hospitality.

As Christians, hospitality is not an option for us: we are to be hospitable
- You shall not mistreat a stranger (Exodus 22:21).
- "Inasmuch as you did not do it to the least of these, you did not do it to me" (Matthew 25:45-46).
- We should be given to "pursuing" hospitality (Romans 12:9-13).
- "A bishop must be...hospitable" (I Timothy 3:2).
- Widows had to show hospitality in order to qualify for support (if she has lodged strangers according to I Timothy 5:10).
- "Gaius my host, and the host of the whole church greets you" (Romans 16:23).

Keep it simple Our homes are remarkable tools to minister to the oppressed. We do not need to serve elaborate meals. Be free to keep it simple. Order pizza! The key is availability.

Recipients of hospitality
- the household of faith (Galatians 6:10)
- the brethren and strangers (III John 1:5-8)
- strangers—they could be angels (Hebrews 13:2)
- the humble (Romans 12:16)
- those who cannot invite you back (Luke 14:12-14)
- a prophet/righteous man (Matthew 10:41)
- a little one (Matthew 10:42)

Atmosphere Jesus said to Simon, "You gave Me no water for My feet, but she has washed My feet with her tears..." (Luke 7:44). Pray that people feel that their feet have been washed; they have been refreshed by being in your home. Take communion together in your home.

The difference between hospitality and entertaining Entertaining says, "I want to impress." It puts things before people. Entertainment looks for payment and compliments. Hospitality says, "I want to minister. This is not my own." It will put people before things and will not look for rewards. Cells that do not practice hospitality only have meetings!

Practical questions regarding hospitality Is it ever right to say "no"? Yes! Jesus did. He knew His priorities (Mark 1:32-38). Remember to not do it alone.

Find people to help you—especially those who have a gift of hospitality. Encourage cell leaders, assistant leaders and all believers to practice hospitality.

What about long-term hospitality? There are different seasons of hospitality for different times of your life. Allow God to show you. Get a clear word from the Lord. Make sure the entire family feels good about it. Write your guidelines and your expectations. Have a pastor or outside person meet with you and with those living in your home to go over these guidelines. This person can serve as an outside court of appeal if any difficulties arise. This helps to avoid misunderstandings and potential personality conflicts.

2. The secret of flexibility and being willing to change

Matthew 9:17 speaks of new wineskins for new wine. We must allow the wineskin to form around the wine. "New wine" can refer to new believers or believers who have experienced a new work of God in their lives. Be open to change in the cell groups. Don't get stuck in a rut!

Birthing is messy A YWAM leader once said, "Either we can keep everything neat and organized, or we can continue to allow the Lord to birth new things among us. Birthing is messy and painful, but there is life!" If you have a mess, clean it up!

Things to remember about flexibility
- Form follows function.
- Blessed are the flexible. They shall not be broken.
- Every snowflake is unique. The same is true with cells.
- The cell often takes on the personality of the cell leader. This is not wrong; it's just a reality. Since there are no two people alike, there should be no two cells alike.

3. The meetings between the meetings (Acts 2:42-47)

There is a danger when we focus on meetings rather than relationships. Instead of a true cell-based church, we end up having a cell program-based church. People should always come before programs and meetings. A cell leader should enjoy being with the people in the cell group.

Relationships In Mark 3:14, Jesus chose twelve men that "they might be with Him." Take people along with you shopping, fishing, or to a football game. Playing games or working on a project together can be a great relationship builder. Have breakfast at a local restaurant before going to work. Remember, the church is built through relationships. Relationship is the key to everything.

4. Prayer—a way of life in cell ministry

In Matthew 14:23, Jesus left the disciples and prayed. They had watched Jesus' example for three and a half years. Prayer was a way of life in the early church.

Prayer in the cell may include:

- **Cover everyone daily in prayer** The cell leader should delegate prayer responsibility to others in the cell so that everyone is prayed for daily.
- **Make early morning prayer** sessions available for cell members. Find out everyone's work schedule first so no one is excluded.
- **If your cells meet biweekly, pray with the men/women during the week you don't meet as a cell** Record your prayer requests and answers to prayer. Don't forget to thank God for answered prayer.
- **Crisis prayer meetings** might be needed. In Acts 12:12, the believers were in Mary's (the mother of John Mark) house praying for Peter who was in prison. Sometimes a cell group or churchwide fast is called during times of crisis, as happened in the Bible when Esther went before the King to appeal for the deliverance of the Jews.
- **A prayer chain** The cell structure is a built-in prayer chain for the local church. Communicate prayer concerns, but avoid gossip.

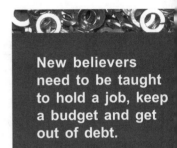

5. Creative ideas for cell life

Don't be predictable! Delegate the responsibility for an outing or picnic to someone in the cell. A section (group of 2-6 cells) may have a volleyball game or a picnic. Relationships are built through playing games and having picnics. Invite unsaved friends! Enjoy life together!

Volunteer time as a cell to serve a local youth center on a regular basis. There might be a work project to participate in or the cell could spend a night building relationships and sharing Jesus with the unsaved youth.

Share meals in each others' homes. Get to know each other by spending time together. Option: Rather than a full-course meal—coffee and dessert is a lot less work!

Weekend cell retreats are great opportunities for the Lord to knit you together to fulfill His purposes.

A great resource for further ideas is the book available through House to House Publications entitled *Creative Ideas for Home Cell Groups* by Karen Ruiz and Sarah Mohler.

6. Discipling new believers

Paul-Timothy relationships A great catalyst to help us grow as Christians is to disciple someone else. Those involved in Paul-Timothy relationships within the cell can meet weekly for breakfast to share about the Word and for practical discipleship.

New believers need to be taught to hold a job, keep a budget and get out of debt. Share what you are learning through discipleship in the cell meetings. In school, we **learn systematically**. The same applies to new believers. They need systematic teaching of the basic truths from the scriptures.

Men should disciple men, and women should disciple women (Titus 2:1-8). We are emotional beings, and discipling someone of the opposite sex can cause unhealthy emotional bonding which can later cause devastating problems.

7. Cells embracing missionaries

Missionaries are members of the cell group living in another area. They are an extension of the cell group. Every missionary in your church should be embraced by a cell group. Notes of encouragement, care packages, phone calls, prayers, and financial support are important to their missionary. When the missionaries are home on furlough, the cell family takes care of them. Missionaries who are embraced by the cell group feel loved! More information concerning "embracing missionaries" is in Module 4, Part C.

8. Homogeneous cells

Definition: of the same or similar nature or kind, of uniform makeup or structure.

Flexible wineskins As children grow, they need new clothes to fit their growing bodies. As the church grows, homogeneous cells provide a flexible "wineskin" for people of all types and backgrounds.

Possible kinds of homogeneous cells Oikos cells focus on reaching those who are a part of our circle of friendships on our jobs, in our neighborhood, family, etc. Same interest cells are those who share similar hobbies. There can be doctor cells, businessmen cells, high school cells, college cells, and ethnic cells. Be sure homogeneous cell members affirm God's grace on other types of cells! Leaders of homogeneous cells should be in relationship with cell leaders who lead different types of cells.

9. Youth cells

Youth cells should not replace youth groups Youth need both a small group (cell group) and a larger group (youth group) to which they can relate. Youth pastors should begin to train a group of young leaders who will start youth cells. Youth cells give opportunity for mature youth to have spiritual responsibility by serving as assistant leaders, etc. Youth cells can meet at school, in a home, or at a worship facility.

Available resource The book *Youth Cells and Youth Ministry,* written by a team of DCFI youth leaders, tells how youth cell groups can provide informal places for youth to develop close relationships and be trained in ministry.

Young and old serve together Encourage youth to glean from the insights of those who are older so they do not fall into pride. The young and the old are called to serve together (Jeremiah 31:13). For more insights on youth cell ministry, see Module 13.

Module 8: Practical Cell Ministry and Cell Life

10. Children's cells

Children's cells can be evangelistic or they can be small groups of children in a Sunday celebration children's ministry. Prayer groups on Sunday mornings can be a type of children's cell. Some children's cells meet at the church facility and some meet in the neighborhood. Children's cells can run simultaneously with the adult cells. More information on children's cells is available in Module 7: C.

11. New believer's cells

If everyone in your cell is a new believer except for the cell leaders and assistant leaders, you can have a new believer's cell. You can use DCFI's *Biblical Foundation Series* books or the *Foundations for Life Video Series* to teach basic Christianity to the new Christians. This cell is focused on helping new believers grow. Another option is for a new believer's cell to be a part of a larger cell and then meet as their own cell at another time.

12. Other types of cells

- **Work cells** a group of fellow employees meet each week over lunch hour at the job site.
- **Midnight cells** for those working second shift.
- **Support groups** These "cells" often meet for a season of time, and then they end because the support group was needed only for a season. These groups must focus on outreach and service as part of the healing process. In most cases, a person in a support group should also be a part of another cell group.

13. The principle of 12: A creative modification

Some believers are involved in two cells. The one cell is a "parent cell" (or leadership cell) where they receive ministry and discipleship while the other is a cell where they are the spiritual parent "fathering" others. Jesus had 12 disciples. If you as a cell leader actually had 12 leaders in your cell and each of these leaders eventually had their own cell of 12 leaders, the multiplication process could continue and hundreds would be discipled. These cells could meet biweekly (meeting in a "parent" cell meeting one week and meeting with those you are parenting the next week). Some cells of this type meet weekly, meaning a cell leader is involved in two cells each week. This modification of cell ministry is often called "the principle of 12" and is presently being used in various parts of the world.

Discussion and Study Questions

1. Explain the statement, "form follows function."
2. What is the reason for same gender discipleship?
3. How is hospitality different from entertaining?
4. What is a homogeneous cell group?
5. Why would a cell group meet at midnight?

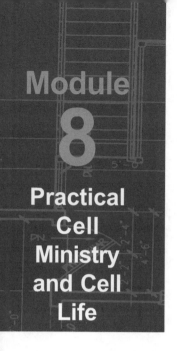

Module

8

Practical Cell Ministry and Cell Life

C. Growing Healthy Cell Groups

1. **Only God can grow a healthy cell group. We sow the seed and cultivate the soil. We trust Him for the increase.**

Jesus said, "The kingdom of God is as if a man should scatter seed on the ground, and should sleep by night and rise by day, and the seed should sprout and grow, he himself does not know how. For the earth yields crops by itself: first the blade, then the head, after that the full grain in the head. But when the grain ripens, immediately he puts in the sickle, because the harvest has come" (Mark 4:26-29).

2. **It all boils down to relationships: prayer, evangelism and discipleship relationships**

The three very basic relational values that every believer, every cell group, and every church should have are prayer, evangelism and discipleship.

Matthew 28:16-20

Prayer is our relationship with our God.

Evangelism is our relationship with the unsaved.

Discipleship is our relationship with other believers.

3. **Understand spiritual mathematics in cell ministry**

In the same way pupils in school learn to add, subtract, multiply and divide, leaders of cell groups and leaders of cell group churches need to understand spiritual mathematics.

Let's look at these four areas and the test that comes with each area

A. Addition

Acts 2:47

Expect people to be added to your cell! Talk about it and pray about it together as a cell group. Without faith it is impossible to please the Lord (Hebrews 11:6). Jesus calls us to be fishers of men (Mark 1:17). We must properly prepare to go fishing. God's will is for your cell to grow.

Who does God want to add to your cell? He wants to add from at least five groups of people:

- **New converts** God desires all to be saved and to come to the knowledge of the truth (I Timothy 2:1-4).
- **New people moving to your area**
- **Christians who have no church home**
- **Babies born into families within the cell group**
- **Misplaced believers in the body of Christ** Some believers are in the wrong cell, and others are in the wrong congregation. If they come from another cell or congregation, it is best if they are commissioned out. Be sure they have pursued peace with their former leadership.

Can we believe for our group to grow?
The test of addition is a test of faith.

B. Subtraction

According to II Timothy 4:10-12, there were those who left Paul's "cell" for various reasons. When people leave, as much as possible, commission them out. This destroys speculation. Some of the reasons people leave:

- **Those who are "sent out" to missions or college** They can still be a part of the cell as you pray for them and encourage them, but for a season they are no longer physically with you.
- **Those who are sent out to another cell or church** Don't take it personally. Allow the Lord to place people in His body (I Corinthians 12:18).
- **Those who just leave or disappear** Jesus left the 99 to search for the one. Pursue them to find out what is happening in their lives.
- **Those who backslide** (James 5:19-20). Again, don't assume you know why they left. Talk to them to find out and communicate clearly with the rest of the cell group.
- **Those who experience church discipline due to unrepented sin** Church elders should help process this scripturally (Galatians 5:19-21, Matthew 18:15-17 and I Corinthians 5).

Are we threatened when someone leaves our cell group or our church? Is our security in Christ?
The test of subtraction is a test of security.

C. Multiplication

In Mark 4:20, Jesus speaks of seed reproducing 30, 60 and 100 fold. We need to expect multiplication to happen in our cell. Acts 9:31 says the early disciples walked in the fear of the Lord, the comfort of the Holy Spirit and were multiplied.

The sower sows in faith See your cell through eyes of faith. Prepare the field/ soil for future multiplication.

- **See future leaders through the eyes of faith** Samuel saw David through eyes of faith. Barnabas saw Saul through eyes of faith. Jesus saw His disciples through eyes of faith. Pour your time into faithful people (II Timothy 2:2).
- **Encourage future leaders** Let them know they can do it (Hebrews 3:13). We all need encouragement.
- **Give future leaders responsibility** (one step at a time). Break responsibility down into simple tasks so people understand it. It is always best to put this in writing.
- **Remember,** the two most important responsibilities of a cell leader is to (1) pray, and (2) train future leaders. Beware of "tunnel vision." See your cell through the eyes of faith.
  Believers multiply by leading others to Christ.
  Cells multiply by starting new cells.
  Churches multiply by starting new churches.
  The test of multiplication is a test of releasing others.

D. Division

I Corinthians 1:10

Division is the enemy's most powerful strategy against the church. Nearly every family, society, nation and church that was destroyed was destroyed from within. Even David had division with his son Absalom. Pray against a divisive spirit and for unity and wisdom (James 1:5).

Be careful to not receive an accusation unless there are two or three witnesses I Timothy 5:19-20 tells us not to receive an accusation against an elder, unless there are two or three witnesses. Titus 3:9-11 says we should "reject a divisive man after the first and second admonition."

Get help from elders and pastors if you are dealing with gossip and division in your cell. The Lord has given them the grace to handle it in a godly manner.

What if you are facing division in your cell? Words of division sow seeds of doubt about the cell group and the cell leader. As a cell leader, face your fears and confront the divisive individual in love. Be sure to bathe the process in prayer and speak with compassion. Maintaining a godly attitude is extremely important (Galatians 6:1-2). Follow Matthew 18:15-19. Division must be confronted. It will not just go away.

Unity does not mean total agreement Unity comes from knowing we are called to serve together. Cell members should appeal to their cell leader and then back his decision. The Moravians taught "in essentials: unity, in nonessentials: diversity, in all things: charity."

Will we respond in loving boldness to situations that could hinder the cell group and our church?

The test of division is a test of character.

Do you believe you have passed these four tests?
Remember, with the Lord we never fail His tests, we just keep taking them over until we pass!

In John 5:19 Jesus said, "The Son only does what He sees the Father doing."
Lord, help us to do the same.

What is the Father doing in your cell group?

> When people leave, as much as possible, commission them out. This destroys speculation.

Discussion and Study Questions

1. Our job to grow a healthy cell group is to _____ the seed, _____ the soil, and _____ Him for the increase.

2. What are the three relational values that every healthy cell group should have?

3. What are the five ways people are added to a cell group?

4. The test of addition is a test of _____.

5. Why is the test of subtraction a test of security?

6. Why would some cell members see multiplication as a negative thing?

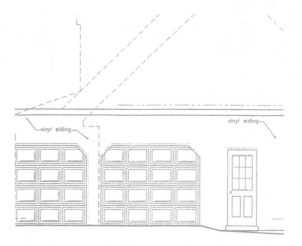

Helping You Build

Module 9

Module 9

Leadership for Cell-Based Churches

T he key to a healthy cell-based church is leadership. In this module, we focus on training and encouraging pastors, elders and others in church leadership as they cast a vision for cell-based ministry, properly pastor the cell leaders, and maintain a clear biblical perspective of a healthy cell-based church.

A. Casting a Vision for a Cell-Based Church

Note: In this Module, we use the terminology of *senior elder* to describe the primary leader of the cell-based church. Some churches may use the term *senior pastor* or another name.

1. Casting vision

Vision comes from values Values must come from the Word of God. You will never change structure until you've changed your values. At the point of crisis, our values will always win out. This is because we naturally return to the things that are deep in our hearts. Our values have to be determined by revelation from the scriptures. The scriptures are the standard for building the cell church. Teach your values from the scriptures. Teach your vision from the values.

"Vision is stretching. Vision is about stretching reality beyond the existing stage. It is not about status quo."—George Barna

Receiving a vision can be difficult It's been said, the Lord gives you a vision and then takes you into the valley of adversity to conform you to that vision. It is in this valley of decision where the future of the vision is determined.

2. The senior elder is the primary vision carrier in the local church

The senior elder must accept the responsibility that *what* he judges to be valuable *will* be valuable. He is called and placed by God to establish the vision of the local church. Acts 20:28 states that as an overseer of a local church, he is to shepherd the church of God. He is called by God to give direction to the local church he oversees.

The senior elder must have the cell vision and be in a cell group himself. He must be convinced that this is the direction for the church to go.

3. The senior elder must have a team around him

A senior elder must realize that he needs a supporting team around him. What God has called us to do, we cannot do alone. What the Lord wants to do is much larger than what we see. There is nothing impossible for the one who doesn't have to do it all by himself. A one man show will never take it as far as it can go. Strong leaders are important, and strong teams are important. It's both!

Acts 13:13

Select and develop other leaders in order to expand the vision You must *develop* them rather than just teach them. *Teaching* is an "impartation of information." *Developing* is "releasing people." In order to release people of like vision, you must impart who you are. It takes *relationship* in order to impart who you are. You must build *relationship* with those you influence.

Acts 20:20; Acts 2:40-47

4. Being in unity with the cell vision

The senior elder's first task in undertaking vision for the cell church is to ensure that each team member has the vision in his heart. This needs to be in place before the vision goes out to the believers in the local church. It will take much time, energy, resource, trust, and patience to do this.

If there is more than one primary vision in the house, there is division. As in the pouring of metal casting (when the molten metal flows into the shape of the mold), there needs to be a melting together of the team—everyone giving up their personal agenda for the purpose of the whole. Any unwillingness or doublemindedness will filter down to the people and breed rebellion and division.

David asked the following three questions of the Benjamites who were coming to join him (I Chronicles 12:17).
1. Have you come peaceably?
2. Have you come to help?
3. Will you betray me to my enemies?

5. Avenues for imparting the vision

You must build through proper communication. Speak clearly and consistently what God is saying. Proper communication is encouraging! Encourage! Encourage! Encourage! Hebrews 3:13

The vision needs to be woven into all aspects of ministry You need to publicly communicate the vision at least 20 times per year for people to grasp it. People need to hear it coming through sermons. It needs to be communicated in various forms of media. Write it in newsletters. Communicate it through testimonies. Declare it visually with banners and overheads. Jacob, in Genesis 30, set branches with white stripes before the flocks, and they reproduced according to the vision they saw. Reinforce the vision in every possible way.

6. Have training and equipping times

Meet together monthly with cell leaders and assistant leaders for training and impartation. Also meet with cell leaders individually to help them apply the vision practically for their cell group.

Continue to provide training for the next step in the leadership process. If the next step is not known, the leadership process will stop. People must know the next step. We must provide it for them—teaching in the classroom setting and, most importantly, on-the-job-training. A clear leadership track gives people incentive.

7. Building with good planning

Set clear attainable goals that can be checked to see if you are on target. It is hard to have unity when there is confusion. Be clear about direction and the speed at which you are going. Timing is the thing most often miscalculated in planning. Be realistic. Have times of evaluation while discerning if you are clearly communicating your heart.

Habakkuk 2:2-3; I Corinthians 1:10;
Luke 10:17-20

Discussion and Study Questions
1. Where do your values come from?
2. Where does your vision come from?
3. How does team unity help to cast the vision?
4. List some practical ways in which vision can be communicated.
5. How does good planning help to cast the vision?

B. Pastoring Cell Leaders

1. Providing a prayer covering for the cell leaders

In a cell-based church, cell leaders become your priority. Next to the Word and prayer, your most important responsibility and privilege is to provide a prayer shield for your cell leaders.

I Samuel 12:23; Galatians 4:19; Philippians 1:9-11; Colossians 1:9-12

2. Spiritual oversight

The role of the elders is to provide spiritual oversight to cell leaders. Cell leaders are an extension of the leadership (eldership) of the local church. A senior elder is like a sheep rancher, having many workers (all leaders) helping him with the flock. Section leaders will give spiritual covering to two or three cells as undershepherds. Although responsibility may be delegated to section leaders, the final responsibility for the people lies with the church eldership.

Hebrews 13:17

3. Communication skills and methods

The responsibility for clear and concise communication lies with church leadership. Both verbal and written communication is necessary to make sure that details are communicated properly. When communication breaks down, there is an opportunity for the enemy to sow distrust. If there is a communication breakdown, leadership needs to take the responsibility to correct it.

If a cell leader misses a cell leaders' meeting, leadership must track them down and give them the information they missed.

I Timothy 4:11-16

When making decisions that affect the church, talk to cell leaders first
This shows that they are valuable. Honor cell leaders by keeping them informed.

4. Church discipline

Church discipline when needed is the eldership's responsibility. Section leaders always need to get the elders involved in this process. Matthew 18:15-20 really works. It has been provided by God to aid in the discipline process. It is important to understand that the goal of any and all discipline is *restoration*. More information on church discipline is included in Module 11:C.

I Corinthians 5:1-13

5. How to deal with problems in cells

Cell leaders are appointed by the elders; therefore, if there are problems, the elders cannot abdicate their responsibility. When dealing with problems within these cells, speak with compassion and confidence. God has given you the grace as a leader to walk through any difficult situation.

Here are six steps to resolve people problems
• Gain agreement that a problem exists
• Discuss alternative solutions
• Mutually agree upon an action
• Identify consequences up front
• Follow up and measure progress
• Reward any achievement or fulfill any consequence—acknowledge the behavior (I Corinthians 1:10-11)

6. Dealing with divisiveness

In the case of divisiveness, the Bible tells us to admonish such an individual. The Lord hates divisiveness (Titus 3:10-11). It is important to understand that God is a reconciling God. He is in the business of restoration. When there is a difficulty, we are to restore "such a one with a spirit of gentleness" (Galatians 6:1). This is important because sometimes people don't even realize their actions are divisive.

7. Practical issues

Baptisms, communion, baby dedications, and hospital visitations can all take place at the cell level. Cell leaders must be trained to be effective in these areas. Even Paul encouraged others to baptize new believers. Good cell overseers will make sure the cell leader has the training to move ahead with confidence in these practical areas.

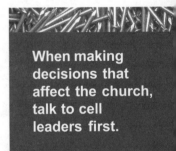

When making decisions that affect the church, talk to cell leaders first.

8. Cell leaders' meetings

Jesus "called His disciples to Him" for training (Matthew 10:1). To train and to maintain vision, there must be regular and consistent impartation given to cell leaders and assistant leaders. This is best accomplished by having monthly cell leaders' meetings. Make these meetings a time of communication, training, and dealing with issues that affect the whole church. As a leader, you should arrive early and stay until the last person leaves. Your cell leaders need to know you are available. Always include prayer in these meetings.

9. The need for specialists and resources

Don't try to do everything yourself. Use specialists and resources available in the body of Christ. Bring in fivefold ministers to train and equip people for the work of ministry. God provides gifts to equip us so that there would be no one lacking among us. Many times a cell leader will receive special revelation by an outside minister you may bring in who says the same thing you have been sharing, but in a different way.

> I Corinthians 12:4-6; Ephesians 4:11-12

10. Premarital and postmarital counseling

Premarital and postmarital counseling provides an excellent opportunity for cell leaders with healthy marriages to minister. When taking couples through premarital counseling, a couple-to-couple mentoring relationship is built that will last for years to come. If a single person is leading the cell, a couple from the church can fulfill this need.

> Titus 2:1-8

An excellent tool for marriage counseling we recommend: *Called Together, A Marriage Preparation Workbook* by Steve Prokopchak.

11. Live the vision

Your cell leaders need to see you practically involved in prayer, evangelism and discipleship. The vision for cell church should come out naturally in conversation. The senior elder or pastor has to be involved in a cell group to model healthy cell group life.

> I Corinthians 11:1

Discussion and Study Questions

1. Why should decisions be communicated to cell leaders before the rest of the church?

2. Why is it appropriate for an elder to be involved in church discipline?

3. How do you deal with divisiveness in a cell group?

4. What is the purpose of cell leaders' meetings?

5. How can a senior leader live the cell vision?

C. A Snapshot of a Healthy Cell-Based Church

"The Eight Essential Qualities of a Healthy Church" was developed by Christian A. Schwarz, from the Institute for Church Development in Germany. They recently gave the findings of the most thorough study to date on the causes for church growth. This study took three years and included data from more than 1000 churches in 32 countries located in five continents. The survey questionnaire, which was translated into 18 languages and completed by 30 members from each participating church, generated 4.2 million responses.

This massive study dealt with the question, **"What are the essential qualities of a healthy growing church, regardless of culture and theological persuasion?"**

An amazing conclusion Christian and his team came to an amazing conclusion. Just as crops grow all by themselves if the weeds are taken out of the way, the same principle applies to our churches. Jesus said, "The kingdom of God is as if a man should scatter seed on the ground, and should sleep by night and rise by day, and the seed should sprout and grow, he himself does not know how. For the earth yields crops by itself: first the blade, then the head, after that the full grain in the head. But when the grain ripens immediately he puts in the sickle, because the harvest has come" (Mark 4:26-29).

It is our task to minimize the obstacles to growth Christian summarizes, "We should not attempt to manufacture church growth, but rather release the biotic potential which God has put into every church. It is our task to minimize the obstacles to growth–both inside and outside the church. Since we have very little control over outside factors, we should concentrate on the removal of obstacles to church growth and multiplication of churches. Then church growth can happen all by itself. God will do what He promised to do. He will grant growth" (I Corinthians 3:6).

What are these obstacles to growth in the church of Jesus Christ? Or perhaps, we might ask, what are the essential qualities of a healthy growing church?

The findings of this research project highlight eight biblical qualities for a healthy growing church:

1. Empowering leadership

Leaders of healthy, growing churches concentrate on empowering other Christians for ministry (II Timothy 2:2). They do not use lay workers as "helpers" in attaining their own goals and fulfilling their own visions. Rather, they invert the pyramid of responsibility for ministry so that the leader assists Christians to attain the spiritual potential God has for them. These pastors equip, support, motivate, and mentor individuals, enabling them to become all that God wants them to be. Cells give a framework providing leadership with a platform to serve.

2. Gift-oriented ministry

The role of church leadership is to help its members to identify their gifts and to integrate them into appropriate ministries. When Christians serve in their areas of giftedness, they generally function less in their own strength and more in the power of the Holy Spirit. Thus ordinary people can accomplish the extraordinary. Cells provide an excellent opportunity for everyone to identify and use their gifts.

> Romans 12:4-8

3. Passionate spirituality

Are Christians in our church "on fire?" Do they live committed lives and practice their faith with joy and enthusiasm? Do they love to pray? The Lord is restoring passionate spirituality to His church in our day. Passionate spirituality comes from every believer realizing his or her responsibility to pray and to reach the lost with the compassion of Christ. Cells encourage personal responsibility and integrity in relationship with God.

> Matthew 5:6

4. Functional structures

There are those who believe structure and life are opposites. The truth is that both are needed. Interestingly enough, biological research reveals that dead matter and living organisms are not distinguished by their substance, as some people might think, but by the specific structure of the relationship of the individual parts to each other. Whenever God breathes His Spirit into formless clay, both life and form spring forth. A comparative creative act occurs whenever God pours out His Spirit within the church today—thus giving it structure and form. New cells are flexible structures in our day for the new life He is bringing to our churches. Both new wine and new wineskins are needed.

> I Corinthians 12:4-6, 28

Do Christians in our church live committed lives and practice their faith with joy and enthusiasm?

5. Inspiring worship service

Is the worship service in your church an inspiring experience for the participants? Cell churches who react to and minimize anointed public worship services are shooting themselves in the foot. Paul taught them publicly, and from house to house (Acts 20:20). We need both! The celebration worship service should be seen as believers in a cluster of cells coming together to celebrate what the Lord is doing in each cell and in the life of each believer.

6. Holistic small groups

Christian Schwarz stated, "If we were to identify any one principle as the most important, then without a doubt it would be the multiplication of small groups. They must be holistic small groups which go beyond just discussing Bible passages to applying its message to daily life. In these groups, members are able to bring up those issues and questions that are immediate personal concerns." Nothing can be more important than having a passion for Jesus and for His kingdom to be built, but healthy cell groups working together as spiritual families provide a tremendous support system for the kingdom of God to be advanced.

>Acts 2:42-47

7. Need-oriented evangelism

C. Peter Wagner, widely recognized as a leading authority in the field of church growth, teaches that the gift of evangelism applies to no more than 10 percent of all Christians. However, we are all called to use our gifts to fulfill the Great Commission. It is the task of each Christian to use his or her gifts to serve non-Christians with whom one has a personal relationship, to see that they hear the gospel, and to encourage contact with the local church. Cells provide both the opportunity for each believer to be encouraged to share his faith regularly and the prayer and accountability base he needs to live a life of obedience to the Great Commission of our Lord.

>II Timothy 4:5

8. Loving relationships

Growing churches possess, on the average, a measurably higher love quotient than stagnant declining ones. Healthy growing churches practice hospitality as believers invite others into their homes as a normal part of their Christian lives. People do not want to hear us *talk* about love, they want to *experience* how Christian love really works. And the cell group provides a natural way for relationships to be developed.

>I John 4:7-12

All of these qualities are essential for a healthy growing church All are needed. Take a quick evaluation of your church and your cell group. Are there any obstacles to be removed for your church to experience healthy growth? The engine, carburetor, and transmission of your car may all be working fine, but if you have a flat tire, you must remove this obstacle in order for your car to function properly. Whether we are focusing on reaching boomers, busters, or the millennial generation, the cell-based church is an ideal model to foster these eight essential qualities. However, it takes more than being a cell church. It takes all of these essential qualities working together to get the job done.

Excerpts taken from *Natural Church Development* by Christian A. Schwarz (Church Smart Resources).

Discussion and Study Questions

1. Why is it important to help people determine their spiritual gifts?
2. Describe "passionate spirituality" in your own words.
3. What is the essential element of small groups that really helps people?
4. Give an example of need-oriented evangelism.
5. Why are loving relationships important to people?

Helping You Build

Module 10

Training Cell Group Leaders

In this module, we discover how pastors and leaders can develop clear training tracks for training cell leaders in their local church. Practical insights are given to train cell members to teach from the Bible effectively as we look at Jesus' model of teaching, training and leadership.

Module 10

A. How to Train Cell Leaders

1. Focus on training faithful assistant leaders to be future cell leaders

This is one of the most crucial things a leader can do to assist a cell leader. Assistant leaders will help carry the leadership load as well as possibly lead a new cell when the cell multiplies. Both make the cell leader's job easier.

An assistant leader needs to feel valued as a person and close to the cell leader. The cell leader needs to feel valued as a person and close to church leadership.
> I Peter 5:2-5

2. Encourage cell leaders to look for assistant leaders with these qualifications

- **A calling** God has spoken to them about leadership. They are not just responding to your invitation.
> Ephesians 4:1

- **Character/Teachability** For them to be trained, they must have good character and be teachable. That means they have a genuine desire to learn and receive from you.
> I Timothy 3:8-13

- **Loyalty** God will take loyal people and anoint them as they grow in God, but there are no guarantees that He will take anointed individuals and make them loyal.
> II Timothy 2:2

- **Servanthood** To be great in the kingdom, you must be a servant. Look for those who come early and stay late.
> Philippians 2:5-8

- **Anointing** There is a discernible anointing in their lives. Anointing is the divine power to do what God has called you to do. It might need developing, but you as a leader can see it.
> Luke 4:18

3. Value cell leaders and assistant leaders

A cell leader or assistant leader's value is the same as any other person, but you are honoring a position. It is important that people feel valued, not for their gifting, but as a person (James 2:9). Be available to spend time with them.

4. Model leadership truths to stimulate their leadership development

The following points are taken from the story of Jonathan and his armor bearer in I Samuel 14:1-23. Please read these scriptures.

Teach them to dream (verse 6). Share with them dreams that you have that might even seem foolish. Realize how foolish Jonathan's plan of attacking the Philistines really was.

Teach them it is the Lord and not you In developing cell leaders, it is crucial that they understand that it is the Lord that does the work. We are just cooperating with Him. If they truly understand this concept, they will be able to be released in a greater capacity in the area of dreams (vision).
  Galatians 2:20

Give them the freedom to choose (verse 7). Let them decide if they want to go with you. If it is not their decision, in the heat of the battle, they may run.

Outline your strategy (verses 8-10). Learn to think out loud with cell leaders and assistant leaders. We do so many things that are second nature to us and we need to remember that someone just learning doesn't always think like we do.

Set the course (verse 12). Define roles and responsibilities. Jonathan told his armor bearer to follow him.

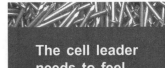

The cell leader needs to feel valued as a person and close to church leadership.

Lead through the tough stuff (verse 13). Jonathan led where it was difficult. Don't be afraid to lead when it gets hard. When you are training, let the assistant leaders start with the easier things. Go before them expecting them to come behind you.

Have a debriefing time Take time with them after a meeting or a ministry time to answer questions and give input. Jesus did this constantly with His disciples.
  Luke 9:10

Teach them to hear the Holy Spirit Many people can hear the devil's voice of doubt clearer than they can the Holy Spirit's. The most important thing you can teach the assistant leaders is to hear what the Holy Spirit is saying so the "communion of the Holy Spirit" is with them (II Corinthians 13:14).

Send them out to fight their own battles Training them without releasing them will cause discouragement and frustration. Send them out to start their own cell group.

5. Watch out for certain things while training leaders

Jealousy Teach them to rejoice with those who rejoice. When someone makes a home run in a baseball game, the whole team benefits. Teach them to have a kingdom mentality.
  Luke 9:49-50

Selfish ambition (James 3:13-17). Our motivation for ministry should not be, "What's in it for me?" but rather, "How is the Holy Spirit asking me to serve?"

Unteachableness Unteachableness will stop growth faster than any other behavior. It cuts off the flow of the Spirit.
James 3:17

Insecurity One of the sure signs of insecurity in future cell leaders is when their lives center around their teacher. We develop others to trust in Jesus, not to be focusing on us.

Holding vs. releasing As leaders, we are called to release people to be who God created them to be. They can only reach their full potential in God as we encourage, equip and release. Jesus said, "Freely you have received, freely give" (Matthew 10:8).

Classroom training It is important that cell leaders receive classroom training as well as on-the-job-training. Conduct weekend training seminars or special cell leaders' training sessions one night a week for a few months. The *DCFI House to House Church Planting and Leadership Video School, Module I*, can be used for this training course. You also may want to teach from this manual to train potential cell leaders.

Discussion and Study Questions
1. What should you look for in an assistant cell leader?
2. How do you practically communicate to a cell leader that you value them?
3. Describe the relationship of Jonathan and his armor bearer.
4. How can you detect insecurity in a future leader?
5. What does classroom training do that mentoring does not?

B. Training Cell Leaders to Teach Effectively

1. An effective teacher loves people

To be an effective teacher, you must have a genuine love for the people you teach. Loving and serving people overflows out of your love for Jesus that floods your heart with caring and compassion for others. While you teach, the warmth of your unique God-given personality will flow out to the group.

> John 13:1

2. Pray, pray, pray

In order for a teaching to become part of our lives so we can impart it to others, it must be bathed in prayer. Luke 6:12 tells us how Jesus prayed: "Now it came to pass in those days that He went out to the mountain to pray, and continued all night in prayer to God." Prayer transforms your teaching from dry information to life-changing impartation.

3. Teach the Word, not your opinions

Someone once said that opinions are like the nose on your face; everyone has one! A teacher needs to teach the Word of God, not ideas and opinions about the Word. The Word is where the authority lies. The fact is, our opinions will never change anyone's life; only the Word of God changes lives.

> John 8:31-32

4. Use visuals and illustrations

Most people are visual learners. Mental pictures always help to focus a message and make it easier to remember. A man in the African bush once asked an American what the Empire State Building looked like. The American used a mental picture to which the African bushman could relate. He said it looked like 200 mud huts stacked on top of each other with a banana leaf sticking out the top. To a man who had never seen a tall building, it was the closet thing he could understand. Be practical in your teaching and use illustrations people can readily understand.

> Mark 4:33-34

5. Please, don't use Christian-eze!

Use plain, everyday language when you teach, not church-y language that only seasoned Christians can understand. Words like "sanctification" and "redemption" will not be understood by a young Christian unless you take the time to explain the words to them.

> Acts 4:13

6. Speak the truth in love

Don't speak down to the people you are teaching. This often happens when a teacher preaches at his audience instead of including them as he teaches. This creates a chasm between him and the group. Instead of saying, "You need to change," say, "We need to change."

Ephesians 4:15

7. Teach with enthusiasm; it's a sin to be boring

Did you ever sit in a Sunday School class, Bible study, or other church meeting while the speaker droned on endlessly and almost put you to sleep? Although what was said concerning God's Word was true, it may have been presented in a rambling fashion, making no sense. Or maybe it was merely a list of facts, like a grocery list, not likely to hold anyone's attention. Make a decision to teach with enthusiasm. Practical, fresh examples from your life will add a spark to your teaching.

Colossians 3:23

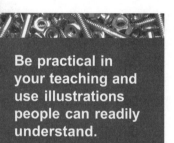

Be practical in your teaching and use illustrations people can readily understand.

8. It's normal to be nervous; teach in faith

A study listing what people are most afraid of showed that speaking before a group is the most fearful thing in life—worse than "death, insects and bugs, flying, sickness, or loneliness." If you have never taught before, it may be scary at first, but even experienced teachers get nervous—it's normal! The experienced teacher has simply learned to make use of his tension and put it to good use. For example, he may turn the nervousness into greater expressiveness.

Hebrews 11:6

9. Speak with authority

You have received authority from God as a believer in Jesus Christ to share His Word. Jesus, the most effective teacher who ever lived, spoke with authority. "...On the Sabbath He entered the synagogue and taught. And they were astonished at His teaching, for He taught them as one having authority, and not as the scribes" (Mark 1:21-22). Jesus amazed the people because He taught differently from the other religious leaders of His day. He knew where He got His authority, and it showed.

10. Be prepared

Please take time to prepare the teaching for the group you are planning to teach. A quick five-minute glance at teaching notes and a hurried prayer does not constitute "preparation." Rambling is distracting and bores people—and we already learned that it is a sin to be boring!

Joshua 1:10-11

11. Be personable

Any audience, including a small group (cell group), usually reflects the attitude and manner of the teacher. Think about it. If you are funny, people will be relaxed and smiling at your humor. If you are stilted and nervous, the audience will be uncomfortable, holding its collective breath. And, of course, if you are boring, they will be fast asleep!

Ephesians 4:29-30

12. Receive constructive criticism

No teacher is beyond the need for improvement. Most teachers want to know if they are using excessive hand gestures or repeating the phrase "you know" constantly. After preaching or teaching, ask people to give you constructive criticism so that you can grow in your ability to teach. There is usually at least a bit of truth in every criticism you receive. A good teacher learns to accept criticism and profit by it. Discovering your weaknesses is the first step to correcting them (I Peter 5:5-6).

13. Teacher Training Course is available

DCFI has a comprehensive *Teacher Training Course* available. This field-tested teaching course is designed to encourage and train those who are new at teaching

God's Word and to help good teachers become even better. It utilizes an apprentice approach designed for a teacher trainer to take four students through a hands-on course to train them to teach. Students critique themselves via videotape and multiply their teaching skills.

Practical and simple, this four-hour long course will help any willing person learn basic principles of teaching from the example of Jesus, the greatest Teacher who ever lived. Along with learning that teaching can be fun, students will learn to teach in a way that will bring life into their cell meetings. Everything you need is in this teaching packet. Expect the Lord to help you and each student to become dynamic teachers of His Word!

The Teacher Training Course is available through *House to House Publications.*

Much of this teaching was taken from the book *Teaching With Confidence* by Larry Kreider. It is available through *House to House Publications.*

Discussion and Study Questions
1. Why do we train cell leaders to teach using practical examples from their lives?
2. How can we overcome nervousness?
3. What role does preparation play in teaching?
4. What role does enthusiasm play in teaching?
5. Why is it important to have faith when you are teaching?

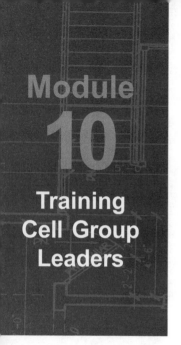

C. Training According to the Jesus Model

1. **Follow Jesus' example and method of training**

    Let's look at Jesus' method of training. Jesus followed a four-step process. First, He **declared** to them the information. Then, He **demonstrated** the task for them to observe. Next, He **directed** them to try it. And last, he **debriefed** them, discussing how it went.

    A scriptural example from the book of Luke "After this, Jesus traveled about from one town and village to another, proclaiming (**He declared**) the Good News of the kingdom of God (Luke 8:1a).

    "The twelve were with Him and also some women who had been cured of evil spirits and diseases..." (**He demonstrated**, Luke 8:1b-2).

    "Then He called His twelve disciples together and gave them power and authority over all demons, and to cure diseases...So they departed and went through the towns, preaching the gospel and healing everywhere" (**He directed them to go**, Luke 9:1, 6).

    "When the apostles returned, they reported to Jesus what they had done..." (**He debriefed** with them, Luke 8:1; 9:1,6,10).

2. **Declare**

    Jesus proclaimed the kingdom of God to the disciples. He taught them what it was and how it worked. This is the kind of training we usually do the most—the how-to, the information, the training seminar or learning about cells from a manual like this. But this is only the beginning.

3. **Demonstrate**

    Demonstration is the practical modeling of the kingdom of God. Jesus modeled healing the sick, casting out demons and raising the dead. The people you are training have to see you minister. Take them along when you are meeting with someone or have them join you for prayer before a cell meeting. Have them sit in with you when you visit a cell that is not growing. Ask them for their input. What would they do differently if they were you? What are their observations?

4. Direct

Jesus commissioned His disciples to go do it: "Okay, boys, it's your turn to try it."
Delegate assignments to those you are training after they have seen you do it.
Start with small things and increase to greater responsibilities. Ask them to pray
at the close of a meeting. Another night, ask them to lead a prayer time. Give
more and more cell responsibility to them. Let them be responsible for the entire
meeting if the cell leader is away.

5. Debrief

Jesus debriefed with His disciples after He sent out the twelve and the seventy-
two. In the latter case, he had to correct them for overconfidence. This time is so
important. Listen to the people tell you about their "new," successful idea that you
have used a dozen times. Help them analyze "why" if they have failed. This
debriefing time shows that you are interested in them as people, not just as potential leaders on whom you can unload some of your responsibility.

6. Hand over the ministry to those you are training

Keep handing the ministry over to those you are training with this mentoring-style
leadership. See people try new things for the first time and succeed. This is how
the Ephesians 4:12 ministry of "equipping the saints for the work of ministry" is
supposed to work.

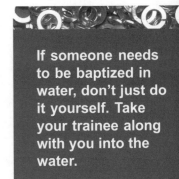

If someone needs to be baptized in water, don't just do it yourself. Take your trainee along with you into the water.

Take your trainee along If there is a need for someone to be baptized in water,
don't just do it yourself. Take your trainee along with you into the water. Then the
next time there is a need for water baptism, you both go in the water, but this time,
your trainee leads and you help him. And finally, the next time he can be
responsible for the baptism himself and take along the next person he is training.
Get the picture?

Discussion and Study Questions

1. Describe how you would use Jesus' model to teach cooking?
2. From your perspective, what part of the Jesus model is most lacking in the body of Christ?
3. What is the significance of the debriefing time?
4. Why do some leaders find it so hard to hand over ministry to others?
5. How does the Jesus model compare to classroom training

C. Training According to the Jesus Model

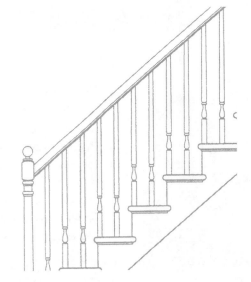

Helping You Build

Module 11

New Testament Church Government

for a Cell-Based Church

In order for cells to function properly in our churches, it is essential to follow the New Testament pattern of church government. In this module, we learn about the New Testament pattern of cell and celebration, leadership and decision-making, and healthy authority and accountability in the local church. Church membership and discipline and restoration are also covered.

Module 11

A. New Testament Church Leadership

1. The need for healthy leadership

The Bible says, "when leaders lead, the people freely volunteer!" (Judges 5:2 Living Bible).

Proper New Testament leadership is essential! In Acts 20:17, Paul called for the elders in Ephesus to hear his final instructions, not the whole church. Elders protect, direct and correct the flock they serve. They are the under shepherds serving under the great Shepherd, our Lord Jesus Christ.

Elders give an account. Hebrews 13:17 tells us elders must give an account to the Lord for how they serve as shepherds and overseers.

2. Servant leadership on three levels

Jesus set the example. He came not to be ministered unto, but to minister (serve) (Matthew 20:25-28). In John 13:1-17, Jesus washed the disciples' feet, modeling servant leadership. He calls us to do the same.

Three levels of New Testament leadership:

• **Cell leaders** give protection, oversight and training to cell members.

• **Local church elders** give protection, oversight and training to cell leaders.

• **Apostolic leaders** give protection, oversight and training to local church elders.

Leadership (on all levels) is characterized by servanthood Each leadership team should model servanthood. The senior leader is appointed by God to serve the team. Leadership principles that apply to any one level of leadership will also apply to the other two levels of leadership.

3. The two categories of New Testament leadership

• **Governmental leadership** In Acts 15, we see apostles and elders mentioned various times. These leaders had positions of governmental leadership in the early church. The governmental leaders have a sphere of authority and responsibility.

   II Corinthians 10:13; I Timothy 3:1

• **Fivefold leadership (equipping)** In Ephesians 4:11-12, we see the equipping leaders mentioned: apostles, prophets, evangelists, pastors and teachers. The fivefold leaders in the New Testament seem to have mainly had a traveling emphasis, and were responsible to equip the saints to minister to others and to encourage the body of Christ.

4. Most fivefold ministers have a mixture of gifts

For example, someone may be an evangelist/teacher or a pastor/evangelist. These vital fivefold ministry gifts equip and minister to individuals both in cells and at the congregational level.

Governmental and fivefold leaders work together Both apostles and elders (governmental) along with apostles, prophets, evangelists, pastors and teachers (fivefold leaders) are needed and must work together for the church to come to maturity. None should disregard or devalue the other.

It is advantageous for fivefold translocal ministers to serve in eldership for a season (if possible) so they can experience local church leadership.

5. Bringing fivefold leadership and governmental leadership together

Since the apostolic gifting is both an equipping gift and a government gift (Ephesians 4:11-12; II Corinthians 10:13-17), the apostolic gift will bring both types of New Testament leadership together.

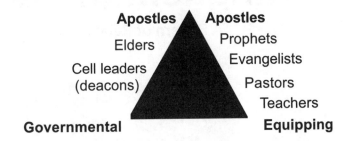

6. Maintaining the balance between the cell and the congregation in the local church

The two legs of the local church are the cell and the congregation. Paul taught the early church both publicly and from house to house (Acts 20:20). Both are needed; they complement one another. Strong cells will cause a congregation to be strong. In the congregation, emphasize the cell; in the cell, emphasize the congregation.

7. Delegation

Moses went up to the mountain to be with his heavenly Father and delegated the administrative/pastoral responsibility to Aaron and Hur (Exodus 24:14).

Delegate as much as possible to others Work yourself out of a job! Remember, people learn by doing.

Delegate to FAITH Christians

F–faithful
A–able and available
I–intimate with God (they love the Lord)
T–teachable
H–holy (those who live lives of purity)

8. Accountability for congregational leaders (elders)

Which field are you in? God's kingdom is made up of tribes for the protection of leaders and God's people (II Corinthians 10:13-17). No congregational leaders should be unconnected and uncovered.

> Vital fivefold ministry gifts equip and minister to individuals both in cells and at the congregational level

If you have had a bad experience with past church oversight do not "throw the baby out with the bath water." God is raising up healthy families of churches all over the world. True apostolic leaders have a father's heart to serve and protect local church leadership.

9. Kingdom clusters

The diagram on this page outlines a pattern of relationships for healthy church leaders on each level of church leadership in the cell-based church. The Lord is building His church through relationships!

Discussion and Study Questions

1. What are the three levels of New Testament church leadership?

2. Why must a leader have a servant leader's heart?

3. Explain the difference between governmental church leadership and fivefold church leadership.

4. Who provides accountability for church elders?

5. What kind of Christians do you delegate to?

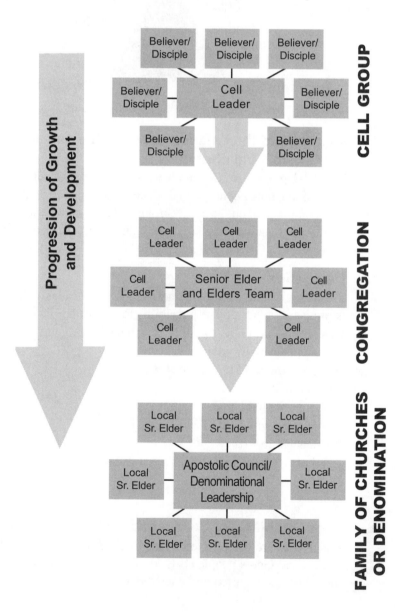

Kingdom Clusters
A Pattern of Relationships

B. Biblical Decision-Making

1. Leaders serve God's people by making decisions

In Acts chapter 15, the early church found themselves in a crisis. But, the apostles and elders, in a healthy way, were able to receive clear, decisive direction from the Lord. This gave great security to the New Testament church.

2. Biblical decision-making

Three principles of Godly leadership

- God calls and anoints someone to lead the way and speaks through this leader.
- God calls and speaks to a team to walk together and speaks through them.
- God speaks through His people in the local church.

Healthy leadership includes each of these three principles These principles apply to cell leadership, congregational leadership and the leadership of a family of churches.

3. God calls a leader who leads the way

Moses asked the Lord to appoint a man over the congregation (Numbers 27:16). God told Moses to take Joshua, the son of Nun, and inaugurate him (Numbers 27:18-23). God always calls someone to lead the way. He speaks to this person in a specific way. Adam, Noah, Abraham, Joseph, Debra, Gideon, David, Daniel, Jesus, Peter, James and Paul are all examples of the Lord speaking to and through a leader.

God calls someone on every team to be the "primary vision carrier" He may be called a senior pastor, presiding elder, senior elder, etc. Regardless of the title, God calls someone on every team to be a PVC (Primary Vision Carrier). There is a primary vision carrier in every sphere of church life, family life, cell, congregation, apostolic movement, etc.

On an airplane, many work together, but only one is the pilot James 3:4 mentions how ships are turned by a very small rudder, going wherever the pilot desires.

Paul and his company Acts 13:13 speaks of Paul and his company (those with him—his companions). He was the clear leader.

James served as the head apostle in Jerusalem Paul went in to James, the head apostle in Jerusalem, and all the elders were present (Acts 21:18). There is always a primary leader in every group.

This is often referred to as episcopal church government.

4. God calls a team to labor together

Many New Testament examples speak of leadership teams. Acts 16:4 speaks of apostles and elders in the plural. In I Peter 5:1, the plural term *elders* is used again. As mentioned before, there needs to be a clear leader on every team so it can function properly.

In Titus 1:5, Paul exhorts Titus to appoint elders in every town. The Lord speaks through teams of leaders who discern His voice together. Husbands and wives serve their families by functioning as a leadership team together.

This is often referred to as presbyterian church government.

5. God speaks through His people in the local church

In Acts 6:1-7, "deacons" were chosen. The people chose seven men and the apostles appointed them. Wise leaders will listen to what God says through His people. We are called to value people! Wise parents will communicate with their children about decisions they need to make that will affect the family. Receive input from those whom you serve before making a decision that affects them.

Deuteronomy 1:21-23 seems to indicate that the idea to send the spies to the promised land came from the people; however, Moses still made the decision. Wise parents won't plan a family vacation without consulting their children. It just makes sense.

This is often referred to as congregational church government.

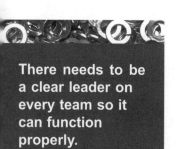

There needs to be a clear leader on every team so it can function properly.

6. Acts 15 gives us a model for healthy decision-making

In Acts 15, the leaders of the New Testament church came together to make a decision that would affect the entire New Testament church. James, in Acts 15:13-21, gave the verdict after listening to the entire team of leadership and discerning what the Lord was saying through the team. The leadership of the church then confirmed his decision.

On a leadership team, the leaders submit to one another, but the spiritual leader of the team is responsible to discern what the Lord is saying through the team "Submitting to one another in the fear of God. Wives, submit to your own husbands, as to the Lord. For the husband is the head of the wife, as also Christ is the head of the church; and He is the Savior of the body" (Ephesians 5:21-23). In families, the Lord has called husbands and wives to submit to each other. God wants husbands and wives to be in unity as a team.

In every team, there's always someone the Lord places as leadership in that team In the case of the husband and wife, the Bible says the husband is the head of the wife. In other words, the husband is the initiator. He's the one who is called to love his wife the same way Jesus Christ loves His church and gave His life for it. He is also the one who, in times of crisis, is responsible to make the final decisions in the home. He does not have absolute authority, but he has final authority.

The same principle applies to church leadership: cell leadership, eldership, and apostolic leadership When a plane is in flight, the pilot, copilot, and flight attendants all work together as a team. But during takeoff, landing and times of crisis, the pilot needs to make the decisions. Wise team leaders recognize the Lord speaks through each of the team members, and discerns what the Lord is saying through the team (Acts 15). The others on the team affirm his decision.

7.   Acknowledge Christ in our midst

We must see Christ in the midst of us as we gather together for decision-making (Matthew 18:20). Each of us has a portion of the Lord's wisdom. The Bible says, "we know in part and we prophesy in part" (I Corinthians 13:9). Together we have the mind of Christ. Listen to what the Lord says through everyone on the team. The primary leader has the grace to discern what the Lord is saying through the entire team.

Prayer and fasting is crucial when making decisions in the local church. Fasting and prayer should be a regular part of a leader's life.

8.   "Head and shoulders" decision-making

The term *head and shoulders government* is sometimes used to describe a healthy leadership team: the head being the primary leader and the shoulders being the others on the team. The body is, of course, the people of God in the local church. God speaks to teams of leaders who, in unity, discern the Lord's direction together and receive input from those whom they serve.

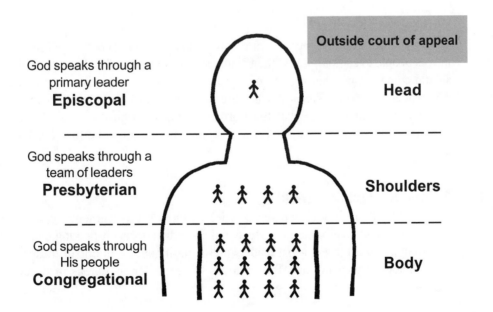

Psalm 133 speaks of the oil being poured down over Aaron's head, beard and collar. Although this scripture is primarily about unity, the analogy of head, shoulders and body is helpful for us to understand this principle. God pours out His wisdom on the head which flows to the shoulders and on to the body. If the head is too far away from the shoulders, we experience a pain in the neck. If the head is pressed down into the shoulders, we experience the same. The shoulders are called by God to support the head. The head protects the shoulders. The head discerns what the Lord is saying through the shoulders (the others on the team). Both the head and the shoulders listen to the wisdom that comes from the body.

9. An outside court of appeal

The head (one in authority) needs to make the final decision. He does not have absolute authority. He has final authority to discern what the Lord is saying through the team. Everyone, including the senior leader of the team, needs to be accountable and under authority. There always needs to be an outside court of appeal. For the cell leaders, this outside court of appeal is the church eldership. For the elders, it is the apostolic leaders who give them oversight. Church members know intrinsically that their pastor should be under authority. When apostolic leaders give Godly oversight to church leaders, the church members are at peace. It gives them a sense of security.

10. Leadership is built on trust

Leadership teams are built on trust. We are better off with a "long neck" for awhile rather than having the wrong "shoulders." In other words, leadership teams should be built slowly, giving time for trust to be built among team members.

In new churches, sometimes leaders try to raise up too many elders too soon Give the Lord time to build you together in a trust relationship. Most church problems are leadership problems that come from unmet expectations and a breakdown in trust.

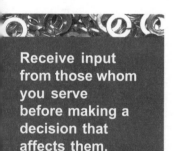

Receive input from those whom you serve before making a decision that affects them.

11. What about voting?

When you take a vote, someone nearly always loses. Voting becomes political and moves people to campaign for "their" side. We want God's side. Decision-making should come through fasting and prayer and spiritual discernment (Acts 13:1-3). The leadership team listens to what the Lord is saying through the body. The primary leader listens to what the Lord is saying through the team. Then the primary leader speaks what the Lord is saying, and the others affirm the Lord's direction.

12. Balanced decision-making

Historically, there have been three types of church government: episcopal, presbyterian and congregational. Head and shoulders decision-making combines the strengths of all three. Most leaders are naturally strong in one of these three areas. They must make an effort to focus on the other two areas of decision-making.

13. Avoid the rule of the negative

Although it is best to reach complete agreement on every decision, we cannot be bound by a requirement of unanimous agreement. This is called "avoiding the rule of the negative." That is, in a team of eight, if seven agree and one disagrees, under unanimous agreement, the negative would carry the decision. If a decision must be made and there is not complete consensus, the team leader must make the decision in light of the input from each team member. To do otherwise would give the final authority on the decision to the lone dissenting member.

14. The basic need of primary leaders

The one in authority (the head on the team) often finds his greatest emotional need is *affirmation* from the shoulders (the team members). Elders need to affirm the call of God on their senior leader's life. Assistant cell leaders need to affirm the call on their cell leader's life.

> I Thessalonians 5:12-13; Ephesians 5:33

15. The basic need of team members

Those who serve as shoulders (under authority) often find their greatest emotional need from the primary leader is *relationship and communication.* Wise leaders will be proactive in "sharing their hearts" with their team. This provides an atmosphere of trust, relationship, openness and security.

> I Peter 5:1-3

16. New Testament church leadership is not a democracy, but a theocracy

Democracy works well for civil government where many are not believers, but it is not a biblical method of church government. Throughout the scriptures, the Lord gave His direction for the people of God through chosen leaders. Both the Old and the New Testament model theocratic leadership. The Lord speaks individually to us about direction for our own lives, but He appoints servant leaders in His body for the direction of His church.

Discussion and Study Questions
1. What are the three kinds of church government?
2. What are the strengths of each?
3. How are all three incorporated into head and shoulders decision-making?
4. Why is an outside court of appeal important?
5. Why is this type of church government called *theocratic*?

C. Authority and Accountability

1. **A proper understanding of authority and accountability is critical for a healthy cell-based church**

    It will bring security into our lives and our churches. Our God is a God of all authority; however, the Lord in His wisdom has also given some of His authority to men and women whom He has placed in our lives. Romans 13:1 tells us, "Let every soul be subject to the governing authorities. For there is no authority except from God, and the authorities that exist are appointed by God...."

2. **Authority and accountability in the church comes through apostles and elders**

    In the New Testament church, we see the Lord giving authority to apostles and elders.

    > Acts 15-16

    Elders oversee the local church, including the cell group leaders Elders have received delegated authority from the Lord to give protection, direction, and correction to the local church. Their first responsibility is to oversee cell group leaders.

    > Acts 20:28-31; I Peter 5:1-4

    Apostles oversee the elders. Apostles have received authority from the Lord to oversee the elders in local churches, especially the senior elder.

    > Philemon 1-2; Philippians 1:1; Acts 21:18

    Anyone who has authority needs to be under authority If you're driving through a town and a police officer stands at an intersection and puts up his hand, every driver will stop because of the authority of the police officer. It is not his own authority, but the authority of the government he represents. If we are not under the authority of God's delegated authorities, we will not have spiritual authority to give oversight to others.

3. **The Lord has set up delegated authorities to help mold us into the image of Christ**

    What does it mean to submit to authority? The word *submit* means *to yield, stand under, defer to the opinion or authority of another.* Submission is an attitude of the heart that desires to obey God and the human authorities that He has placed in our lives. According to Webster's Dictionary, the word *authority* means *a right to command or act.*

    In other words, authority is a right given by God to men and women to build, to mold, and to adjust and structure the lives of others An authority is a person who has been given responsibility for our lives. Whenever I resist any authority the Lord has placed in my life—parents, employer, police, church authority—I am actually resisting God. (Unless, of course, the authority is causing me to sin: Acts 5:29).

Unless we learn to submit to the authorities the Lord has placed in our lives, we cannot respond appropriately as an authority to others Children who do not obey their parents and never repent for their disobedience grow up with an unwholesome understanding of authority. They are often domineering toward their own children. The same principle applies to church leadership.

We do not submit to the authorities the Lord has placed in our lives because they are perfect, but because the Lord has placed them there Wherever we go, one of the first questions we should ask ourselves is, "Who has the Lord placed in authority here?" People who are truly under God's authority see authority everywhere they go. They realize these authorities have been delegated and appointed by the Lord. Secure people have no problem with submitting to the authorities the Lord has placed in their lives.
>Hebrews 13:17

Relational authority The church must be built on relational authority. If we are not in relationship with those over us in the Lord, we fall into the trap of bureaucracy. Whatever is not of faith is sin (Romans 14:23).

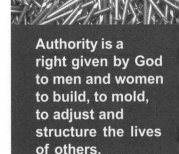

Authority is a right given by God to men and women to build, to mold, to adjust and structure the lives of others.

4. What if we don't agree with the direction of our spiritual leadership?

Pray for them People who say, "I don't agree with my pastor or my church leadership," need to first be encouraged to pray for God's blessing and wisdom on their spiritual leaders. It is unscriptural and wrong for us to pray for them to fail so they will see things our way. Genuinely pray for God's will, not ours, to be done.
>I Timothy 2:1-4

Appeal to them in love Keep in mind that we are not called to change our leaders—that is God's responsibility.

Check our heart s for any rebellion If the differences persist, we also may need to consider other possibilities—maybe we have rebellion in our lives we need to deal with.

The Lord may be calling us to another church In some cases, the Lord may be calling us to another local church sharing the same vision we have.

So then, what should our response be to those who give leadership to our local church? We are called to pray for them, support them, submit to them and appeal to them. To be in submission is "to be under the mission" or the authority the Lord has placed in our lives. So then, at work we are under the mission of our employer. In school, we are under the mission of our teacher. On a basketball team, we are under the mission of the coach. In our homes, we are under the mission of the head of our home. And in the church, we are under the mission of the spiritual leadership the Lord has placed in our lives.

I Thessalonians 5:12-13

5. The Lord is concerned about our heart attitudes

Wherever you're committed in the body of Christ—in a small group (cell group) or a local congregation—the Lord has called you to actively support and submit to the leadership He has placed there. If you hear an accusation against a cell group leader or church leader, send the accuser to the leader. Do not allow gossip or slander to hinder the work of God in your midst. Having an attitude of submission toward the authorities God has placed in our lives will protect us from many mistakes. It also is a protection against the influence of the devil. The nature of the devil is rebellion and deceit. In the universe there are two major forces. The one is submission to the authority of God; the other is rebellion. Whenever we allow an attitude of rebellion into our lives, we are beginning to be motivated by the enemy.

The principle of faith When we submit to the authorities in our lives, we learn the principle of faith. The Bible tells us in Matthew 8:8-10, "The centurion answered and said, 'Lord, I am not worthy that You should come under my roof. But only speak a word, and my servant will be healed. For I also am a man under authority'...[Jesus said], 'Assuredly, I say to you, I have not found such great faith, not even in Israel!'" In order for us to be people of faith who see miracles happen in our lives, we must understand the principles of authority. This centurion received a miracle from Jesus because he understood authority.

6. The blessing of accountability

In Hebrews 13:17, we read that spiritual leaders "watch out for your souls, as those who must give account." What is accountability? It is *to give an account to others for what God has called us to do.* In our lives we are accountable to the Lord regarding how we live out our commitment to Christ. Our lives need to line up with the Word of God. Our spiritual leaders are also accountable to God for our lives. There is also a tremendous blessing and freedom that comes when we ask others to "hold us accountable" for certain personal areas in our lives needing encouragement and support.

Personal accountability is finding out from God what He wants us to do and then asking others to hold us accountable to do those things Personal accountability is not having others tell us what to do.

Safety in a multitude of counselors The scriptures tell us in Proverbs 11:14, "in the multitude of counselors there is safety." Other people can see things in our lives that we often miss. Many of us have "blind spots" that we may miss but others can see. We need to have a small group of people to whom we can be accountable.

Module 11: New Testament Church Government

Admonishing one another "Now I myself am confident concerning you, my brethren, that you also are full of goodness, filled with all knowledge, able also to admonish one another" (Romans 15:14). According to Webster's Dictionary "to admonish" means *to counsel against wrong practices, to caution or advise and to teach with correction.* We all need people in our lives to admonish us and hold us accountable.

We need to ask people to hold us accountable It doesn't just happen. It takes humility to ask others to hold us accountable for the way we live our Christian lives, but God gives grace (His favor and divine energy) to those who are humble and willing to open their lives to others. God resists the proud, but gives grace to the humble (I Peter 5:5b).

Jesus held the disciples accountable The disciples were accountable to Jesus. He sent them out on a task and they reported back to Him what they experienced. This is an example of true accountability in operation. Mark 6:7,30 tells us, "And He called the twelve to Him, and began to send them out two by two, and gave them power over unclean spirits. Then the apostles gathered to Jesus and told Him all things, both what they had done and what they had taught." If the early disciples needed to be accountable to Jesus, the One who had sent them out, how much more do we need to be accountable, not only to our Lord Jesus Christ, but to those who train us and equip us and encourage us in the things of God? Who are the authorities the Lord has placed in your life?

Who is holding you accountable? We are not called to live our Christian lives alone! It is not enough for believers to belong to an invisible, mystical church. **The church is a local, visible church with practical commitment.** We see this modeled in the church in Antioch, Lystra and Jerusalem.

7. Church membership in a cell-based church

The basic commitment to Christian community in a cell-based church must include commitment to believers in a cell group.

There are at least **two options for membership in a cell-based church.**

- Some cell-based churches have no formal membership, but every person committed to the church is committed to the Lord, His Word, accountability, local church leadership, to the vision of the church, and to other believers **in a cell group setting.**
- Other cell-based churches have a formal written membership, but the believers are committed to the Lord, His Word, accountability, local church leadership, to the vision of the church, and to other believers in a cell group setting as a requirement for membership.

8. The Lord has placed elders and pastors in the church to protect, direct and correct His people

Hebrews 13:17 tells us, "Obey those who rule over you, and be submissive, for they watch out for your souls, as those who must give account. Let them do so with joy and not with grief, for that would be unprofitable for you." According to the scriptures, the Lord places spiritual authorities in our lives who rule over us and must give an account to the Lord for our spiritual lives. They are accountable to God for us and are given spiritual oversight by apostolic leaders.

- **Protection** That's why it is so important for every believer to be connected to the local church; it brings spiritual protection to us from the powers of darkness. This is also why every senior elder needs to be given oversight by apostolic leadership; it gives him spiritual protection from the powers of darkness.
- **Direction** Our leaders listen to the Father's voice and give leadership to the vision and direction of the local church.
- **Correction** There are various forms of correction. There is public teaching which will bring correction and adjustment in our lives. There is also personal warning and admonishment when an elder sees a believer approaching danger. The most severe correction happens in the form of church discipline.

The goal is restoration Our elders are responsible before God to bring church discipline into the life of any believer in the church who lives in unrepented sin. The goal of all discipline is restoration. Cell leaders should always involve church elders in church discipline regarding cell members.

9. **Scriptural insights for church discipline**

If believers have sin in their lives, the Lord instructs church leaders to lovingly discipline them and restore them to again walk in truth (I Corinthians 5, Galatians 6:1, Matthew 18:17). Earthly fathers will discipline their children in love, because they care for their children. God has chosen to use men and women as His rod to discipline us in love (II Samuel 7:14). In fact, the Lord tells us in Hebrews 12:8, "But if you are without chastening, of which all have become partakers, then you are illegitimate and not sons."

If a spiritual authority (elder, pastor, etc.) is disobedient to the Lord, those whom the Lord has placed over him are responsible to discipline him Local churches should be a part of a larger "family of churches" or a denomination. The leadership of this family of churches has the responsibility, along with the other elders, to administer proper discipline. In fact, the Bible says he should be rebuked in the presence of everyone in the church (I Timothy 5:19-20). This is why all local elders should also have spiritual authorities who will give them the protection, direction, and correction they need as they serve the Lord in the local church.

See Appendix C–Scriptural Insights For Church Discipline for scriptural insights and practical biblical steps for church discipline in a cell-based church.

Discussion and Study Questions

1. Why has the Lord set up delegated authorities in our lives?

2. Define biblical accountability.

3. Why does it give people confidence to know someone is keeping their leaders accountable?

4. How is this confidence in the people's hearts a blessing to the church leaders?

5. How can church discipline be done in a loving and redemptive manner? Read Appendix C and give a paragraph summary.

Helping You Build

Module
12

Module 12

The Fivefold Ministry and Cell Groups

The Lord is restoring the ministries of apostles, prophets, evangelists, pastors and teachers to His church in these days. The cell-based church is an ideal model for the training and release of these vital ministries in the church. In this module, we look at the role, function, and practical application of each of these ministries within the cell-based church.

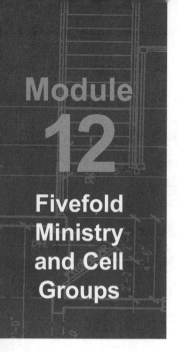

A. The Fivefold Ministry

1. The fivefold or ascension gifts (Ephesians 4:11-12)

It is the Lord's plan for His people to be equipped to do the work of ministry. The Lord has given the gifts of apostle, prophet, evangelist, pastor and teacher to equip His people to minister and to build up and encourage the body of Christ. These five gifts to the body of Christ are often referred to as the *fivefold ministry.*

Ascension gifts The fivefold gifts are sometimes also called the ascension gifts because they were released to earth when Jesus ascended into heaven (Ephesians 4:9-11).

2. Impartation from these gifts

These fivefold ministry gifts are provided by Jesus Christ so that His body may be equipped, be encouraged and grow to maturity.

It is God's desire that there is no lack in the kingdom that every believer might have an impartation from each of these gifted ministries in order to better fulfill the Lord's call in his or her life.

    Ephesians 4:13-14

3. Origin of the fivefold ministry

The fivefold ministry consists of **apostle, prophet, evangelist, pastor and teacher**

The fivefold gifts are from Jesus Christ Himself We know the origin of the fivefold ministry gifts is from the person of Jesus Christ. Ephesians 4:11 says, "He gave." It is a direct reference to our Lord and Savior Jesus Christ. All of these gifts were functioning to their fullest in Jesus Christ. He sent these gifts to us that we might be complete, lacking nothing.

Jesus was

The Apostle of apostles "As the Father has sent me" (John 20:21).

The Prophet of prophets At first His disciples did not understand all of this (John 12:16).

The Evangelist of evangelists "I am the way, the truth and the life, no man can come to the Father except through me" (John 14:6).

The Teacher of teachers "You call Me Teacher and Lord, and you say well, for so I am" (John 13:13).

The Pastor of pastors "I am the Good Shepherd" (John 10:11).

Using the human hand symbolically, you could say that:

The index finger represents the prophet points the direction that the Lord is speaking.

The middle finger represents the evangelist reaching out the farthermost to bring others to Christ.

The ring finger represents the pastor married to the church.

The little finger represents the teacher able to dig out the detailed truth of God's Word.

The thumb represents the apostle He is the only one who can touch all of the other four gifts. He is the one to bring to unity all the fivefold ministers to cause them to work together effectively.

Make a fist with your hand. The four fingers come under the thumb. As the other ministries submit to the apostle, great power and force is released to advance the church.

Many fivefold ministers are a gift mix Some fivefold ministers are prophetic teachers, others are pastoral teachers, others are apostolic evangelists, etc. Paul was an apostle, a prophet and a teacher.

I Corinthians 9:1-2; I Corinthians 15:9; Acts 13:1; II Timothy 1:11

4. Purpose of the fivefold ministry (Ephesians 4:12-15)

The purpose of the fivefold ministry is to equip the saints for the work of ministry and encourage the body of Christ. Their goal as fivefold ministers is to train, equip and prepare the Lord's body to be functional in everyday life as ministers of the gospel of Jesus Christ.

Goals of the fivefold ministry

Edification Their ministry is one of edification to the body of Christ.

Unification The goal is to bring us to the unity of the faith and the knowledge of the Son of God.

Preparation They minister to bring us to the full measure of the stature of the fullness of Christ.

Reconciliation to the Word They ground us in the Word so that we are not tossed to and fro by every wind of doctrine.

Conformation Their ministry is one of love so that we might be conformed to the image of Christ.

5. The difference between a fivefold ministry gift and a fully developed fivefold ministry

Many people have one or more of the fivefold gifts in seed form and yet are not considered a fivefold minister. For example, someone may really be an evangelist at his workplace and see many people come to know Christ, but that does not mean he is a fully developed fivefold evangelist. Many have a fivefold gift in "seed form" (Mark 4:28) that is presently being developed. When a fivefold ministry is fully developed, it will be recognized and affirmed by other fivefold ministers and apostolic church leaders.

The fivefold ministry is one of equipping A proven fivefold evangelist will meet the character requirements of an elder (Titus 1:6-9) and be released to equip the saints for the work of evangelism.

A fivefold minister has a proven ministry A true Ephesians 4:11 fivefold minister has a proven ministry. This means he carries within himself the ability to train and release others of like gifts and calling.

6. All fivefold ministers are not in governmental leadership

While all fivefold ministers carry spiritual authority, not all fivefold ministers carry governmental authority. In other words, some fivefold ministers will not hold a governmental position such as an elder in a local church or an apostolic governmental position of leadership in a family of churches. However, many governmental leaders (elders) will be gifted by the Lord in one or more of the fivefold ministry gifts. The non-governmental fivefold ministers will function as "circuit riders," ministering from cell to cell and from church to church. This is sometimes called translocal ministry.

Acts 15:30-35

7. Requirements of a fivefold minister

Since a fivefold ministry gift carries spiritual authority and is a representation of one of the ministry gifts of Jesus Christ, it is imperative that all fivefold ministers carry the heart of Jesus and meet the same character requirements set forth for elders and deacons in I Timothy 3:1-13.

They must be able to equip the saints for the work of ministry This is one of the key aspects of their ministry. They must do more than preach good sermons. People will be motivated, changed, equipped and empowered through their ministry.

They need to carry the authority of Jesus They will speak with the Lord's authority, and there will be spiritual fruit, changed lives and signs following their ministry. Jesus will always validate those whom He has placed in fivefold leadership and ministry.

Recognized by local leadership To be released into the fivefold ministry, they must be recognized by their local senior elder (pastor) and leadership team as having one or more of these gifts. If we can be trusted in our local church, the Lord can trust us in a broader sphere of ministry (Luke 16:10).

8. Different levels of fivefold ministry

It all starts at the cell level! The seed of these fivefold ministry gifts dwells in many of God's people at the cell level. This is where they can begin to exercise their spiritual gifts and minister to others. The cell is a safe environment for ministry.

Local church This is the next level of fivefold ministry. A local pastor (senior elder) and leadership team will identify and release someone into their ministry gift for that local congregation. Their sphere of ministry is within that local church.

Acts 13:1

Family of churches This is another sphere of development for a fivefold minister. When a local pastor (senior elder) and leadership team (elders), discern that the gifts and anointing of an individual has grown beyond the scope of the local congregation, they recommend them to the next level of authority (the apostolic leadership of their family of churches), to be commissioned and released as a translocal minister. The term "translocal" refers to a minister who travels from church to church and from cell to cell.

Translocal ministers then have the authority to move from congregation to congregation (including cells in various churches), to train, equip and release the saints for the work of ministry. To be released in this level, they must have the affirmation of those who have governmental authority over the family of churches.

Acts 15:2, 30-35, 40-41

The whole body of Christ To be released in this sphere, a translocal fivefold minister must carry the affirmation of the overseers of the family of churches and the affirmation of other translocal fivefold ministers in the body of Christ.

Their sphere of ministry extends to the body of Christ and these fivefold ministers carry within themselves the character, authority and signs that are recognized by the larger sphere, namely the body of Christ at large.

Galatians 1:1, 8-9; Galatians 2:1-2, 7-8

9.   What about accountability?

Since accountability is such an important aspect of the Christian walk, it is important that clear lines of accountability are established for every fivefold minister.

Accountability for the individual's personal walk with the Lord and interpersonal relationships (both his family and the local church) comes from his local pastor (senior elder) and eldership team.

Hebrews 13:17

Accountability for their ministry then depends upon those who are responsible for that sphere of their ministry:

- **Fivefold minister in a local church**—accountability for their ministry comes from the local leadership team.
- **Fivefold translocal minister in a family of churches**—accountability for their ministry comes from the leadership of that family of churches.
- **Fivefold translocal minister to the body of Christ at large**—accountability for their ministry must still come from the leadership of the family of churches that they are part of as well as from apostolic fathers in the church at large.

10. Financing the fivefold ministers

Some who have been called as fivefold ministers plant churches to provide a financial base for their ministry. The end result is that they move away from their anointing, equipping the believers in many churches to be effective ministers and focus on one church because of needing a financial base.

Financing for fivefold ministers needs to come from those who are being blessed by their ministry I Timothy 5:18 says, "You shall not muzzle an ox while it treads the grain..." (while it works for you). I Corinthians 9:1-14 tells us that God has commanded those who preach the gospel to live from the gospel.

Wherever fivefold ministers are ministering, they should be given financial remuneration for ministry This includes their ministry in cells, local churches, seminars, and one-to-one equipping and ministry.
Galatians 6:6

Many fivefold ministers are called by the Lord to build a support team of family, friends and churches who give financially on a regular basis to support them in their calling and ministry.

The Lord is giving fresh wisdom in these days for fivefold translocal ministers to be properly supported financially. Read "Covering the Bases," Module 15:C, for more insights on financial support.

11. Longevity of the fivefold minister

These gifts have been given to the church until the purpose laid out in Ephesians 4 is fully accomplished. They have been given by Christ to function until His return. Each one has a part to play in bringing about the whole purpose of God for their lives and for His church.

12. How the fivefold minister functions in a cell-based church

The same vision of house to house and temple gatherings (Acts 20:20) set forth for the cell church is set forth for the fivefold minister. Wherever the church is gathering, there is opportunity for them to impart to others.

- **Serves the congregation** Fivefold ministers help the pastor equip the saints. When the church meets as a congregation, the fivefold minister comes alongside the pastor (senior elder) and elders to equip the saints and assist them in bringing the believers to maturity.
- **Serves the cell** Fivefold ministers assist the cell leaders. In the cell setting, they are assisting the cell leader and ultimately the local leadership by practically equipping the saints for the work of ministry.
- **Serves individual believers** Fivefold ministers mentor, equip and train individual believers to be effective ministers through consultation, mentoring and one-on-one ministry training (I Corinthians 4:15-17).
Whether fivefold ministers are serving our local church, our cell, or us as individuals, it is important to provide financially for their ministry.

13. Fivefold ministers and church planting

The model developed in the early church, according to the book of Acts, has the fivefold ministry intimately involved in church planting (Acts 13-14).

Apostles, prophets and evangelists are essential in the early days of a church plant Apostles lay foundations, prophets break through spiritual strongholds, and evangelists bring in the unsaved. Pastors and teachers are more involved in the long term care and nurture of the church as it grows. This pattern in church planting does not negate the fact that existing churches benefit from all the fivefold ministries in reaching maturity.

The fivefold ministry will never be fully developed unless it is released in church planting. This is the biblical model.

14. Ephesians 4 teaches us that "some" are apostles, prophets, evangelists, pastors and teachers

Not all believers have a fivefold anointing that will grow into a fully developed fivefold ministry. However, most believers will have a fivefold tendency which can be identified by completing the Fivefold Minister Survey in Appendix D.

Discussion and Study Questions

1. What is the biblical basis for the fivefold ministry?

2. How do fivefold ministers equip the saints to do the work of ministry?

3. How can you remember the strength of each ministry from the fingers on your hand?

4. How are fivefold ministers recognized and developed?

5. Who gives accountability to the fivefold ministers?

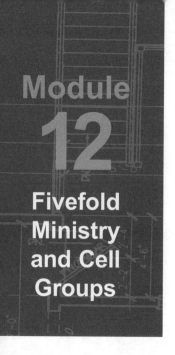

B. The Role and Function of Apostles and Prophets

1. The term "apostle" carries some important definitions

Definition of apostle One who is sent by God with a mandate from the Lord Jesus to build, plant, nurture, correct and oversee His church. Apostles are foundation layers.

> Ephesians 4:11; I Corinthians 12:28; I Corinthians 12:29; I Corinthians 3:10

There are various types of apostles mentioned in scripture The twelve apostles of Christ are in a special category all by themselves. The New Testament mentions more than 20 apostles who served the early church. Some examples are Paul (I Timothy 1:1), Junias (Romans 16:7) and Apollos (I Corinthians 4:6, 9). God is raising up modern-day apostles who love His church and who serve as fathers in the body of Christ.

2. The apostle's authority comes from the Lord and is confirmed by men

His greatest responsibility is to the Lord who has called him. However, his call must be affirmed by those whom the Lord brings to him (Romans 1:1), by other apostles, and spiritual leaders in the body of Christ (Acts 13:1-4).

3. The apostle's calling is not self-appointed—it is the Lord who calls

The ministry of an apostle is evidenced by his call from the Lord, the commissioning of his local church, the leaders of his family of churches, and the affirmation of other leaders within the body of Christ.

4. Apostles are called to build and plant churches

An apostle is an "architect." He is one called by God to design and lay foundations. Paul was commissioned by the Lord and by other apostles in the early church to build and to plant churches among the Gentiles (Romans 11:13). Peter was commissioned by the Lord to build and to plant churches among the Jews (Galatians 2:8).

5. Two types of modern-day apostles

The Paul-type apostle

The Paul-type apostle is sent by the Lord with a vision burning on his heart to establish a family of churches, and it will burn on his heart until he fulfills it. The blueprint and vision come from the Lord. His call is affirmed by other apostles and spiritual leaders in the body of Christ (Galatians 1:18-22). He is sometimes referred to as an overseeing apostle.

- His authority is from the Lord (Galatians 1:1).
- God equips him for this work.
- The Lord supplies him with the supernatural faith and perseverance to see this vision become a reality.
- The Lord brings others alongside this apostle to fill in what is lacking in his gifts so the vision can be fulfilled. Paul was called by God to build the church among the Gentiles, but a team of apostles served with him (I Thessalonians 1:1).

The Timothy-type apostle

The Timothy-type apostle is affirmed and commissioned to help fulfill the vision received by the Paul-type apostle from the Lord.

- A Timothy-type apostle receives his authority from the Lord and from the Paul-type apostle.
- He is sent out by the Paul-type apostle with specific instructions and mandates that will contribute to the main goal the Lord has given to the apostolic team.
- His sphere of ministry is given to him by the Lord and by the overseeing (senior) apostle with whom he serves.
- Timothy and Titus were sent by Paul to establish elders and oversee churches (I Timothy 1:1-4; Titus 1:5).

6. Seal of apostleship

The seal of apostleship (I Corinthians 9:1-2) is one of the Lord's vision being built and fulfilled and lives being changed. The proof is in the tangible results. An apostle's field of ministry is limited to that which he was sent to do (I Corinthians 3:5-15). He is the father to the churches he plants.

> II Corinthians 10:13-18

The marks of an apostle Supernatural signs, wonders, miracles and perseverance (II Corinthians 12:12) are all indicative of modern-day apostles.

7. An apostle normally carries a measure of the gifts of prophet, evangelist, pastor and teacher

Most apostles have been used by the Lord at some time in their lives and ministry in the ministry gifts of prophet, evangelist, pastor and teacher. Paul, the apostle, is an example of this truth.

> Acts 13:1

8. The qualifications of an apostle

- An apostle must have the **character qualifications of an elder** (I Timothy 3:2-7).
- Christ, the Apostle, came with a servant's heart; therefore, a modern-day apostle must **have a servant's heart** (Matthew 20:26-28).
- As a representative of Christ, an apostle must **be clothed with humility**. He has been sent by Christ to do Christ's work (Philippians 2:5-8).
- An apostle must **have a father's heart**. This means he has a desire to see his spiritual sons far exceed him in ministry (I Corinthians 4:15-21).
- An apostle will **have a heart to release others**. Since his work is to build, he is not afraid to release others to the work of God. He sees others as helping to bring *completion* not *competition* to the ministry the Lord is building (John 3:30).
- An apostle will be **someone leaders will want to follow** and give themselves to (Acts 13:13).
- An apostle is **willing to sacrificially suffer for the church** (I Corinthians 4:9-13; II Corinthians 6:3-10). As the father, he gives no thought to himself but is concerned that the vision of God goes forward.

An apostle has the God-given ability to walk with the prophet, evangelist, pastor and teacher, drawing them together in a common vision and purpose.

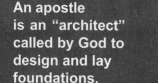

An apostle is an "architect" called by God to design and lay foundations.

9. The prophet/prophetess

"He gave some prophets" (Ephesians 4:11; I Corinthians 12:28).

Definition A prophet is someone who has the ability to consistently speak forth God's heart to His people. As with every other fivefold gift, there are different levels of prophetic gifts. A prophet is one who has fluency in speaking forth God's heart and mind maturely and who has a proven record of accuracy.

Seek the prophetic word and receive a blessing We are admonished by the Lord to seek the prophetic word of the Lord. The Bible tells us in Matthew 10:41 that if we are open to a prophet and receive him, we will receive a prophet's reward. This is saying, at the very least, if we are open to the prophetic gift, we will receive a blessing from God.

10. The calling and affirmation of a prophet

Prophets, just like any other fivefold ministry gift, receive their call from the Lord. They must know that God has set them in the church. The affirmation of prophets comes from the eldership of their local church where they serve. Theirs is a "time tested" ministry and one that requires a time of maturing and proving. A translocal prophet also receives affirmation from apostolic leadership in the family of churches with which he serves.

Acts 15:30-32

11. The qualifications of a prophet

The qualifications of a prophet are the same as that of an elder (Titus 1:6-9) Revelation 19:10 tells us that the spirit of prophecy is the testimony of Jesus. Therefore a true prophet will speak forth the Lord's words with the Lord's heart.

A prophet needs to **carry an anointing for signs and wonders** to follow this ministry. He will often minister prophetically through visions, dreams, and prophetic utterances (Acts 21:10-11).

A prophet needs to have an **anointing for the ministry in the Word of God.** Lives will be changed when he ministers God's Word in cells and in local churches (Acts 15:32).

12. The ministry of the prophet

The ministry of the prophet is to **"mature and perfect" the saints.** Their heart is to bring attention to areas of weakness in the body of Christ and minister until they see a strengthening in those areas.

They are to **bring the saints into their ministry and see them released.** Often a prophet will be used to either confirm a known gift in an individual or identify a gift "in waiting."

They are called to **edify the body of Christ through the teaching and preaching of the Word of God.**

They are used to confirm and/or **give direction from the Lord** for an individual, a cell group, a local church, a family of churches, or the church in a given community. New direction from the Lord will be confirmed by the individual or by the leaders responsible for the cell, local church or family of churches.
    Acts 21:10-14

Prophets who minister usually **will deliver a prophetic word that will minister in one of the following ways:**
- Exhortation—to stir up
- Edification—to build up
- Comfort—to strengthen
- Conviction—to correct
    I Corinthians 14:3,4,37

> A prophet is called to edify the body of Christ through teaching and preaching.

13. Prophets are not infallible in their ministry

Prophets hear in part and prophesy in part (I Corinthians 13:9). It is up to the individual person to affirm the word of the Lord coming from the prophet. All believers are in a position to hear from the Lord. The ministry of the prophet needs to have the affirmation of the Holy Spirit in our own lives.

14. False prophets

A false prophet is someone who knowingly or unknowingly (if they are blinded by the enemy) tries to lead someone astray. Since we all prophesy in part, just because a prophetic word has some inaccuracy in it *does not* mean that the individual is a false prophet. False prophets will tend to bring division in churches and leadership and hinder the building of the church.

> Matthew 7:15-23; Titus 3:9-11

15. Distinction between Old Testament prophets and New Testament prophets

Old Testament prophets

The way the Lord spoke to His people in the Old Testament was through the prophets (Hebrews 1:1). They needed to be infallible in their ministry and were used to give direction and guidance to God's people. Many Old Testament prophets were used to write scripture.

New Testament prophets

The prophets of today are often used to confirm the word of the Lord which He is speaking to the hearts of individuals (Hebrews 1:2; Hebrews 2:1-4). They may also be used by the Lord to ignite a vision or calling in an individual. This must be confirmed by the witness of the Holy Spirit in this person's own life and/or the affirmation of their church leadership. Every believer has an "anointing from the Holy One" and can hear from God (I John 2:20).

16. Apostles and prophets are called to work together

It is essential for modern-day apostles to have proven prophets working alongside them (Ephesians 2:19-22).

Together they form a check and balance Although scripture assigns apostles the role of leadership, apostles and prophets must work together. The apostle keeps the church in a forward thrust, and the prophet helps the apostle to see the current "word of the Lord" so he is building properly (I Corinthians 12:28-29).

The apostle and prophet not only compliment each other by working together in the unity of the Spirit, but they also need each other for the enhancement of each of their ministries.

Discussion and Study Questions

1. What does the apostle impart to the church?

2. What are some of the key qualifications of an apostle?

3. What does the prophet impart to the church?

4. How are Old Testament prophets and New Testament prophets different?

5. How do apostles and prophets work together?

Module 12: The Fivefold Ministry and Cell Groups

C. The Role and Function of Evangelists, Pastors and Teachers

1. The evangelist (Ephesians 4:11)

Evangelism means *to announce the Good News*. Jesus Christ is the Evangelist and His ministry on earth was to spread the Good News that He had come to save mankind from their sins.

2. The calling of an evangelist

Fivefold evangelists have more than a desire to see people saved. They carry within themselves a call of the Lord that has supernaturally equipped them with the ability to lead others to Christ and to train other believers to effectively reach the lost. Jesus, the evangelist, trained His disciples to reach the lost of their day.
Matthew 10:1-20

3. The qualifications of an evangelist

The qualifications of an evangelist are the same as that of any other fivefold minister (I Timothy 3:2-7).

- An evangelist must be full of the Holy Spirit and power. Philip, the evangelist (Acts 21:8), was full of the Holy Spirit (Acts 6:5).
- They must be sound in doctrine since a large part of their ministry is preaching the Word (I Timothy 2:15).

4. The affirmation of an evangelist

A fivefold evangelist must first be **affirmed by the eldership team** in his local church and serve his local church in modeling evangelism as a life-style. Some evangelists have a broader field of ministry beyond the scope of ministering only under the authority of their local church. They are also accountable to the apostolic leadership in the family of churches of which they are a part.

The Lord affirms evangelists by signs and wonders that follow them These signs and wonders are for setting captives free and for drawing people to Christ (Acts 8:6,13). Individuals with a strong emphasis on signs and wonders are often called *power evangelists*.

5. The ministry of an evangelist

A large part of their ministry is to bring people to the Lord.
Evangelists have a supernatural ability of knowing where an individual stands spiritually, and starting from that point, they begin to preach Jesus to him or her (Acts 8:35).

Evangelists also have the God-given supernatural ability to bring the conviction of Christ, individually, and in large crowds to the point where people feel compelled by God, the Father, to come to Christ (Acts 8:37).

Another aspect of their ministry is to stir up the body of Christ to reach the lost. Their desire is to see others in the church receive a burden for evangelism. It is important to note that people will not feel condemned for not evangelizing but empowered and motivated to evangelize. This can often happen at the cell group level. If your cell lacks an evangelistic fervor, invite an evangelist to come to your cell to stir up God's people in evangelism and give practical training in reaching the lost.

The third aspect of their ministry is to disciple other evangelists and see them released for the harvest. There is a fivefold evangelist in New Zealand presently discipling more than 20 young evangelists.

Evangelists are also called alongside the other fivefold ministers to bring the body of Christ to a place of maturity and perfection (Ephesians 4:13).

6. Pastor

Another name the Bible gives for a pastor is a *shepherd*. Two aspects of their ministry are to feed and protect the sheep (I Peter 5:1-4).

7. The calling of a pastor

A pastor's calling comes from the Chief Shepherd (I Peter 5:4). He is an undershepherd serving under our Lord Jesus Christ. A pastor's calling is affirmed by the fact that people are following him.

8. Qualifications of a pastor

A pastor must have the heart of a shepherd, which means he cares for the sheep. Character qualifications are the same as the other fivefold ministries (I Timothy 3:2-7).

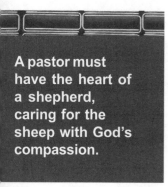

A pastor must have the heart of a shepherd, caring for the sheep with God's compassion.

- Pastors must know their sheep. Jesus, the Chief Shepherd, calls us by name (John 10:3-4).
- Pastors love people. They carry God's heart and compassion for the sheep and will not run when adversity comes (John 10:10-15).

9. Characteristics of a pastor

Pastors have the God-given ability to **assume long-term personal responsibility** for the spiritual welfare of a group of believers. Those who give long-term direct oversight to cell leaders need to have a pastoral gift operating in their lives.

Module 12: The Fivefold Ministry and Cell Groups

The pastors' **authority is limited to those who have been entrusted into their care.** In a cell-based church, pastors spend much of their time equipping, training, and serving cell group leaders.

A true fivefold pastoral minister **carries a father's heart** and therefore has a desire to see people released in their spiritual gifts.

True pastors are **not threatened** by others who have the same spiritual gift (or a greater measure of grace than they have). Instead, they have a genuine desire to see the body of Christ becoming all it can be. Some fivefold pastors also have an apostolic gift and serve as apostolic pastors to church leaders in the body of Christ. This could be called a pastor to pastors.

A pastor will go before his sheep to **lead them, and they will gladly follow** (I Corinthians 11:1; John 10:4). He has a supernatural ability to gather people and go after strays. Walls come down and people feel protected and thus open their hearts to a pastor.

A pastor **carries the genuine God-given desire to bring healing to the flock.** Psalms 23 gives a clear picture of the role of a shepherd in the church.

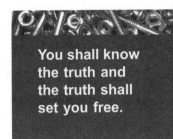

You shall know the truth and the truth shall set you free.

A pastor will not rule by lording over others but **in humility will lift the people before the Lord.** The pastoral gift in Paul comes out in I Thessalonians 2:6-12.

10. Teachers (Ephesians 4:11)

Definition: the supernatural, God-given ability to teach the principles and doctrine of God in a life-giving way that can easily be understood and applied to everyday life. It is an anointing that imparts God's divine life. The leadership of the church of Antioch was made up of prophets and teachers (Acts 13:1).

11. The calling of a teacher

Teachers are called by God. A teacher is called by the Lord and affirmed by his spiritual leadership and has the God-given ability to teach the Word of God accurately.
The fivefold teacher gifting is to rightly divide the Word of Truth (II Timothy 2:15). A teacher's motto is, "You shall know the truth, and the truth shall set you free" (John 8:32).
Romans 12:7

12. The qualifications of a teacher

The qualifications of a teacher are the same as with other fivefold gifts. Character is a qualifier (I Timothy 3:2-7). The Bible tells us that those who teach will be judged more strictly (James 3:1).

A teacher must be **called by God, filled with the Holy Ghost and power and must be able to teach in a life-giving way** that brings grace to those who hear him teach the Word of God.

I Corinthians 12:28-29

Fivefold teachers **must live what they teach,** being an example to the body of Christ in word and sound doctrine.

I Corinthians 11:1

13.   The characteristics of a teacher

They will validate truth A teacher has the need to validate truth, particularly doctrinal and theological truth. They often have a desire to spend large amounts of time studying and meditating on the Word of God.

Teachers speak with authority Teachers speak with authority, knowing Who gave them the words to speak.

Mark 1:21-22

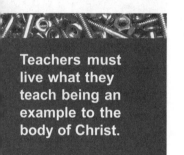

Teachers must live what they teach being an example to the body of Christ.

They have the ability to articulate and express thoughts Teachers have the divine ability to articulate and express thoughts well as they teach the Word of God. A teacher is not easily persuaded nor blown about by every wind of doctrine (Ephesians 4:14).

A teacher trains and releases A fivefold teacher desires to train and release other teaching ministries (II Timothy 2:2). They mentor future teachers.

They possess a passion for God's Word A teacher's passion is the Word, the Word, the Word. They carry a God given desire to see the body of Christ reach a place of maturity so as to be able to handle the "meat" of the Word.

Some teachers serve only within the spiritual field of their own local church while others serve in the broader body of Christ.

Discussion and Study Questions

1.   What does the evangelist impart to the church?
2.   What does the teacher impart to the church?
3.   What does the pastor impart to the church?
4.   How do all the fivefold ministries help to bring the church to maturity?
5.   How do they work together?

14. God matures His church through the fivefold ministry

The fivefold ministry is called by God to work together as a team. Each ministry gift is needed. The church of our generation will only come to maturity in Christ as we receive from each of these gifts and as they walk together in unity (Ephesians 4:11-16).

Module 12: The Fivefold Ministry and Cell Groups

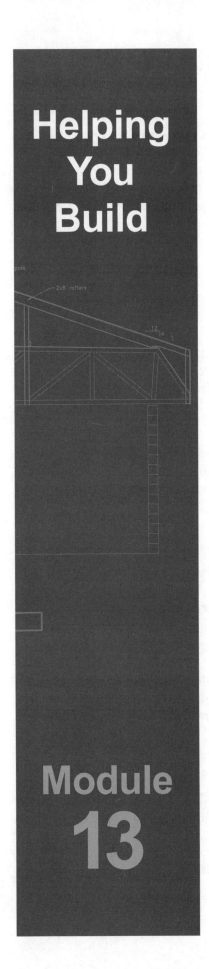

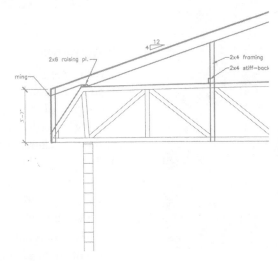

Helping You Build

Module 13

Youth in a Cell-Based Church

The training and releasing of young people is vital to the cell-based church. In this module we look at youth cells, youth groups and youth ministries and how they can all function together. We also look at youth cell values along with practical training to lead a healthy youth cell meeting.

Module 13

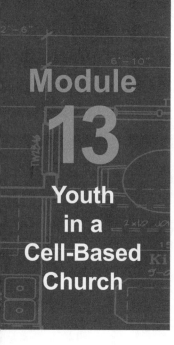

Module 13

Youth in a Cell-Based Church

A. Youth Cells and Youth Ministry

1. Why youth cells?

Family cells don't always meet the needs of youth Unless a leader in a family cell group has a real heart to be involved with the youth, the youth won't be a real part of the group and their needs won't be met. The teens end up outside playing basketball, taking care of the children or sitting in the cell meeting staring at their sneakers. Within a youth cell, issues, problems and interests are similar and can be addressed.

Teenagers tend to cluster in groups of:
- 2-3 close friends
- 10-15 peer relationships
- 15-40 youth group or team
- 40+ large crowds

They draw life and energy from all of these groupings. Youth cells include the first two groups of relationships. **For Christian teens, it is important that those primary relationships are with other Christians.**

2. How do we start?

It is best to **start with one prototype youth cell** and see that cell work properly and multiply. This way all the youth will see it modeled. DCFI's complete story of transition into youth cells is documented in the book *Youth Cells and Youth Ministry* written by a team of youth leaders.

3. Who leads?

Youth are generally attracted to anyone who has an open heart, is real, and has a home that is open. Generally, our youth cell leaders are at least one level of maturity above the group they are leading. For example, a middle school youth cell leader will be someone who is senior high age. There will often be junior high assistant leaders in that cell group.

We definitely need to believe in young leaders and give them a chance to lead In some cases, it works for youth cell leaders to lead a group of their peers. However, there needs to be a strong relationship and prayer covering from youth leaders (Jeremiah 1:7-8).

4. Who teaches?

Youth have the gift of teaching (Romans 12:7) as well as gray-haired adults The process of encouraging youth to step out in faith and teach will help you recognize their spiritual gifts (I Timothy 4:12).

Resource DCFI has a *Teacher Training Course* which provides a simple, practical, tangible method to train youth to teach and stimulate them in their spiritual growth.

This postmodern generation of youth does not have the basic Bible foundations or a Christian worldview. **Teaching is essential** DCFI recommends *The Biblical Foundation Series* books from *House to House Publications*, which are excellent for teaching youth. The simple pattern of scripture, key truths and examples make it easy for youth to understand God's Word and apply it to their lives. The video series *Foundations for Life* is also an excellent tool to use to teach youth the basic scriptural foundations of the Christian life.

5. Youth cell leaders' and assistant leaders' job descriptions

We write a job description for youth cell leaders and assistant leaders so they can know what is expected from them. It is not appropriate to assume that youth cell leaders know what to do.

Here is a sample youth cell leader's job description:

• **Pray for the youth in your cell group regularly** and communicate with your assistant cell leader to see each individual covered daily in prayer.

• **Your goal is to see all the youth walking with God** and in the vision of their church. Encourage each youth to be living an accountable life, involved in prayer, evangelism and discipleship.

• **Speak the vision of your local church**
  For example, DCFI's vision is *to build a relationship with Jesus, with one another, and to reach the world, from house to house, city to city, nation to nation.*

• **Meet with the other leaders in your cell to pray and plan** cell meetings and activities. Pray to see new leaders released and for your cell to multiply.

• **Keep in touch with your youth pastor, youth leaders** or other overseers with prayer concerns and growth strategy.

• **Attend all cell group leaders' meetings and training days** You are modeling leadership for future youth cell leaders.

• **You are also encouraged to support the youth group activities and meetings** by both encouraging the youth from your cell to attend and by attending them yourself.

6. Youth cell tips

• In a youth cell, the energy level is much higher. Be prepared for this!
• The youth need to know that they are important.
• Encourage them to help plan youth cell meetings and activities.
• Encourage them to help teach.
• Encourage them to help lead prayer times.
• Have as much discussion as possible.
• Talk openly about key issues.
• Help the youth discover how biblical truth applies to these issues.

- Allow plenty of time for ministry and waiting in God's presence.
- Keep a prayer journal complete with a list of answered prayer.
- Youth often wear masks, but their hearts are soft. They will not necessarily accept everything the leaders say at face value. There needs to be an atmosphere of love and acceptance. Expect the best, but accept the worst from them.

The three key issues in the life of a teenager
- Their relationship with God
- Their relationship with friends
- Their relationship with parents

If there is a problem in any one of these areas, it will affect the other two. A youth cell should help peers keep all these relationships healthy. **Open communication with parents is essential.**

7. Each generation of youth need a revelation of God

As much as parents and youth leaders enjoy their own relationship with God and worship expression, it will not be reproduced in the next generation in exactly the same way. God never changes, but how He is expressed through each generation will vary according to the personality of the generation. See Acts 2:17-18.

Jesus' disciples were young and Paul exhorts Timothy to not let anyone look down on him because he is young. Youth make tremendous spiritual leaders in the church today (Acts 2:17-18; I Timothy 4:12).

8. The youth culture is postmodern

The youth culture today is that which comes after a belief in modernism. Youth do not expect the world to get better. They feel the world they are being handed is a mess and there is no hope for it to improve. This international youth culture values honesty, relationship and community and is ripe for youth cells.

This generation of youth has had their beliefs formed by moving every few years, divorce and remarriage, and a rationalistic society. Fortunately, the things they are looking for—relationships, community, fathers—can be found in youth cells and the church. This generation of youth has it within their hearts to commit all and radically follow a cause. They are ripe for a spiritual awakening.

9. Youth cell ideas

There are many different kinds of outreach services and activities youth cells can participate in. The Lord leads us into creativity (I Corinthians 12:4-6). A complete list of ideas that have been successfully used is included in the book *Youth Cells and Youth Ministry.*

Discussion and Study Questions

1. Why are the youth of today ripe for a youth cell revival?

2. What do youth cells do that family cells do not?

3. Why should we give youth the freedom to decide along with their parents if they want to come to a youth cell or a family cell?

4. What three areas of relationships are essential to a teenager?

5. Why does each generation need its own revelation of God?

B. Creative Youth Cell Models

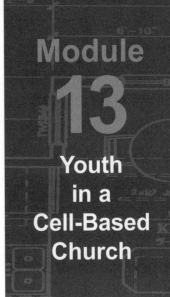

1. A word of caution

Please do not take this youth cell information as a pattern and start to implement it at your youth group without understanding the values behind it. Ask the question, "Why are we doing what we are doing?" We believe the church should be built on relationship and trust, releasing the youth to do the work of ministry. But the way you implement these values in youth cells could look different from our model. "Where the spirit of the Lord is, there is liberty" (II Corinthians 3:17).

2. The basics–youth cells and celebrations

Whatever model is used, the two essential ingredients are the same—that is, youth cells and a celebration of those cells in a corporate youth meeting. In these two components, the youth mirror what the rest of the church is doing. The creativity comes in the frequency, location, type of cells, leadership and celebration. These vary according to the needs of the group and the vision of the youth leadership and local church leadership.

Acts 20:20

3. Youth cells in homes and corporate youth gatherings

The primary method that is used in youth groups is to have the youth cells meet in homes during the week and have a corporate youth gathering at the church facility on a regular basis.

Youth cells in homes The youth seem to enjoy the natural relationships and community that a home allows. A home (though not their own) provides a relaxed environment where walls can come down. Youth are used to spending time with friends in homes and are encouraged to bring friends. Beware, they will stay late (if curfews allow!) The youth cells in homes meet every week or every other week. This depends on the desire of the youth to get together and the endurance of the leaders! The cells can be either gender-based or coed.

Corporate youth gatherings The corporate youth meeting is where the cells come together. It can be held every week, but many times will be held every other week or once a month. This meeting is generally at the church facility or youth room, a place where instruments and a sound system can be used as the group size dictates. This youth celebration appears similar to a traditional youth meeting, except the teaching is probably parallel to what is being taught in the cells. Depending on the current emphasis in the youth group, this corporate meeting can take on an evangelistic nature.

4. Youth cells at the church building

A creatively different model was developed where the youth cells and celebrations both take place on a Sunday night at the church building or youth room. The night starts with all the youth together for an informal social time of about 45 minutes. This is followed by roughly 30 minutes of worship. Next there is a teaching of approximately 30 minutes. Then the youth go with their cell leaders to different rooms and have a cell meeting. This cell meeting usually lasts 65 minutes. It all happens in one place on one night, solving transportation problems, especially for younger teens. It also gives greater accountability for the cell meetings.

5. Leadership

As mentioned earlier, in many of our youth cell groups, the leaders are at least one level of maturity ahead of the rest of the group. For example, we have a junior high youth cell led by a senior high leader with junior highers as assistant leaders. The youth still feel strong ownership of the cell because their peers are assistant leaders. This works well but it is not the only way to do it.

In some youth cell groups, peers or even younger youth lead the group
You have to work with the leaders God gives you. In this case, these young cell leaders need much more contact and closer oversight from the youth pastor, youth leaders or your pastor. This is essential to protect the young leaders, and it does work.

Jeremiah 1:4-10

6. Be creative

So, please allow the Holy Spirit to direct you as you consider implementing youth cells in your youth group. It can be accomplished in a variety of ways. You serve a creative God who understands the needs of your youth. But remember, youth cells must remain "outward focused" to be healthy.

7. Observe

Start observing what God has given you. What is God putting in the hearts of the youth you already have? What are the spiritual gifts of the youth already involved? Do a "spiritual gift survey" and find out. Use this as a starting point to start your first youth cell. "Spiritual Gift Surveys" can be ordered from your local Christian bookstore or *House to House Publications.* Call 800.848.5892.

Proverbs 27:23

Discussion and Study Questions
1. How do values lead to actions?
2. How does a cell-based youth ministry mirror a cell-based church?
3. What are the advantages of having youth cell groups in homes?
4. What are the advantages of having youth cell groups in a central location?
5. How can teens lead a cell of their peers?

C. What We Value in Youth Cells

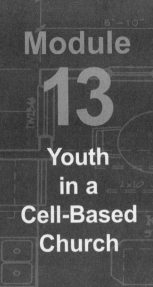

Much of the material in this section is adapted from Student Impact, 1993, Keith Kreuger.

Every "program" or activity we plan must run through these filters:
1. Does it build the cells?
2. Does it service the cells?
3. Is it done through the cells?
4. Does it fit in the philosophy of cells?

The word *value* means *a principle, standard, or quality considered worthwhile or desirable*. In ministry, there are many events, programs, meetings, and gatherings that come and go quickly. It is our responsibility to bring common direction, purpose, or "value" to some of these gatherings. The following are five basic building blocks that you can use creatively to hold high the value of cells.

1. Friends: connecting with each other

Teens are "relational beings." You see it on their school campuses—clusters of friends, gangs of friends. Build on this; don't fight them. Students feel most comfortable and open to truth when they have friendships or common bonds with people or have come to Christ on the arm of a trusted friend in the cell. Help students feel welcome. Help them bond themselves with other students. Remember, life change occurs best and is communicated best within the context of relationships and small groups. When students have shared and cared for each other, then you have had a successful cell.

Tips Joke around, have some fun, feed them food, take the time to break down any apprehensions a student brings to the meeting.
We want to build Godly cliques The only bad cliques are "exclusive" cliques.

2. Participation: connecting with each other

Imagine yourself as a young junior high or high school student having to "sit and listen" five days of your week at school, then coming to cells and having to "sit and listen." Learning can happen in many ways other than straight teaching. It is at this time that participation needs to take place. Participation can happen in many different ways. "Friends bringing friends" is their best and most valuable participation by bringing their friends to a relationship with Jesus. Some other suggestions follow:
- Don't just sit! Your students' attention span is short.
- Don't be predictable. Pre-plan and try different ideas.
- Listen to your students. What issues are they struggling with? What issues do they need addressed?
- Meet their needs and interests.

3. Student ownership: connecting with each other

Let go of the pressure that you must create a "killer" program in your cells. You must get students to own this time. The best way to get them to do this is to invest in it. People don't usually walk away from investments:

- Friends bring friends. This is an evidence of ownership.
- Let cell members do different parts of your cell meeting. Remember students will more readily listen to one another than listen to someone older than themselves.
- Let students assist in the planning. They can help plan activities, small group topics, etc.
- Listen, listen, and listen. Watch, watch, and watch. The Lord and the students will tell you what they need.

4. Communicate a biblical truth: connecting with God

Students don't need our thoughts ("milk"); they need God's Word (solid food).
> Hebrews 5:12-13

Suggestions:

- You can still communicate information and motivation; just springboard off the truth.
- This generation is very visually stimulated. Use videos to illustrate and clarify.
- Scripture, prayer, and worship are the best "teambuilders" you will ever find.
- Take the Word of God and apply it to the issues that your students are struggling with.
- Don't shy away from worship. Worship doesn't always involve singing, but does involve a heart of praising the goodness of God.
- Aggressively look for "teachable" moments.

5. Prayer: connecting with God

Pray! Pray! Pray! It gives Christ the credit, the glory, and the proper place in our walk with Him.

- Don't always pray in a large group.
- One on one is effective.
- Give a direction for prayer.
- Find out from the students what to pray for.

Discussion and Study Questions

1. Name the five building blocks of youth cells.
2. Tell how participation can happen in the youth cell.
3. How will youth connect with each other?
4. Name one evidence of ownership youth have to their cell.
5. How can you encourage youth to connect with God?

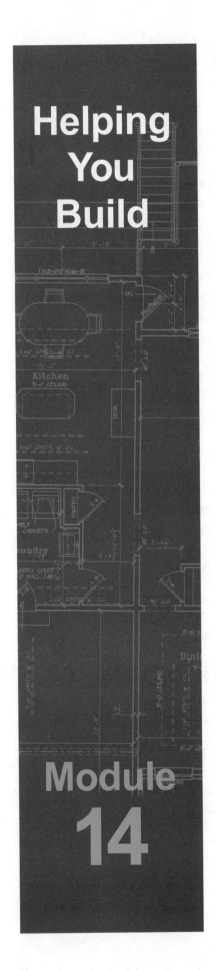

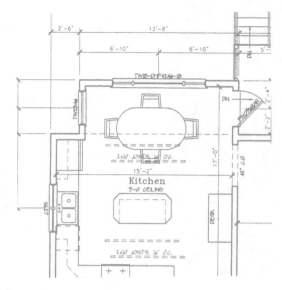

Module 14

Cell-Based Church Planting I

This module focuses on the practical aspects of planting a new cell-based church. Emphasis will be placed on effectively casting a vision for cell-based church planting and various methods to consider. We will also expound on the scriptural teaching of "fields" of ministry, which is important to understand before planting a new cell-based church.

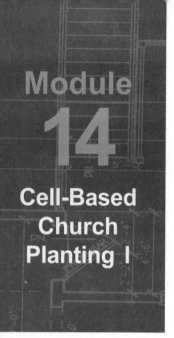

A. Casting a Vision for Church Planting

1. Cells multiply; churches multiply

Examples from nature Anything that is healthy and has life will reproduce and multiply. Obviously, the examples in nature are endless (Genesis 1:28).

Healthy reproduction In John 17:4, Jesus said He had completed the work that the Father gave Him to do. The Father has a similar work for each believer, each cell group and each local church. Each should multiply. A healthy cell group will grow and multiply into two cell groups. The same would then be true for a healthy local church. It will reproduce and plant other churches.

2. Church planting is the New Testament pattern

The New Testament church was a church planting movement. In Acts 2:37-47 the Jerusalem church was planted. In Acts 8:1-25 the Samaritan church was birthed. In Acts 9:20-22, the Damascus church came to life. Acts 9:31 reports churches throughout Judea, Galilee and Samaria. In Acts 19:9, we find out about a church planting school Paul ran in the lecture hall of Tyrannus. And the list goes on—Joppa, Caesarea, Antioch—**the book of Acts reads like a church planting manual.**

3. Church planting develops new leadership

It provides the opportunity for new and young leaders to stretch their wings and fly. We use the example of parents owning a house with different rooms. As they have children, each child may have a different room in the house to call their own bedroom. **But there will come a time when just a room in their parent's house is not enough. They will want their own house.**

Healthy parents will release their children to get their own place. It will be a stretching, learning experience for the children. Church planting allows our spiritual children to reach a new level of maturity they won't reach if they continue to live in our house.

4. Church planting prevents church splits

Could it be that one of the reasons that churches split is because the next generation of leaders is not released and sent out to establish its own churches? Insecure spiritual leaders frustrate developing leaders by not releasing them. What if the new church plant grew to be larger than the sending church? Frustrated by a glass ceiling, sometimes young leaders eventually leave disgruntled and take people with them.

When you send out a new cell leader, you are not always sure that he will be ready. It will sometimes be like this for church planters. In fact, they might not be ready, but the challenge of the church plant might be the very thing that will develop them to the next level of leadership. **Remember, someone took a chance on us!**

5. Church planting is efficient

C. Peter Wagner states, "There is no more practical or cost effective way of bringing unbelievers to Christ in a given geographic area than planting new churches." This statement is the result of extensive research and analysis of church growth.

Church planting provides the infrastructure to support and maintain the fruit that is coming forth Teaching the biblical financial principles of tithing and giving provides the substance to continue to extend the kingdom of God further.

6. Church planting stimulates existing churches

A new church in an area tends to raise the spiritual interest of the people, and if it is handled correctly, it can be a benefit to existing churches. Any new church that truly has a heart to reach a community it is targeting will want all the churches in the community to be blessed, prosperous and overflowing.

Some of the new converts from church planting evangelism will go to the existing churches because they already have relationships there.

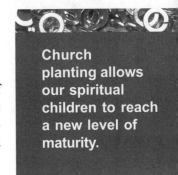

Church planting allows our spiritual children to reach a new level of maturity.

7. Not all churches are supposed to be mega-churches

A German church growth researcher, Christian Schwarz, reported the results of his research on church growth. He showed that statistically, small churches are 16 times more effective at winning new members than mega-churches. For example, two churches of 200 generally win twice as many people for Jesus as a single 400 member church.

So let's not be mesmerized by thinking every church is supposed to have thousands of people. **Maybe some churches are just supposed to grow to around two hundred people (addition) and then start planting churches (multiplication).**

8. Church planting is the only way to fulfill the Great Commission

Conversions alone will not fulfill the Great Commission. Matthew 28:18-20 is very specific about teaching, baptizing and making disciples. This is church activity: teaching, baptizing and making disciples.

9. Church planting reaches Christians who are currently not in churches

In almost any community in the western world, there are some Christians who have not been growing in their spiritual lives and who are not contributing to the kingdom of God simply because they do not fit into the present churches in their area. What they really need is a new church where they can feel at home. **A new church provides an entry point for people.** They don't have to break into an already established group.

10. Church planting provides more options for the unchurched

As long as there are unsaved people in our communities who are not being reached there is a need for new churches. New churches provide more options for the unchurched. They are a key to outreach and generally grow better than old ones. It is easier to have a baby than to raise the dead. This is not to say that existing churches are dead. It is just to point out that **the maternity ward is the most exciting place in a hospital.**

Discussion and Study Questions

1. Describe one of the church plants found in the book of Acts.
2. How does church planting develop new leadership?
3. How does church planting stimulate existing churches?
4. How does church planting fulfill the Great Commission in a way that conversions do not?
5. Why do we know that more churches are needed?

B. Methods of Church Planting

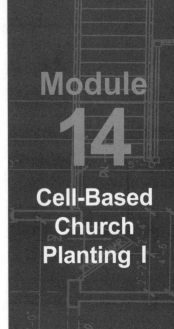

There are many models and methods of cell-based church planting. The book of Acts, our church planter's manual, gives us many examples. Here are some methods of church planting we have seen used both in the scriptures and in the body of Christ. **Sometimes two or more of these methods are combined in church planting.**

1.   One cell

A church planter and team will target an area and believe God for people to come in and join a cell group through some creative and divinely inspired methods. **The one cell becomes two, two becomes four and the church multiplies from there.**

2.   Hiving off

Hiving off is a common way to plant a church. **One or more cell groups from an existing church will be commissioned to start a new church.** Hiving off usually occurs with a cluster of cell groups in an area that is not very close geographically to the sending church, but this is not always the case. DOVE Christian Fellowship has used this method many times.

3.   Colonization

Colonization is a radical form of hiving off. In this case, **a cell group or a group of people from the sending church actually become a church planting team that relocates to a different geographical area.** They will move, find new homes, and new jobs in the target community and plant a church.

4.   Adoption

Adoption involves **a church that was started by someone else that for some reason wants or needs to be adopted.** In some cases, crisis in leadership or a change in vision may lead to these adoptions.

5.   Accidental parenthood

No one likes it, but church splits do produce new churches This would not be a planned church plant. But, sometimes the core group of a new church plant will separate for reasons that are mostly carnal. Personality conflicts, different visions, and theological disagreement can all cause church splits. However, if reconciliation occurs, God does seem to prosper both groups. This could be compared with a baby born out of wedlock. God loves the baby and has a plan for its life!

6. Satellite model

The satellite model is best described as a branch church A separate celebration of cells is sent out but still remains under the authority and leadership of the sending church. Generally a satellite church plant has its finances pooled with the original church. Eventually satellite churches could become their own churches.

7. Multi-congregational churches

In some multi-congregational churches, the same building will be used for different congregations Each congregation will appeal to a specific group based on music, culture, age, church tradition, etc. Each congregation will be a network of cell groups. A church building could be used Saturday night for a youth church, Sunday morning for a traditional church, Sunday afternoon for an ethnic group church, and Sunday night for another group.

8. Multiple campuses (circuit rider)

A circuit rider is a leader who will start clusters of cells in different geographic locations and travel to visit and encourage them John Wesley made this strategy famous as an effective way to plant churches. The blanket of Methodist churches covering the northeastern United States is testimony to its effectiveness.

9. Mission board

A mission board will recruit, sponsor, finance and send a team of church planters to another location, usually another nation. The mission board is usually supported by a group of churches.

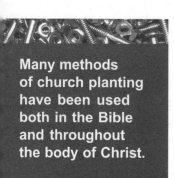

Many methods of church planting have been used both in the Bible and throughout the body of Christ.

10. Catalytic church planter

A catalytic church planter is a pioneer He likes to go into an area, clear new ground (plant a church) and then turn it over to someone else to maintain. He will then go into a new area to plant another church. Pioneers tend to plant many smaller churches which will grow according to the spiritual gifts of the leader he turns the church over to. It is important to not require the catalytic church planter to stay in one place too long.

11. Homestead church planter

The homestead church planter likes to go into a new area, plant a church and continue to build it up for a long period of time He will farm his ranch and it will grow and become a place of great strength over a period of time in a community. He will raise up spiritual sons whom he will send out to plant churches. It is important to not require the homestead church planter to move on to a new location.

12. Independent church planter

An independent church planter goes out on his own to start new churches This is an option but is not recommended. We believe churches need spiritual protection and correction.

160

13. The apostolic church planter

A group of churches in relationship with apostolic spiritual covering and oversight will send out church plants with an emphasis on spiritual gifts and the ministries mentioned in Ephesians 4:11-12. The new churches will usually have separate legal standing and have their own property, but the pastor will be under the spiritual authority of an apostle or apostolic team in the movement. The apostle's authority is not legal but spiritual. The Holy Spirit produces and sustains this mentoring relationship.

14. Spontaneous church

Believe it or not, some **churches just happen without any intention or plan.** The Holy Spirit is poured out in a home or workplace, and people start to come to faith in Christ. Eventually a leader emerges from the group.

Listen to this story: A man in Nepal received a piece of gospel literature and decided to send for a correspondence course to learn more about Jesus. He walked five hours to a post office, where he met another man mailing a request for the same material. As they headed toward home, they met a group of men headed for the post office to request the same course. The 15 men agreed to gather for worship on Saturday, and when the Holy Spirit moved in their midst at that meeting, they decided to gather weekly.

15. Outpost preaching points

In the outpost preaching points method **a gifted individual will draw people to public places for preaching or teaching by returning to the same geographic places a number of times** At first, this seems to be the opposite of the cell vision, but with care, a large group can be taught cell values and be assimilated into cells over a period of time. This does work, but it can be awkward.

16. The phone's for you

The "phone's for you" is basically **a tele-market strategy to reach people in a community** The church planter will need a solid core group with a number of cell leaders and assistant leaders already trained and ready to go. The phone strategy will draw a crowd, but the challenge is to see everyone get involved with cell groups. This strategy has been very effective in planting new churches.

17. Mission Sunday School

The mission Sunday School starts out by reaching the children in a community When children get involved in Sunday School, church, and children's cells, the parents and other relatives tend to follow. Household salvation was very common in the early church. Acts 16:31-34

18. Regional presbytery church plant

A regional presbytery church plant is a group of churches in an area working together to plant a church Two, three or more churches pool their resources, talents and money to see the new church established. The sending churches should be of the same spiritual family of churches but could come from different church families.

19. Bible study group

Many churches started out as a Bible study in a living room This can be very effective in intellectual communities (close to universities). The concept of a cell group might be new for people, but often they will come to an "issues" kind of Bible study. The Bible study then can become a cell group, or the Bible study continues as an outreach and the first cell starts on another night. The Alpha Course is a good example of an inductive Bible study that has been used very effectively in church planting.

20. Signs and wonders

The signs and wonders model is simple and profoundly effective. **Look for a home where someone is sick. Pray for the sick person and see them healed. Then start a cell group right in that home.** Very often the whole family and extended family will get saved. Other supernatural aspects of the gospel, like spiritual gifts and deliverance, will also be effective as people have a hunger for the supernatural power of God.

21. Youth ministry

Many times youth ministries will become churches. As new converts and new leaders mature, the youth ministry will mature into a church. The first DOVE Christian Fellowship church started out of a youth ministry.

22. Micro churches

Sometimes new churches are planted in homes, and rather than eventually renting or purchasing a larger building for a celebration, leaders are sent out to start new micro churches in homes. These churches can be cell-based and give the opportunity for more leadership to be trained and released. To be the most effective, micro churches need to network together with other micro churches and with the body of Christ. Possibly, micro churches could meet together bimonthly for a larger celebration.

23. Other methods

We believe that in the season of church planting ahead, the Lord will raise up new methods not yet identified or used. We need to be sensitive to creative, new ideas for church planting. Some people have opened bookstores, coffee shops, medical clinics and drilled wells all in the name of church planting.

Discussion and Study Questions

1. How is a church planted by hiving off?
2. Is a church split a church plant?
3. What is the difference between a pioneer and a homesteader church planter?
4. Why is an independent church plant undesirable?
5. Describe a possible new method for church planting.

C. Fields of Ministry

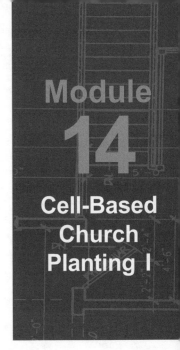

1. Understanding fields of ministry

A scriptural understanding of "fields of ministry" is essential for successful church planting and all leadership. II Corinthians 10:13 states, "We, however will not boast beyond measure, but within the limits of the sphere which God appointed us—a sphere which especially includes you."

Metron—field of ministry The Greek word for "field" in the New Testament is "metron." It means *a measure or sphere of activity that defines the limits of one's power and influence.* Verses 14 and 15 of II Corinthians 10 define this even more.

Special grace is given for a field of ministry Ephesians 4:7 (NIV) translates metron differently: "But to each one of us grace has been given as Christ apportioned it." Here the word *apportioned* is a translation of the same word "metron." So, it seems that for each metron or field of ministry, there is a special grace given for that field. A simple definition of grace is "the enabling power to do what God has called us to do."

Fields of ministry make us fruitful within those areas Psalm 16:5-6 (NIV) teaches us more: "Lord, you have assigned me my portion and my cup: you have made my lot secure. The boundary lines have fallen for me in pleasant places; surely I have a delightful inheritance." Boundary lines don't limit us, but allow us to be fruitful in certain areas. Fields that God assigns to us are secure, protected places of learning. We grow and learn how to receive our inheritance there. If we are out of our field, we are out of grace.

Christians are wrong to wait around for God's additional, external direction when they already have the internal anointing guiding them in the areas of their metron. In Exodus 14:15, God rebuked Moses for not leading and using the authority he had been given as the leader of the children of Israel.

2. Examples of fields of ministry
All of us have different fields of ministry

Our marriage	Our family
Our home	Our cell group
Our local church	Church plant
Our neighborhood	Our community

Adam and Eve surrendered their "field" to Satan In Genesis 1:26 God gave Adam and Eve authority over the whole world, but first their stewardship had to be proven in the garden of Eden. Satan came into Adam and Eve's field, and they surrendered their authority to him.

This is an example of how **not everyone who comes into our field is from the Lord.** The usurper will come to take your field away from you. Stand firm against him with great wisdom and strength. Do not stand for the enemy interfering in your field. Rise up in faith and throw the enemy out in Jesus' name!

3. God determines and expands our fields

It is Jesus who determines and expands our fields of ministry. Psalm 75:6-7 (NIV) states, "No one from the east or the west or from the desert can exalt a man. But it is God who judges: He brings one down, he exalts another." **Fields of ministry are areas in which God gives us stewardship.**

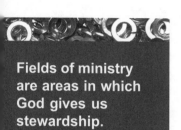

Fields of ministry are areas in which God gives us stewardship.

He gives grace and anointing to us to rule our fields In Matthew 10:1, Jesus gave authority to His disciples as He was opening up a new field for them. He didn't send them out without first giving them the authority. God gives His authority through delegated individuals.

Specific fields It seems that God gave Paul and Peter specific fields. Paul's call and anointing was to the Gentiles, and Peter's call and anointing was to the Jews. These lines were so clearly drawn that Paul confronted Peter when he crossed over into his field. In ignorance, Peter's ideas were undermining what God was doing at Antioch. Paul came under the Jerusalem elders when he was in their field (Acts 15), but he was over others in his own field. (Galatians 2:7-9,11-13 describes this confrontation.) **We cannot assume the field that is ours.** Paul seemed more qualified to reach the Jews, and Peter seemed more qualified to reach the Gentiles. But God crossed them over to the group unlike themselves.

You can delegate authority in your field You can temporarily delegate to others the authority God has given you in a field of ministry. I Timothy 1:1-4 describes how Timothy was assigned a portion of Paul's authority in Ephesus, even to the point of bringing correction to false teachers and doctrines.

An example of this is the elders of a local church assigning authority to a cell leader for a cell group. There will be confusion if that cell leader then tries to take that authority beyond the cell into other areas of the church.

Another example: When parents are away from home, they might ask the oldest child to be responsible for the house. This child has received delegated authority for his parent's field. When the parents return, they are in charge of the house again.

Module 14: Cell-Based Church Planting I

Stay in your field! You will have great authority and confidence in your field. But, if you leave your field, you are outside of the grace given to you. According to James 4:6, God will oppose you. Don't presume the anointing and authority you have is a general anointing for you to use anywhere and at any time. This is dangerous, even when done in ignorance. When you move out of your field, it can open you up to spiritual deception. Fields do not limit you; many times they keep you from getting beaten by the enemy.

4. How to determine your fields

Acts, chapters 17-21, describes the process by which Paul "discerned" his field. This happened by Paul recognizing the area where he did not have grace—namely in relating the gospel to the Jews (Acts 17:5-6). In Acts 18:5-8, Paul made a conscious decision to give up on ministering to the Jews and endeavoring to reach the Gentiles. He saw almost immediate success. In Acts 21:17-19, he was responsible to give a report from his field. Romans 1:5 has Paul again clearly stating his field.

Paul understood fields of ministry well He often appealed to those in authority when he was in their field. In Acts 22:25-29, he appealed to the Roman guards, stating that in their field he should not be beaten because he was a Roman citizen. **Allow God to assign you fields through his delegated authority, and expect He will expand them as you are faithful.** You have stewardship of the field, not ownership. A symptom that you are taking ownership occurs if you get depressed when someone leaves your field.

Don't stand for the enemy's activity in your field Paul had a sense of responsibility for the Corinthian church (II Corinthians 11:28-29). Do spiritual warfare for your fields. God has given you authority.

5. Application for church planting

Be responsible within your present field, build it and God will enhance it Allow God to promote you. You need a sending base (Luke 16:10; Acts 13:1-4). Timing is everything. Ecclesiastes 8:5-6 indicates there is a proper time and procedure for every matter. David is the classic example—he was called and anointed to be King, but there was already a king. David did not seize or usurp authority. He allowed God to promote him (Psalm 78:70-72).

Recognize the importance of defining a territory as a metron and giving yourself for it To plant a church, you need to make some type of personal investment in the territory. Do spiritual warfare for it. Carve out something new. In Romans 15:20, Paul said he did not want to build on another's foundation.

Avoid infringing on the spiritual territory of another. Work cooperatively and respectfully with existing efforts within one's geographical sphere. If you are sent out from a church and have a spiritual covering, this will calm the fears of pastors in the area. Have your apostolic overseer meet with you and the other area pastors together.

Evil powers take advantage when there is confusion over authority when one intrudes into the field of another. This can happen in relating to people. It can also happen in prayer. A person can pray for things to go the way they think they should go rather than the way the person responsible for that metron is led by the Spirit to take them. If intercessors are not taught about fields of ministry, it can be dangerous.

We must recognize what fields are and faithfully work within them. It is important to teach our church planting teams and future leadership how fields of ministry work.

Discussion and Study Questions

1. What is the meaning of metron?

2. What does Jesus give you for your metron according to Ephesians 4:7?

3. How do fields of ministry expand?

4. What is the key in determining our fields?

5. Give an example of how you crossed out of your field and how you knew it.

Module 14: Cell-Based Church Planting I

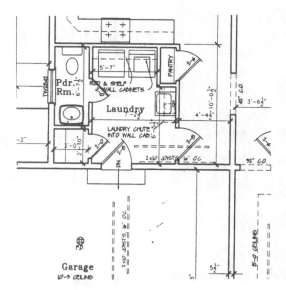

Module 15

Cell-Based Church Planting II

Building a healthy team for church planting is essential. In this module, we walk you through the steps to planting a cell-based church. In addition, we will "cover the bases" of principles to understand before you launch a church planting endeavor.

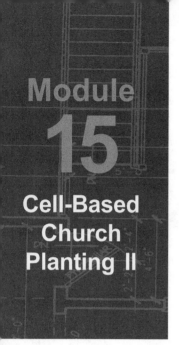

A. Building a Church Planting Team

It takes longer to plant a church without a team, and the likelihood of success is smaller. A team helps to carry the load and see the project to completion.

1. Build with vision

God has a vision for His people. Vision always precedes reality. It is a gift God places in the church to inspire people to see something they would not otherwise see and to believe what they would not otherwise believe. Every church planter must lead with vision. It will motivate the group to make the required sacrifices. Write the vision down so the team can run together (Habakkuk 2:1-4). An exercise to help you develop a vision statement is included in Appendix E.

Visionary leaders can expect to be criticized Many people resist change. Initiate the general vision, but allow the team to help develop the final vision. Don't criticize the vision of others on the team, but look for a way to implement it within the context of the overall vision.

Common vision is essential for the success of any team.

2. Build in holiness

We want to welcome diversity of personalities on our church planting team, but we must confront sin if there are conflicts Sin (especially rebellion) divides and opens the door for more sin. Confront sin prayerfully, gently and firmly. Confront sin by teaching the truth (Romans 2:4). Set a biblical standard and teach it clearly. Announce your expectation, then hold people to it. Focus on the nature and holiness of God. Leaders do have a higher standard.

3. Build a diverse team with unity

You want diverse personalities to be included in your team. You want a variety of gifts, especially the ones you don't have. Encourage diversity. Unity does not come from uniformity. A diverse team reflects the character of God. Don't think unity is a nebulous concept that we either have or don't have. Teach people how to walk in unity. Matthew 18:15-17 dictates how conflicts should be resolved. Unity begins by every team member affirming every other person on the team (I Corinthians 1:10). Unity should be built around common values not common personalities.

Common values are essential for the success of every team.

4. Build through inclusiveness

Teach your team that the Great Commission is more important than our pet minor doctrines. We want to major on majors and minor on minors. Seek leaders from different cultures and races to be involved on your team.

Listen, respect and accept

Be inclusive in how you make your decisions. The first step in clear communication is listening and respecting what you hear and taking it seriously. Accept all team members, understand them, and value their input.

James 1:19

5. Build by following

Build team unity by being under authority If you can't come under authority, you can't be in authority. The more mature you become, the more people you are willing to come under. Authority doesn't mean anything in our lives until we have to give something up.

Authority is not a title; it flows out of who you are It is the reflection of maturity, wisdom, character, experiences and spiritual gifts. People will submit to your authority if you submit to those God places over you (Romans 13:1-7).

6. Build team unity joyfully

The kingdom of God is supposed to be fun. Church planting is no different. Yes, it is a serious task, but it is not to be a drudgery. Include celebration in the life of the church planting team. God made us with the capacity to laugh. The spirit of celebration is part of how God created us to mark those things that are special in our lives. If this kind of joyful celebration does not come to you naturally, be sure to release others on the team to initiate it.

Enjoy your team

The people of Israel had seven times of celebration as they served together. Worship should be a joyful celebration of God's goodness. Life should be celebrated.

Nehemiah 8:10

Common relationships are essential for the success of any team.

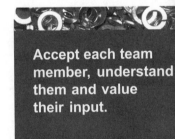

Accept each team member, understand them and value their input.

7. Build with discernment

We are fighting against the powers of darkness. Discern the tactics of the enemy that are specifically aimed at your church planting team. We must saturate our minds with the truths of God's Word to discern what is of God and what is not. There is no manual that has the pattern for every decision.

Ephesians 6:12; John 8:32

There is a protective role given to leaders to watch over the team This is your field. Don't open the door to everyone who comes along. Get to know them first. Help people discern the impact of the culture they are living in and how that keeps them from developing community on the team. Continue to ask the Lord for wisdom and discernment (James 1:5).

8. Build as learners

Ask questions. Identify your own (biblical) presuppositions and test other ideas by your presuppositions and your ministry philosophy. A primary way to lead people is to ask questions. Be learners from others in their spiritual walk. Never stop learning. Go to retreats, get alone, take days off to give you time to rest, to reflect, to pray. Stretch your mind. Read books you don't always agree with. Take your team to a conference where you can learn and discern together.

9. Build with good communication

Speak consistently and clearly and stick with what God says. Speak lovingly; inspire people; encourage people. Sound a sure, steady note. Get the people together who are having conflict. Help them to work it through. Develop skills to manage conflict. Conflict can be a gift to help people work out character flaws (Acts 15).

Respond to manipulators with righteous speech Don't take responsibility for others' problems. Set the tone on your team by only talking about that which edifies other people (Ephesians 4:29) unless you are directly involved in helping a person solve a problem or if someone comes to you with a problem. Use only the details that are needed and keep it to the smallest group possible. Don't correct the whole group when only one person is the problem. Go to them.

10. Build with good planning

Good planning will avoid confusion and increase unity. Nehemiah gave clear job descriptions as they built the wall (Nehemiah 4:13-14). Every vision should include: who you will reach, how you will reach them, and what will happen when you reach them. Write it down.

Develop your planning and administration skills Good management builds team unity. Communicate clearly with people when they are not doing their job. Implement regular evaluations. Budgets and staff positions should be planned in advance. The book of Nehemiah contains much instruction in people management and healthy, godly leadership.
Common procedures are essential for the success of any team.

Discussion and Study Questions
1. How can vision help develop a team?
2. What are three qualifications you personally would like to see in a team member?
3. How does diversity develop team strength?
4. How can you teach your team unity?
5. How can you teach your team good communication?

Module 15: Cell-Based Church Planting II

B. Steps to Planting a New Cell-Based Church

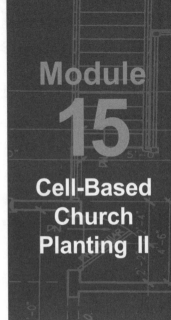

1. **The three legs to establish a church plant**
   It is helpful to look at the end product you are desiring in a church plant and then make sure you are doing the right things to achieve the desired result.

   There are three things that define a cell-based church in Acts 20:20
   • House to house (cell groups)
   • Temple meetings (public celebration)
   • Leadership (In this case it was Paul addressing the elders at Ephesus.)
   We want to see these three legs established in the church plant.

2. **Pray, pray, pray**
   The primary leader must increase his prayer life. Hold group prayer meetings and recruit intercessors who will support the work in prayer. From this initiative of prayer will come guidance concerning location, a target people, timing, evangelistic strategies and future reproduction of the new church. There are helpful resources concerning demographics and church planting/evangelism techniques, but these only supplement prayer. The first church plant in the book of Acts was preceded by much prayer (Acts 1-2). **Prayer and fasting is what plants the church.** It would be beneficial to include three to five extended fasts in the first two years of the church plant. **Recruit an intercession team that is not a part of the church plant.**

3. **Assembling a team (read Acts 13-14)**
   Church planting without a team takes longer and is less successful. A team is essential, although it can be a small one. Speak vision to the people. It is okay to recruit people as long as they respond because they feel a genuine call from the Lord. Jesus recruited the disciples. **Note that recruiting is a military term because it will be warfare to start a new church.** Assemble the group and start meetings to pray. As you meet with those you have, God will add to your team. It is appropriate to fast when selecting those who will be on your church planting team.

4. **Developing a vision and mission statement**
   If people are going to commit their time, effort, and lives to this church plant, they need to know what the vision is and be able to consider it in written form. See Appendix E for a step-by-step procedure to develop a vision and mission statement.

5. Spiritual warfare

There are some very good books and resources available on the subject of spiritual warfare. We will not go into great detail here other than to say that spiritual warfare needs to happen. You are carving out something new in enemy territory so the strongman of the territory must be bound in order to take his goods (the people). This again is an appropriate time to fast with your prayers.

Matthew 12:29; Ephesians 6:12

Do spiritual warfare from a posture of victory After World War II was over and a peace treaty was signed, the fighting still continued in remote Pacific islands. They had not yet received the news that the victory was won. The victory has been won for all people by the blood of Jesus on the cross. The price has been paid, and the enemy is defeated. But this new area where we are planting a church has not yet received the word that the battle is over and that Jesus won the victory. It needs to be proclaimed!

6. Finding people willing to listen

This is where your church planting techniques, demographic studies and evangelism tools come into play. Appendix E contains demographic information to help you select the target group. Especially look for divine contacts with people and believe God for heads of households to be saved. Look for the "man of peace" who might open up a whole neighborhood. Perhaps you may connect with scattered or backslidden Christians. If you target the unsaved, these other Christians will also come. **Call in all the reinforcements from the sending church at this point.**

7. Beginning networking

Now is the time to start contacting other pastors and leaders in the area. Let them know who you are and what you are doing. They may not initially receive you, but keep blessing them. **Relationship takes time.**

8. Starting cell groups

You might consider the team your first cell group and add to it or look to establish a cell group in the home of one of your initial contacts. The first cell will include a lot of sharing Christ, laying foundations in peoples' lives, and sharing vision.
The oikos evangelism principle should be taught and now kicked into action, leading to growth and a multiplication of cell groups. See Module 4:A for insights on oikos evangelism. Your team members should be already trained to lead these cell groups. Water baptism and Holy Spirit baptism should happen in these cell groups.

9. Starting a temple meeting

It is possible to bring two cell groups together for a celebration. However if you wait until there are at least three, there may be a broader base to support the celebration. It takes children's workers, greeters, worship leaders, administrative leaders and others to run a celebration meeting effectively.

Things to remember when selecting your celebration place:
- It should be an easy-to-find location near your target group.
- You should balance the needs of worship, nursery, children and parking.
- Is the location available for other meetings, cell leaders, etc.?
- Are the acoustics and lighting adequate?
- Leave room to grow. Can you have multiple services there?
- Is it cost-effective?

The key to the timing of starting a celebration is the amount of key laborers and cell leaders, rather than the number of people or the number of cells. Also, you should have a clear sense it is the Lord's timing.

Give the church a name Around this time you should be settled on a name for the church, if not before. Names are important, so the team should pray and ask God to reveal what it should be. The name should be distinctive, relevant to people, easy to remember and inclusive. But most importantly, it must be God's name.

Set up your organization legally with the government There is a set of sample cell church bylaws in Appendix E.

10. Teaching and identifying spiritual gifts

This is a new church paradigm. Membership in the local church is now equal to ministry. Every member ministers according to Ephesians 4:11-16. Guide people to where they can use their spiritual gifts. **Each one is held to the body by what they contribute.**

11. Training leaders

Provide a clear cell leadership track for people to be trained It should be visible and recognizable for people to get started. Also provide a clear discipleship track for new Christians.

After the public meeting is functioning alongside the cell groups, it is time to determine the long-term leadership of the church. This is a good time to evaluate the original team. In a lot of cases, a number of the original team won't be there anymore. They were just called to help birth the new church. They provided the scaffolding to build the wall. They were never called to be part of the wall, but only to help build it. This is one reason why, in most cases, elders should not be appointed in the beginning of the church plant. In Acts 14:22-23, Paul and Barnabas appointed elders about two years after the church was birthed.

Is the church planter a homesteader or a pioneer? That is, will he stay there and continue to build a sending base for future church plants, or will he move on and start the next church plant?

In either case, the elders of the local church must be trained and commissioned Apostolic overseers need to be involved in this process. The elders are responsible to protect, direct and correct the local church and thus see it grow and prosper.

Acts 14:23; Titus 1:5

Discussion and Study Questions

1. What are the three essential elements to establish the church plant according to Acts 20:20?
2. What role does prayer play in a church plant?
4. What role does spiritual warfare have in a church plant?
5. When should you start a celebration meeting?
6. How should the long-term leadership of a church plant be chosen?

C. Covering the Bases

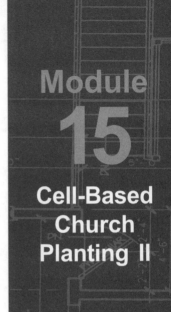

1. Cover your bases before launching out to plant a church or starting a new ministry

This teaching contains basic principles, not laws. Many sincere church planters and missionaries, after a few years of pioneering, seem to hit a brick wall. They are praying and believing, yet something does not seem to be working the way they anticipated.

There are spiritual bases for us to cover to be properly prepared to plant a church or launch out into a new area of ministry. In order to score in the game of baseball, the player must touch all the bases. If we learn to start out correctly, it is easier to finish properly. Paul said, "I have finished the race" (II Timothy 4:7). May we all do the same!

Timing is crucial! There is a price to pay in preparation for church planting. Moses initially missed the timing of God by forty years. The Lord trained him to lead the children of Israel out of Egypt as he took care of his father-in-law's sheep.

2. The playing field is built on the foundation of the grace of God (I Corinthians 15:10)

We are completely dependent upon the grace of God. We are responsible (as the Lord's sons and daughters) to hit the ball and run. Others may assist us, but we are responsible before the Lord.

3. Home plate

Home plate is the sending base (Ephesians 4:16) Where is your primary connection to the body of Christ? Who is sending you out? II Corinthians 10:12-17 speaks of fields of ministry and responsibility in the body of Christ. Which field are you in?

- In Titus 1:5, we see Titus as an apostle commissioned by Paul to appoint local elders in every city.
- In Acts 13:1-4, Barnabas and Saul were sent out of their local church at Antioch to plant churches and then reported back to their church a few years later (Acts 14:26-28).

If you do not have a local church, find a connection somewhere for both apostolic and pastoral accountability and protection According to Hebrews 13:17, our spiritual leaders are called by God to watch out for our souls. Who is watching out for your soul? In Acts 15:1-4, Barnabas and Saul reported to the apostolic leadership of the early church.

4. First base

First base is the training/preparation base Initially, we need to have a deep personal relationship with Jesus. This is our first area of preparation.

    John 17:3

Then, we should be trained in a cell group setting We need to learn to be faithful in little, so we can be faithful in much (Luke 16:10). We should lead a cell and see it multiply as a part of our hands-on training.

Learning from others with experience More than 90% of all missionary and leadership problems concern relationships with other leaders. We can learn so much about working with people in a cell group setting. Questions we must ask ourselves.

- Do we recognize our limitations and strengths?
- Do we have a ministry gift or a ruling gift, or both?
- Do we recognize our need for a team with various gifts?
- Do we understand healthy church government and decision-making?
- Do we know our role in leadership?
- Are we a primary leader or a supportive leader?
- Do we understand group dynamics?

A school like the *House to House Church Planting and Leadership Video Correspondence School* may be vital for you as a part of your preparation.

A biblical training base has a two-pronged focus:
- **Impartation of knowledge and inspiration in a classroom setting** (Paul taught future leaders in the School of Tyrannus: Acts 19:9).
- **Experiencing practical ministry through a mentoring** (internship) relationship. Paul mentored Timothy (Acts 16:1-5).

We should lead a cell and see it multiply as a part of our hands-on training.

5. Second base

Second base is the prayer base You must break through the spiritual strongholds in the potential church planting area. You need a team of dedicated prayer partners/intercessors who will stand in the gap for you and with you.

- In Acts 12:12-16, we see Peter getting out of prison as Mary and the "cell group" were praying for him.
- In Luke 6:12, Jesus prayed all night and then chose His disciples.

See Module 2 for a more extensive study on the prayer life of a church planter.

6. Third base

Third base is the financial base God's plan to finance the local church is through the tithes (10%) and offerings (Malachi 3:8-11; Matthew 23:23). However, when a church is being planted, there usually are not enough tithes to support a leader for the church. We need to prayerfully consider various options and take personal responsibility for our finances.

How does the Lord desire to fill your cup to provide for you and for your family? Luke 6:38 tells us that men will "give into our laps" (fill our cups) as we, in obedience, give to others. We must allow the Lord to fill our cup any way He chooses. Luke 16:10-11 teaches us that God uses our proper handling of money to prepare us for spiritual ministry.

Our cups may be filled by a combination of sources Here are some of the ways (potential sources of provision) the Lord may choose to fill our cups:

• **Tent making** "He stayed with them and worked..." (Acts 18:1-3). Tent-making is working at a job or business to earn income to finance our family and the new church plant as the church is being planted.

• **Supernatural provision** In Matthew 17:27, Peter found a coin in the mouth of a fish to pay his taxes and Jesus' taxes. This was not normal for Jesus' provision; however, the Lord did feed the 5,000 supernaturally.

• **Support team of family and friends** In Luke 8:1-3, we read that Jesus had a team who supported Him from their substance. Many para-church ministries encourage missionaries and church planters to build a support team, send out newsletters, etc. This is a scriptural way for the Lord to provide for us.

• **Local church support** In II Corinthians 8:3-4, a gift was given to Paul from the local church. Some missionaries and church planters are blessed by the support of their local church as God's way of providing for them.

• **Living from the gospel** I Corinthians 9:7-14 teaches us that those who preach the gospel should live from the gospel. Galatians 6:6 says, "Let him who is taught the word share in all good things with him who teaches." If a traveling fivefold minister (Ephesians 4:11-12) preaches the Word to a cell group or local church, the believers should bless him financially. This helps to fill his cup.

• **"Honor" given to an elder who is sent out** I Timothy 5:17-18 tells us the laborer is worthy of his wages. Sometimes a local church leader will be supported as a local elder as he ministers for a season in another part of the world.

• **Inheritance** Proverbs 13:22 says a good man leaves an inheritance to his children's children. Some families have used inheritance money as God's provision to support them as short-term missionaries and church planters.

• **Investments and business** In Matthew 25:14-18, Jesus gives the Parable of the Talents. Some successful businessmen who have been blessed to use their talents wisely give a season of their lives to missions and church planting. Retired military personnel have at times used their pension to support them financially in church planting and missions.

• **The ant method (work and save)** Proverbs 6:6-8 tells us that ants "labor hard in the summer, gathering food for the winter" (Living Bible). Some church planters work hard and save for a season and then use the money that is saved to support them on the mission field and in church planting.

- **Kingdom breadwinning** Luke 10:7 tells us the laborer is worthy of his wages. "Kingdom breadwinning" is to be paid by the church or Christian ministry as a staff member of the church or ministry.

Count the cost (Luke 14:28-30) Count the cost with these questions regarding the Lord filling your financial cup in the way that He chooses:
- Lord, have you called me to be a church planter, a missionary, a local or a translocal minister or an elder?
- Lord, how do you desire to fill my cup?
- Lord, what can I do now to start?
- Am I willing to count the cost and "bear the cross"? (God's choice of provision not being the same as ours can be our cross.)
- When one door of provision closes, am I willing to allow God to open another?
Unmet expectations bring a death blow to many church planters, spiritual leaders, translocal fivefold ministries, and missionaries.

Here are some danger signs to avoid:
- Dictating to God how to fill your cup
- Comparing how God is filling our cup with how He fills others' cups (II Corinthians 10:12; John 21:21-22)
- Seeing one area of provision as more spiritual than another with it becoming an idol in our hearts (Ezekiel 14:3). If I trust any one area as being more spiritual, I get my eyes off the Lord!
- Not being willing to pay the "timing price" (The Lord uses the process of filling our cups to prepare us spiritually for service)
- Expecting another person, mission agency, or church to take the responsibility to provide the funds to fulfill my vision

7. **A home run**
   A home run is being sent out to plant a church or launching into a new ministry God's timing is crucial. Some initial team members may serve as a "scaffolding" but not a part of the permanent spiritual building. Move slowly in building a leadership team. The sending church can rejoice with you as the new church is established. The order of these bases can be changed. The key is for us to cover them all.

Discussion and Study Questions
1. What role does grace play in covering the bases?
2. Why do we need to be sent from somewhere?
3. How would you go about recruiting intercessors for a church plant?
4. Which of the financial sources of provision have you seen in your life?
5. How can unmet expectations discourage people?

Module 15: Cell-Based Church Planting II

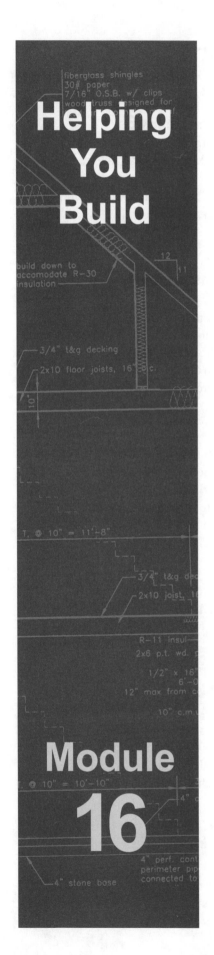

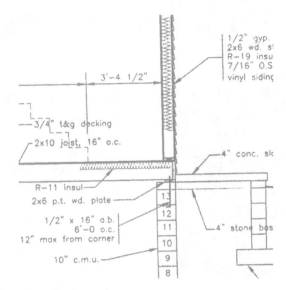

Module 16

Transitioning to a Cell-Based Church

This module gives basic steps to take regarding sharing the vision, timing, training cell leaders and a healthy approach to dismantling some of the programs that may no longer be needed in your church. Examples and insights from a church that has successfully transitioned will be shared.

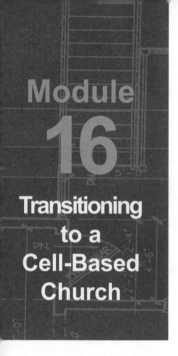

A. Basic Transition Steps

1. **Don't be in a hurry: Give God the time He needs**
    The scriptures teach us to be as wise as serpents and as harmless as doves (Matthew 10:16). Matthew 13:33 speaks of the kingdom being like leaven (yeast). In this case, it is positive leaven.
    We must give time for the yeast to rise Don't be in a hurry. Give God enough time to grow the vision to transition in the hearts of His people.

2. **The primary vision carrier (senior pastor) must have this vision**
    Cell ministry cannot be a side program. The senior pastor must have these scriptural values in his heart and be committed to implement them. A cell-based church is as different from a program-based church as salt is from pepper. We must choose how we are called to build. Don't try to change your pastor. He is responsible before the Lord for the vision of the church he oversees.

3. **The senior pastor must be willing to lead the way**
    He needs to teach values from the Word of God on cell-based ministry. Otherwise, people will not have faith for the change. He will need to speak the vision over and over again. Taking the key leaders to a conference or seminar on cell ministry can help others in leadership to "catch the vision."

4. **The senior pastor must model this concept**
    It takes time! He must give himself to this model; it is caught more than taught. He must be willing to be in a cell group.

5. **The primary leader of the church should choose a few leaders to start a cell**
    Choose key people who will soon be able to start their own cells (Mark 3:14). Having a cell group meeting "underground" is a bit like a baby growing within his mother. At first the baby is unseen, but eventually it "shows" as the baby continues to grow. You will have a church within a church for a season of time.

    Give books concerning cell ministry to the people in this initial cell Reading them will help to strengthen the cell vision in their hearts.

    Do not abruptly stop all programs (Some may be good!) Discontinue any programs that you can without causing the believers in the church to overly react. Move slowly and prayerfully!

6. **After a few months, these leaders should each start their own cell (by relationship)**

Continue to meet with the leaders *at least* monthly for training and discipleship. Watch the cell leaders grow as they start their own cells.

7. **Continue meeting with the leaders (all underground)**

Care about them as individuals. Pastor the cell leaders. Meet with them individually. Bring people in to equip and encourage them (fivefold ministers, etc.). Make sure the cell leaders feel valued. We need to encourage one another daily (Hebrews 3:13). Encourage these new cell leaders regularly.

8. **Teach values of cell ministry from the scriptures for a season**

Let the people know why you are encouraging every believer to be a minister. It is in the Word! Beware of using cell group buzz words. Find new ways from scripture to share the same truth. Module 1 of the *DCFI Church Planting & Leadership Video Correspondence School* gives many scriptural truths regarding cell ministry which you can use to teach God's people.

> Give books about cell ministry to the people...reading them will help to strengthen the cell vision in their hearts.

9. **Make sure all of the elders embrace the cell group vision**

Everyone in leadership must make the paradigm shift or there will eventually be frustration and division. This transition is like going from horses to cars. You are not adding a program. If the elders are not all at the same place, do not "go public" until they are. Otherwise you open the door for the devil to cause a church split and division.

10. **When enough leaders are available, encourage cell involvement publicly**

To encourage cell involvement without enough trained leaders frustrates God's people. Have believers in cells share at the celebration meetings about what the Lord is doing in the cells.

11. **Stay flexible and encourage many kinds of cells**

Provide whatever new wineskins are needed for everyone to "connect" to a small group of people. Have cell groups for those who have common interests. If you are a small church, meet in a home rather than at the church building for your weeknight meeting. This meeting can become a cell group that will multiply into two cells.

12. Bathe the entire process in prayer

Move slowly and prayerfully. The larger the church, the longer it will probably take you to make a full transition.

I Thessalonians 5:17

13. After you have made your decision to transition, refuse to look back!

Most pastors who begin the process of transitioning to become a cell-based church are tempted to quit midway through the process. Trust the Lord for grace to complete that which He has started.

Luke 9:62; Philippians 1:6

14. Everyone eventually will need to make a decision

D-day will come. Some may need to find another church if they cannot embrace cell ministry. To be cell-based means every church member is connected to other believers in a cell, and every member is also a part of the life of the congregation.

15. Commission/affirm those who go to other churches

For those who do not have a conviction for cell ministry, commission them out to other local churches with a blessing. We are building *His* kingdom, not *ours*!

16. Make sure your church government and decision-making policies are based on New Testament theocracy

Without a New Testament church government, you cannot give clear scriptural leadership to the church. Be sure your church constitution and bylaws reflect a New Testament pattern of church government. For more instruction on New Testament church government and decision-making, see Module 11:A&B.

Discussion and Study Questions

1. Is it possible to transition a church without losing people?
2. Why does it take so long to transition a church?
3. What are the keys to people "getting" the vision?
4. Who has to make the initial decision about embracing the vision?
5. Why is it important to model a prototype cell rather than having a shotgun start with a bunch of cells?

B. Surviving Transition Trauma

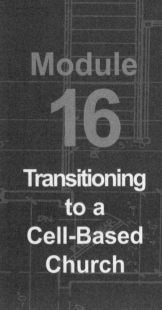

1.   "The call will be tested" trauma

Be sure that you know God is telling you to transition into a cell-based church. This calling will be tested along the way, just like it happened to Nehemiah when the wall was halfway built. You need to know that God wants you to transition and have it completely settled in your heart, your spouse's heart and your leadership team's (elders') hearts (Nehemiah 4:1-15).

2.   "People are slow to change" trauma

This is just human nature. Personality tests show that two thirds of people do not like change and, in fact, resist it. It only takes a quick flip of an oar to change directions in a row boat, but an ocean liner makes a long, slow, gradual turn. Pray for six months before starting the first model cell. Pray! Pray! Pray!

3.   "People are not getting the vision" trauma

The vision of a cell-based church must be taught from the Word or else it will be just another program in the church. If the scriptural basis for cell ministry is taught, the Holy Spirit can illuminate it in the hearts of the people. This is where prayer is such a key.

The vision must be articulated and reinforced in many ways Use writing, banners, video, biblical teaching, question and answer and open forum discussion to help people get a grip of the vision. Share the vision you have at this point in time. It will become clearer to you as you take steps of obedience. Keep sharing the vision; there are new people coming in who have not heard. Pray! Pray! Pray!

4.   "Unity of leadership" trauma

The unity in your leadership team will be tested. Pray for unity. Even your most trusted leaders will have questions you need to take extra time to answer. Trust will be important because you will not have answers for all the questions. The next transition trauma # 5 will be something that will test your unity as leaders.

5.   "People leave the church" trauma–ouch!

You don't want this, but it probably will happen. Not everyone is called to cell-based ministry or will find it easy to change years of tradition and incomplete teaching. It is okay if people want to leave. It happened to Jesus.

6. "Cells become ingrown" trauma–help!

Cells must be outreach oriented in purpose and focus. Fellowship and community happen as a by-product of reaching out. It is human nature to become self-centered, so this trauma will happen to your cells unless you constantly reinforce and prompt (guide) the cells to reach out. Teach "oikos" evangelism; give tools and examples of how this works. Have cells give testimonies at your public meetings of outreaches they have done. Conduct whole church outreaches. **This is probably the most dangerous trauma that could stall your transition.**

7. "Not enough leaders" trauma

This is a recurring trauma. Remember, most of the people are just beginning to learn that they are called to do the work of ministry. It is essential to keep the groups from getting too large. People are even less likely to lead a large group, but on the other hand, if you don't have leaders, you cannot multiply.

We believe there is a vast, untapped reserve of cell leaders in our churches. This group could very well be the key to see your cell ministry prosper and grow. It has been overlooked for hundreds of years by the church. Are you ready for the big secret?

The vast, untapped group of cell leaders in our churches are normal, average Christians! Most of our cell leaders are not super-gifted, charismatic, guitar playing, solo singing, Billy Graham-preaching, "Ken & Barbie" look-a-likes. They are normal people who originally might not even have enough confidence to think they could help with a cell group.

They need someone to come alongside of them and encourage them. Paul told Timothy whom he should train, "And the things you have heard from me among many witnesses, commit to these faithful men who will be able to teach others also" (II Timothy 2:2).

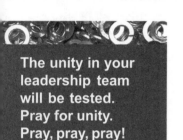

The unity in your leadership team will be tested. Pray for unity. Pray, pray, pray!

8. "Inadequate training and equipping" trauma–oops!

You must have personal one-on-one mentoring as well as structured, classroom training. Try to be as flexible as possible to fit training sessions into people's schedules. For example, recently a cell group of four families started going through the *House to House* book, chapter by chapter. The cell doubled to eight families by the time they were at Chapter Eight.

9. "Old small group mentality" trauma

This is especially a problem if you previously had some form of pastoral small groups at your church that were not true cell groups. The best way to break this pattern is to shut down these groups completely for at least six months before your first model cell group begins. Use new terminology for the new small group (cell).

Module 16: Transitioning to a Cell-Based Church

10. "Budget" trauma–oh no!

The rubber will hit the road when you make budgetary changes. Hear from God for a fresh vision and budget accordingly. Budget money for meals with cell leaders, section leaders, retreats and training conferences (a must), and new church training materials. If some of your present programs are being discontinued, it should free up some money.

11. "Church government" trauma

The biblical vision for cells is a unique vision that requires a biblical church government and decision-making policies. You may want to examine your church government. Some governmental changes might need to take place in your church to enhance cell ministry. Unbiblical church government can hinder or stall transition to a cell-based church. (Examine Module 11:B and Appendix E.)

12. "Stopping programs too quickly" trauma

Trauma can happen when you discontinue programs, but your cells have not yet come into full implementation. You need to be aware that this will frustrate people and discourage them. Keep speaking the vision and be sure your cells are replacing the ministry of the programs as they are phasing out. Have cells serve in practical areas of setup, cleanup, nursery, greeters, children's ministry, etc.

13. "Discouragement" trauma–I feel like quitting

The feeling of "will this transition ever be complete?" can make you feel like quitting. Discouragement will come. Stir yourselves up by praying, meditating on the Word, listening to teaching tapes and rereading books. Call on experienced cell church pastors for input and encouragement.

Discussion and Study Questions

1. Which do you feel is the most serious trauma a transitioning church could encounter?

2. What is the way to overcome this trauma?

3. Where are all the cell leaders?

4. Describe how church government and budget really could derail a transitioning church.

5. Is there any way to speed up the transition of a church?

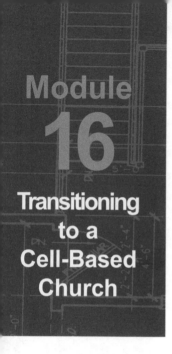

C. A Success Story and What They Learned

*The following is the story of Indianapolis Christian Fellowship in India-
napolis, Indiana, USA, as told by senior elder, Paul Gustitus. Indianapolis
Christian Fellowship has fully transitioned from a program-based church to
a healthy cell-based church.*

Introduction

Seeing people birthed into His kingdom and growing up spiritually is Christ's will.
He desires fruitful people who live the gospel (Isaiah 58). As a pastor, I had
become frustrated with the ministry. I was tired of working hard—investing my
life and not seeing lives change. My desire was to see people conformed to the
image of Christ, to see Jesus formed in them. This just did not seem to be happening in the church.

**I realized that we, as a church, had not done a very good job of making
disciples** If anyone was being "discipled," it was a sovereign work of the Holy
Spirit. It wasn't that we didn't want to make disciples; we just didn't know how.
We had small groups for years. These groups met in homes and were good at
"fellowship" and Bible study, but they were ingrown and became lifeless. In 1991,
I was given the book by Dr. Ralph Neighbor, *Where Do We Go From Here?* This
planted the seed in my heart for the cell-based church. **Here are some of the
keys we used to open the doors to transition to a cell-based church.**

1. Prayer

Prayer is the master key; it unlocks all the rest It is needed more now, as
you begin and proceed with the transition to cells, than ever before. As the senior
servant-leader, I started praying, asking God for direction. My wife and I prayed
together for some time.

I went to our elders and shared with them what I felt God was saying to us
I shared a vision of the church being like a man on a gurney in a hospital emer-
gency room with all kinds of tubes and monitors running from him. Doctors and
nurses were scrambling around as they worked feverishly to keep the patient
alive. I said, "This isn't what God wants for His body." He wants a church that is
strong and powerful, a body that is becoming a mighty army!

Then the elders and their wives began praying with us We all prayed for
several months before we shared with the deacons what the Lord was doing.
Then we prayed with the deacons for one or two months before we shared with
the congregation.

2. Assurance

The vision must be settled in your heart and the hearts of the servant leadership I remember telling the elders that we needed to be so convinced that transitioning is of God that we wouldn't turn back when we found ourselves in the wilderness. We were in agreement that if everyone left and we had to sell our property and meet in our home, that is what we would do.

It may not be the popular thing to do, but God's will is not determined by a vote of the people A lady called and asked, "Are you sure this is God? Look at all the people who are leaving." My response to her was, "God's will is not determined by a popular vote of the people or by how many people are in agreement." If that were the case, then Jesus could not possibly have been in the will of God because no one followed Jesus to the cross—all forsook Him. Moses also had to make decisions that the children of Israel did not like.

3. Unity

It is important to have **unity with your spouse.** I talked with a pastor who had a vision and desire to transition his church to cells. His wife did not. Since you are in ministry together, this could be real trouble.

Next, you need to have **unity with your eldership team** or key leaders. No matter what form of government you have, there are some folks who are the main influencers or who make decisions for the church. These folks need to be "on board" before you proceed further.

Unity with the deacons These next level of influencers need to at least say, "We don't completely understand, but we are willing to trust you and the other leaders. We recognize you as the primary vision carrier and we know you hear from God. We will walk with you in this." The deacons as a group were willing to move ahead with the vision God had given even though they didn't understand the vision. (This is partly because I didn't have the complete vision and wasn't able to clearly articulate the vision I did have.) But because we had a good relationship and a trust established, they were willing to follow the eldership team.

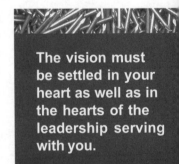

The vision must be settled in your heart as well as in the hearts of the leadership serving with you.

4. Vision

During this time, the vision for the cell church, for me, was like driving a car in a thick fog. I remember when I was in high school, living in a suburb of Chicago, Illinois, a friend's parents had a summer house on Lake Delavan in Wisconsin. We used to drive up there and go sledding and tobogganing. Once I had to drive home in a very thick fog. Because I could only see a few feet in front of the car, I drove about 30 mph in a 55 mph zone.

Proceed with caution You need to go 30 mph when you would like to go 55 mph. Since you can only see part of the vision, you should move forward slowly. You also need to go slowly to allow the Holy Spirit time to change people's values.

The Holy Spirit must change values People, as a rule, resist change. They don't like it. This requires a work of the Holy Spirit. Be patient! Dr. Ralph Neighbor says in his book *Where Do We Go From Here?* that it can take from three to seven years to transition to a cell-based church.

5. Communicate

Communicate where you are going and how you are going to get there When we began to share with the people what God was saying about transitioning to a cell-based church, the people wanted to know exactly where we were going and how we were going to get there. It reminded me of Abraham as he told his household that they were going to leave their homes and head for the promised land. I imagine they wanted to know what the promised land was like and how they would get there. They wondered if it would be safe and which route they would take.

Many people wondered where we were going and even why we needed to leave in the first place. They were content where we were. They saw no need to change from a program-based church to a cell-based church. They didn't know what a cell-based church was—neither did I, completely—but I knew God was telling us to pack up and go to the place He was leading us.

They wanted to know how their children would adjust They wanted to know what would happen to our Wednesday night children's program. (We had a full program: people even drove up and dropped their children off so we could baby-sit them while they went shopping or out to dinner.) They wanted to see the maps and photos of our "Trip-Tic" (the plan an automobile agency provides for those going on a road trip) that would show this "promised land" called cell church. They wanted to know where we would be staying along the way; where did we have our motel reservations?

6. Be teachable

Learn from others This is a continual learning process. Ask Dr. Neighbor, Larry Kreider or Larry Stockstill. No one has all the truth. You must find and apply what God wants in your particular local area.

Editors note: Transitioning is possible!

Before transitioning, membership at Indianapolis Christian Fellowship was 220. During its transitioning, membership dropped to 180. After the church had fully transitioned, it quickly grew to 240.

Discussion and Study Questions

1. What part of Paul's story stuck out to you the most?

2. What was the most serious obstacle Paul faced?

3. What role did effective communication play in Paul's successful transition?

4. What did Paul do when he didn't have all the answers to the questions people had?

5. What was the key to the successful transition of Indianapolis Christian

Module 16: Transitioning to a Cell-Based Church

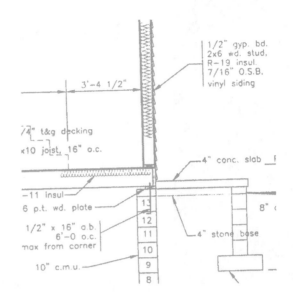

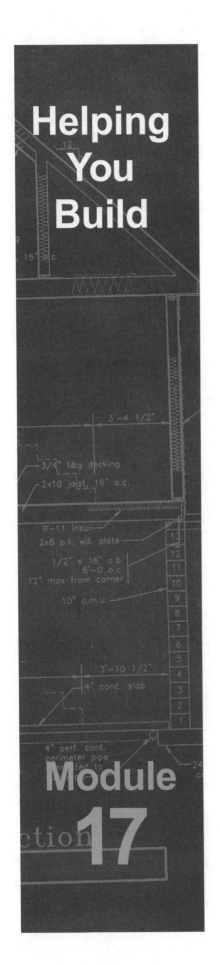

Module 17

Advanced Cell Leadership

This module focuses first on giving clear, practical, biblical training to handle crisis situations in cell ministry. Then it takes a look at the different kinds of church structures on today's church landscape and how God uses this variety for His purposes as we minister and reach out in our postmodern society.

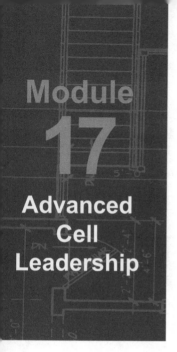

A. Handling Crisis in Cell Ministry

When crisis situations come into the cell group, healthy leaders will know the difference between **exercising healthy authority vs. unhealthy control** in their counsel. A cell leader will not tell cell members what to do, but instead gently point them to Jesus so they can make the right decisions. For this to happen, cell leaders need to have a healthy view of themselves and of those they lead. They understand the difference between power, control and love in counseling cell members in crisis.

I Peter 5:1-6

1. Marriage struggles
Cell leaders, assistants and cell members are all susceptible to struggles in their marriages. Ongoing problems in this area can cause crisis in a cell group. For biblical methods of resolving marriage struggles, we use an excellent booklet for cell groups called, *Resolving Conflicts in Marriage.*

2. Handling crisis financial needs
Cell groups are the first level of financial support to the person in need. Cells can take regular offerings and keep for emergencies or collect special offerings. If the cell is unable to meet a need, a specific fund above the cell level could help (e.g., a deacon's fund). A cell leader also needs to be available to offer advice to help a struggling member handle his finances.

Galatians 2:10

3. Discouragement
All Christians, including cell leaders, undergo discouragement at some time in their Christian walk. Struggling cell members (or cell leaders) can cause a crisis in the cell. In most cases, discouragement comes from believing lies from the enemy. We must speak the truth of what God's word says about us to break through the enemy's lies. In our cell groups, we use a pamphlet entitled *Who I Am In Christ* that contains dozens of scripture verses to encourage personal commitment.

4. Hidden agendas
Beware of those who attend a cell group in order to promote their personal agenda that may include, but not be limited to: politics, theology, evangelism, dress, school preference, social action, personal business, sales, etc. Calmly share that you would like to talk more with them about their ideas after the cell meeting is over. "Speak the truth in love" (Ephesians 4:15). Lead the cell; it is your field!

5. Codependency and emotional dependency

Codependency is when we try to "rescue" others because of our own need to be needed. In codependency, you replace Jesus as a person's savior.

A simple definition of emotional dependency is *meeting your own needs by drawing life from others*. This kind of behavior leads to unhealthy relationships and is dangerous in cell ministry.

Both codependency (rescuing others) and emotional dependency (depending on others) are unhealthy. For additional help with emotional dependency, a booklet called *Recognizing Emotional Dependency* defines, identifies and reveals how to be free of dependent relationships.

6. Dissolving a cell group

If a cell has failed to grow and multiply or if the leader is stepping down and there are no new leaders, the cell may need to dissolve. Pastors and church leadership must assist in the process. Take plenty of time to dissolve a cell. It is vital to not rush the process of cell members locating another cell to be committed to. It is important for leadership to follow everyone up to be sure they connect with a new cell group.

I Peter 5:2-3

7. People struggling with change

Many people struggle with change. When a cell group changes vision or direction, it can cause a crisis in the cell. We need to teach everyone from the word of God how to handle change. This includes change in the world around them as well as change in their hearts. A cell leader's overseer will almost always have insight into how fast change can happen and how to help people handle it. The booklet *Thinking Right in a World That Thinks Wrong* can help people deal with change in a positive way.

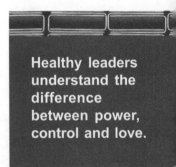

Healthy leaders understand the difference between power, control and love.

8. Divisiveness in the cell

Two visions in a cell is called "di-vision" Division brings discord among the cell members. God's Word tells us to warn the divisive person (Titus 3:9-11).

Division will cause a split in the cell rather than a healthy multiplication In love, confront those who sow discord as soon as possible.

9. Church discipline

The goal of discipline for believers is to provide restoration to God, to others and to themselves. The cell group level is an excellent place to begin the process of discipline. A church elder should always be involved with the cell leader in cases of church discipline. Matthew 18:15-20

10. Burnout

Proper delegation will keep a cell leader from burnout. Delegation is caring enough about others to help them learn to operate in their gifts. Delegation is caring enough about yourself so that you do not burn out while trying to "do it all." Effective ministry through the cell happens when each cell member does his part.

Luke 10:1-2

11. Unresolved anger

Life experiences can lead to unresolved anger in cell members and new Christians. This can also lead to conflict in the cell or may inhibit the development of your assistant leaders. People need to be taught to move beyond self-justification and anger to forgiveness and healing according to the word of God. Teach the Word, ask people to repent and pray for freedom. An excellent booklet entitled *Be Angry and Sin Not* is a helpful tool for use in the cell group.

Psalm 30:5

12. Other types of potential crisis

Disruptive life changes like death, illness, hospitalization, change of jobs, a life-controlling problem or giving birth can affect cell members. This is an important time of ministry to that person or persons by the whole cell. Everyone can minister in some way in these situations.

I Thessalonians 5:14

Discussion and Study Questions
1. How should financial needs be met in a cell?
2. Complete this sentence. The best way to handle divisiveness in a cell is....
3. How can you determine when someone has a hidden agenda for a cell group?
4. When dissolving a cell, who should follow up with the people?
5, How should the people of a dissolved cell be followed up?

B. Three Kinds of Churches

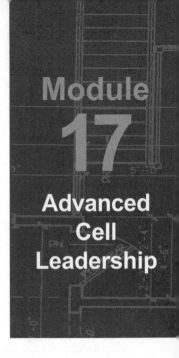

The Lord is using diversified types of structures and methods to build His church today—from the traditional churches to the emerging house (micro) church networks. Both those churches that operate within a more traditional setting and those that operate outside of traditional structures are needed. Let's examine three kinds of churches found in the nations today:

- Community churches
- Mega-churches
- Micro churches

1. Community churches

These churches appear in nearly every community around the world. They meet in a church facility each Sunday morning, in addition to holding various meetings at the building throughout the week. Their specific target area they are reaching is the local community.

There are many styles and flavors of community churches—the Methodist flavor, Baptist flavor, Congregational flavor, Episcopal flavor, Presbyterian flavor, Assembly of God flavor, non-denominational flavor: the list goes on.

They usually average between 50-200 members, some higher. When they reach 1,000 attendees, they fall into another classification—mega church.

Community churches are like community stores Most people buy groceries in a store in close proximity to where they live. Proximity and ease of access are a big part of the nature of the community church.

2. Mega churches

Thirty years ago, nearly every church in America was a community church. Then Pastor Cho from Korea encouraged American churches to hear the voice of the Holy Spirit to train small group leaders and release the ministry of the church to these trained leaders. Through the help of small groups, rapid multiplication and growth occurred.

This new mentality led to a wave of mega-churches mushrooming across America. These churches often have 1,000 and upwards members.

Mega churches are like Wal-Mart superstores They have much to offer. Mega-churches, like the Wal-Mart superstores, are large and they offer an abundance of services to the churchgoer. However, unlike the community church where you may know nearly everyone, at a mega-church you probably know only a few people. Yet, church members thoroughly enjoy a mega-church since everything is easily accessible in one location. Today is not unusual for people to drive an hour or more to attend worship services at a mega-church.

3. Micro churches

The entire concept of micro churches requires a different way of thinking than we have been used to. Believers in micro churches do not focus on growing larger like the community church or the mega-church. They focus on growth by starting new micro churches by multiplication. Micro churches are small; therefore they can meet anywhere—in a house, in a college dorm room, in a coffee shop, in a corporate boardroom. They meet in these locations and do not think of growing larger requiring the construction of a building to accommodate the larger group.

A micro church is meant to be a complete little church Each church is led not by a cell leader and a team of assistant leaders, but by a spiritual father or mother who functions as the elder along with a small eldership team for the little church. He or she does not simply lead a meeting in a house, but rather provides an environment for people to grow spiritually in the context of everyday life. There is no need for a church building in which to meet because each house church is a fully functioning church in itself, meeting in a home.

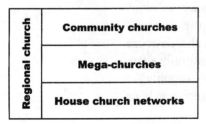

| Community churches |
| like a community store |
| **Mega-churches** |
| like a Wal-Mart superstore |
| **House church networks** |
| like a shopping mall |

This is not to say that a house church consists of only one group meeting in a house A house church should encourage smaller "cells" within the group to meet for prayer, encouragement and accountability outside of the actual house church meeting. One "cell" of people could regularly meet for breakfast before work and another "cell" could meet together to disciple a few new Christians in the house church.

When micro churches network together, they function like a shopping mall In describing a micro church network, the analogy would be equivalent to the stores in a shopping mall. If the average store found in a shopping mall was taken out of the mall and let to stand on its own, it would die within a year. The normal store in a shopping mall needs the others to survive. Each specialized store flourishes together within the cluster of the others. Yet each store is fully a "store" in its own right, despite being in a mall. The house churches function like these shopping mall stores. They are individual and specialized, yet they flourish when they network together with other house churches.

Regional Church

We believe the Lord is restoring the unity He prayed for in John 17:21: "That all of them may be one, Father, just as you are in me and I am in you. May they also be in us so that the world may believe that you have sent me."

The regional church includes the three kinds of churches in a geographical area

Regional church	Community churches
	Mega-churches
	House church networks

Walls that have divided denominations and churches for centuries are coming down throughout the world at an increasing rate. Pastors in the same town who never knew one another are now finding each other, praying together regularly, and supporting each other. This kind of church unity is exciting!

Module 17: Advanced Cell Leadership

Unity like this makes room for the regional church to emerge What is the regional church? I believe it will be comprised of all types of churches—community churches, mega-churches, and micro churches in a particular geographical area. These churches, of many different denominations, will work together to represent the church (the body of Christ) in a region.

In the New Testament, each church was identified by its geographical location—there were no denominations back then! The body of Christ met in house churches within a city, and they were unified by their specific city boundaries: the church of Antioch, the church of Corinth, the church of Jerusalem, the church of Smyrna. However, today, the church has been divided into many different denominations within one geographical area. Many times, such things as doctrinal interpretations and worship styles were the cause of these divisions in the body of Christ.

The regional church is not an attempt to do away with denominations and get back to separating believers on the basis of geographical distance exclusively. I believe we have to work with what we have today. This means that the local churches within a collective regional church will probably each maintain their denominational flavor, while working in a unified manner to more effectively share Christ in their geographical area. In short, I believe when unbelievers see the unity of churches in their community, they will be attracted to Christianity.

Apostolic fathers and mothers will unify to lead the regional church
Over the next years, I believe there will be an emergence of spiritual leaders from various backgrounds and denominations who will form teams of spiritual leadership to "father" this collective, regional church. These apostolic fathers will serve the church in towns, cities and regions to resource the body of Christ. They will not think only in terms of pastoring a church or churches, but will think and pray in terms of sensing a responsibility with other fellow servant-leaders throughout the body of Christ to pastor their region.

This initiative will not be contrary to their denomination's vision, but will bring wholeness. Although these "fathers of the region" will be concerned about unity, it will not be their focus. Their main focus will be on the Lord and on His mandate to reach the lost as the Lord brings in His harvest. Again, the regional church will include all the types of churches in a geographical location—the community churches, the mega-churches, and the house church networks. All denominations and church movements operating in a region have a redemptive purpose to meet the needs of that particular region.

Discussion and Study Questions
1. Why do you think God builds with both traditional and non-traditional church structures?
2. What is the greatest difference between the community/mega churches and the micro churches?
3. What can pave the way for the regional church to emerge?
4. Which kind of church is God calling you to?

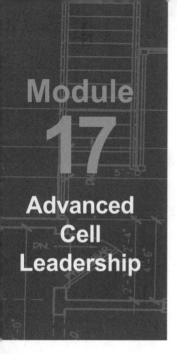

C. Ministering in a Postmodern Society

1. Time frames in history

As we look at the history of the world, we find different "worlds" or ages that were characterized by vastly different socio-economic conditions.

2500 BC - Ancient World

500 AD - Medieval World
Life expectancy was 35.
Life was hard.
Church preached there was a better life to come.

1500 AD - Modern World
World view changed
Could get in ship, travel and come back
Telescope developed
The earth was not the center of the universe.

1950 - Present - Postmodern World
Information expansion
We can build and fix things.
We can wipe out disease.
We can make things better.

2. How people view the world today

We cannot fix everything.
We are not getting better.
We have cured some diseases but there are new strains developing that we are powerless over.
People are losing hope.
The world is not a better place, and there is not much hope for the future.

3. Traits in this postmodern society

An ideology that is searching to give meaning to life
A suspicion of any authority
There are no objective truths, no absolutes.
Instead of an *either/or* mentality, it has become a *both/and* mentality.
There is the feeling that the inhabitants of the world have ruined the world.

The understanding becomes that we cannot understand things with our minds.
Rationalism is thrown out of the window.
We talk not to find truth but to have conversation.
There is a move from individuality to community.
We must remain in relationship so that we can talk.

4. We can give up and wish to go back to a previous world view or we can ask the Holy Spirit how we can relate to this world and address the issues and obstacles

We will probably have to change our language, but knowing that they want to communicate will keep the door open.

1. We need to understand the importance of relationship.
2. We must listen to their story and then they will be able to connect with our story. The best evangelistic tool is "this is what Jesus has done for me."
3. Can we tear down the walls that separate us? We think in terms of *us* being saved and *they* are not. Change the tactic to make them feel like they belong, then they will believe. Postmodern people are not aware of guilt, since there are no absolutes, but they are aware of shame.
4. Understand that people come to Christ through a process. We stress the Damascus Road experience vs. the Emmaus Road where Jesus was with them and they weren't aware of it.
5. We need to help them see how the Holy Spirit has been working in their lives reaching out to them.
6. We need to reach out to them in humility knowing that they may be able to teach us something. Most people are not ready to listen to you until they know that you have really listened to them.
7. We must really shift to serving people with a servant's heart.
8. We must become more life affirming. In the past, we stressed, "If you were to die tonight...." The question for today is, "If you were to live tomorrow, what would you really want to live for?

Much of the above "Ministering in a Postmodern Society" was adapted from a message by Peter Bunton.

5. How to speak so people listen[2]
First pray and

> Ask God for the gift of communication.
> Ask God for the gift of conviction.
> Ask God for the gift of compassion.

Establish common ground

Let them know that you do not know everything. Try and find something that they know a lot about and ask them questions. Allow them to educate you. Reach them on their level. If there is something that you have in common, talk about it for awhile before you talk about Jesus.

Tell them what they know to be true

Use media, songs, news, etc.
Tell them ten things they know are true first, then they will tend to believe you.
Remember all truth is God's truth.
Just tell stories.

Bring it all back to Jesus

He loves us. He wants to and has the power to take away our shame.

[2] "How to speak so people listen" was adapted from a message by Winkie Pratney.

Discussion and Study Questions

1. What worldviews changed to set the stage for postmodern society?

2. Explain how the postmodern person views the world today.

3. How can you change your language to keep the door of communication open to pre-Christians?

4. Name three things you can do to help you communicate better to a postmodern pre-Christian.

C. Ministering in a Postmodern Society

DOVE Christian Fellowship International

Who are we?

DOVE Christian Fellowship International (DCFI) started with a group of young Christian believers who had a burden to reach the unchurched youth in their community in northern Lancaster County, Pennsylvania.

It was the early 1970's and the time of a nationwide awakening among young people in the United States. The nation had been through tumultuous times in the 1960's with rapid changes tearing at the fabric of our society, including the sexual revolution and the Vietnam war. After a decade of young people dabbling in the occult and drug culture seeking answers for life but being disillusioned, they were now turning to God in great numbers.

It was in these times that we started an organization called "The Lost But Found." Through friendship evangelism, we saw many young people come to know Jesus as their Lord. A Bible study under the direction of Larry Kreider called "Rhema Youth Ministries" nurtured many of these young Christians.

Although we tried to get the new believers involved in the established churches in our community, they simply didn't fit. It seemed clear there was a need for new church structures flexible enough to relate to new converts from a variety of backgrounds. That's why Jesus said we need to put new wine into new wineskins (Matthew 9:16-17).

Increasingly, there became a need for a flexible New Testament-style church (new wineskin) that could relate to and assist these new believers (new wine) in their spiritual growth. In 1978, God spoke to Larry about being "willing to be involved with the underground church."

Our adventure into cell groups

So began our church's adventure into cell groups. A cell group was started in Larry and LaVerne Kreider's home and when their living room was filled to capacity, they turned over the responsibility to leaders they had trained and started a second cell in another home. The roots began to grow for this "underground church" where believers were nourished in these "underground" cell groups as they gathered together to pray, evangelize and build relationships with each other.

By the time our church, DOVE Christian Fellowship, officially began in October, 1980, there were approximately 25 of us meeting in a large living room on Sunday mornings and in three cell groups during the week. We discovered

cell groups to be places where people have the opportunity to experience and demonstrate a Christianity built on relationships, not simply on meetings. In the cell groups, people could readily share their lives with each other and reach out to a broken world. We desired to follow the pattern in the New Testament church as modeled in the book of Acts, as the believers met from house to house.

Twelve years later, as these cell groups continued to grow and to multiply, more than 2,300 believers were meeting in over 125 cell groups throughout south-central Pennsylvania. Churches were planted in Scotland, Brazil, Kenya, and New Zealand. Believers met in cell groups in homes during the week and in clusters of cells in geographical areas for celebration meetings each Sunday morning. Here believers received teaching, worshiped together and celebrated what the Lord was doing during the week through the cell groups.

We made our share of mistakes

Although the church had grown rapidly in a relatively short span, we made our share of mistakes. The Lord began to deal with pride and unhealthy control in our lives. We found the Lord's purpose for cell groups was to release and empower His people, not to control them. We repented before the Lord and before His church.

Our cell-based church had reached a crossroads. We were experiencing the pain of gridlock among some of our leadership. There was an exodus of some good leaders from our ranks. It was painful, and Larry Kreider, who was serving as the senior elder, almost quit.

In retrospect, we feel the mistakes we made were partly due to our immaturity as leaders and partly due to our not having an outside accountability team to help us when we ran into conflicts in decision-making. And perhaps the Lord in His providence was repositioning some of His players elsewhere in the body of Christ.

But the Lord kept taking us back to the original vision He had given, calling us to be involved with the "underground church." Today we walk with a spiritual limp, but we are so grateful to the Lord for what He taught us during those days.

Transition to several churches

It became clear that in order for DOVE (an acronym for "Declaring Our Victory Emmanuel") to accomplish what we were originally called to accomplish, we needed to adjust our church government and "give the church away." The vision the Lord had given us, "to build a relationship with Jesus, with one another, and reach the world from house to house, city to city and nation to nation," could not be fulfilled under our current church structure. We recognized the Lord had called us to be an apostolic movement, but we did not know how it should be structured.

It took more than two years to prepare for this transition. On January 1, 1996, our church became eight individual churches, each with their own eldership team. We formed an Apostolic Council to give spiritual oversight to DCFI, and Larry Kreider was asked to serve as its International Director. The Apostolic Council gave each church eldership team the option of becoming a part of the DCFI family of churches and ministries or connecting to another part of the body of Christ. Each of these eight churches expressed a desire to work together to plant churches throughout the world and became a part of the DCFI family. The majority of the overseas church plants also desired to become a part of the DCFI family of churches.

We have found apostolic ministry provides a safe environment for each congregation and ministry partnering with DCFI to grow and reproduce themselves. This new model emphasizes leading by relationship and influence rather than hands-on-management. A senior elder and team has a leadership gift to equip believers to do the work of ministry in cell groups within a congregation. The Apostolic Council members are responsible to spend time in prayer and the ministry of the Word and give training, oversight and mentoring to local church leadership. They also are called to give clear vision and direction to the entire movement.

Becoming an apostolic movement

Unlike an "association of churches," which gives ordination and general accountability to church leaders, we see an "apostolic movement" as a family of churches with a common focus—a mandate from God to labor together to plant and establish churches throughout the world.

As a cell-based and house church planting movement, we are intent on training a new generation of church planters and leaders just waiting for a chance to spread their wings and fly! We are called to mobilize and empower God's people (individuals, families, cells and congregations) at the grass roots level to fulfill His purposes. Every cell group should have a vision to plant new cells. Every church with its team of elders should have a God-given vision to plant new churches.

In addition to church planting and multiplication, the Lord has given us a process of adopting churches who are called to partner with us. After going through a one-year engagement process of discernment, churches with similar values and vision are becoming partner churches with the DCFI family.

Our desire is to see congregations of cell groups clustered together in the same area so leaders can easily meet as regional presbyteries for prayer and mutual encouragement, and to find ways to be more effective in building His kingdom together. Senior elders of DCFI churches in Pennsylvania have the blessing of meeting together each month for prayer and mutual encouragement. An Apostolic Council member also meets each month individually with each senior elder. Each DCFI partner church is governed by a team of elders and consists of believers committed to one another in cell groups. Each cell and each local church has its own identity while being interdependent with the rest of the DCFI family.

Networking with the body of Christ

We believe another important aspect to kingdom building is networking with other churches and ministries outside of the DCFI family. In this way, we can resource one other.

God has given us a wonderful support team at DCFI consisting of the Apostolic Council, a team of Fivefold Translocal Ministers, a Stewardship Team which handles the administration of financial details and legalities, and various ministries who are committed to resource the leadership and believers in DCFI partner churches and serve the greater body of Christ.

These various ministries offer leadership training and ministry development on many levels. An essential twenty-four-hour Prayer Ministry includes a team of "prayer generals" who recruit, train and encourage a team of "prayer warriors" responsible to cover segments of time each week while praying for the entire DCFI family twenty-four hours a day. Nelson Martin oversees this vital prayer ministry.

The Apostolic Council and leadership from DCFI partner churches throughout the world meet together each March for our annual DCFI International Leadership Conference for the purpose of mutual encouragement, leadership training, relationship building, and to receive a common vision from the Lord. We believe the Lord has called us to work as a team together—*with a shared vision, shared values, a shared procedure, and to build together by relationship.*

In order for the DCFI family of churches and ministries to be effective in laboring together, we wrote our procedure in a DCFI Handbook. This handbook is available by contacting the DCFI Office.

Training and releasing God's people

An important philosophy of ministry at DCFI is to release each believer and local leadership in order to provide a delegation of authority and responsibility to all believers. Unless elders can release responsibility and authority to the cell leaders at a cell group level, this principle will not work. In this way, the Lord releases every believer to be a minister.

Every church elder is encouraged to maintain his security in the Lord and take the risk of empowering and releasing cell leaders to minister to others by performing water baptisms, serving communion, praying for the sick, giving premarital counseling, and discipling new believers. A major aspect of cell ministry is preparing and training future spiritual fathers and mothers. And many of these cell leaders will be future elders and church planters. They are experiencing "on the job training."

The *Church Planting and Leadership School* is now being used to train cell leaders, pastors and elders in cell-based churches throughout the body of Christ. It is both a live school and a video correspondence school used as a satellite school in churches throughout the world. We expect the believers in our cell groups and churches to soon have their own families—new cell groups and new churches that they plant.

Fivefold translocal ministry

According to Ephesians 4:11-12, the five ministry gifts of the apostle, prophet, evangelist, pastor and teacher are called by the Lord to equip the saints to minister and encourage the body of Christ. Within the DCFI family, fivefold ministers, who have proven ministries and are recommended by their elders as having a larger sphere of ministry than their own cell and congregation, are recognized and affirmed by the Apostolic Council to serve translocally. These translocal ministers are often invited by other cell groups and congregations for ministry.

DCFI missions outreaches

During the past 20 years, DOVE has sent hundreds of short and long term missionaries to the nations. Each long term missionary is "embraced" by a cell group, a congregation, and by individuals from DCFI partner churches. A team of people join a missionary's support team by giving financially and praying for the missionary. Cells who "embrace" a missionary or missionary family pray for them, write to them, and serve practically while on furlough or during times of crisis.

The DOVE Mission International team endeavors to serve all DCFI missionaries who are sent out from DCFI partner churches regardless of which "field" they serve on. Some missionaries are directly involved in the DCFI church planting "field," while others may serve instead with the YWAM "field" or with some other missions agency. We are called to build the kingdom, not just our own network of churches. Yet, as a network of churches, we are called by the Lord to plant new cell-based churches together in the unreached areas of the world.

Looking unto Jesus, the Lord of the harvest

We believe as we continue to commune with the Lord and obey His voice, build together as a family of churches, and reach the lost in our generation, there is going to be a need for thousands of new houses (new churches) and new rooms (new cell groups). Every generation is different and has different needs and preferences. We are committed to empowering, releasing, and supporting the next generation among us as they fulfill their call in God. As Elisha received a double portion of Elijah's anointing, we want to see our spiritual children far exceeding us in their depth of spiritual experience and church leadership. Believers will be called to various areas of leadership: some are called to cell group leadership, others to local church leadership, others to fivefold ministry, and others will serve in apostolic leadership.

Our long term goal is to establish many apostolic councils in various regions of the world. There are already apostolic leadership teams who are responsible for oversight of DCFI churches in seven regions of the world. Eventually, we believe the leadership for the DCFI movement will be a true DCFI International Apostolic Council, whose members will include apostolic leaders from many nations. This International Apostolic Council will be responsible for the spiritual oversight and mentoring of apostolic leaders and councils located around the world.

The vision continues

The Bible tells us without a vision the people perish. The DCFI family is called to keep actively involved in what the Lord is doing in the world and participate in the present expressions of His anointing. We desire to empower, train, and release God's people at the grass roots level to fulfill His purposes. Jesus values people. He has called us to look at people and see the Father working in those whom the Lord has placed in our lives.

Simply put, these are our "roots," and our continued focus today. You could say that the very DNA of who we are as an international family of believers in Jesus Christ today includes our specific calling as an "underground church" to reach our world from house to house, city to city and nation to nation. May Jesus Christ be honored and glorified!

To learn more about DCFI, read the book *House to House* by Larry Kreider which can be purchased from *House to House Publications*.

Our Vision

To build a relationship with Jesus, with one another, and to reach the world from house to house, city to city, nation to nation.

Our Mission

To exalt Jesus Christ as Lord, obey His Word, and encourage and equip each believer for the work of ministry. We are called to build the church from house to house, city to city, and nation to nation through small groups. This "underground church" is built through prayer, reaching the lost, and making disciples. Our mission includes reaching adults, youth and children for Christ. We are also called to church planting, proclaiming the gospel through media, and building unity in the body of Christ. As a spiritual army, we will cooperate with the church that Jesus is building throughout the world in fulfilling the Great Commission.

Our Plan

By the grace of God we will accomplish our mission by:

1. **Strengthening** our faith through the daily meditation of the Word of God and **developing** an intimate relationship with Jesus.

2. **Committing** ourselves to other believers in a cell group.

3. **Praying** to the Lord of the harvest to send out laborers into the harvest fields: locally, nationally and internationally.

4. **Encouraging** every believer to be involved in prayer, reaching the lost, and making disciples.

5. **Helping** each believer to learn to serve and discover the gifts and callings within his life.

6. **Teaching** the Word of God with power and authority in a way that is practical and applicable to everyday life.

7. **Releasing** apostles, prophets, evangelists, pastors and teachers to equip the saints for the work of ministry and to build up the body of Christ.

8. **Training** and **equipping** leadership in home cell groups and congregations to minister to others and to plant new churches.

9. **Planting** and **multiplying** home cell groups and congregations locally, nationally and internationally.

10. **Sending** laborers to identified harvest fields.

11. **Caring** for, **loving, healing** and **restoring** those who are wounded and need deliverance, healing and restoration.

12. **Promoting** unity by **supporting, networking** together and **laboring** with other churches and ministries locally, nationally and internationally.

13. **Mobilizing** and **challenging** adults, youth, and children to be radically committed laborers for the harvest.

14. **Utilizing** all forms of media to proclaim the gospel.

15. **Resourcing** each believer through the ministry of helps, administration and communication.

16. **Ministering** to the poor and needy.

17. **Encouraging** each child, young person and adult to be a worshiper.

18. **Giving** of tithes, offerings, material possessions and our time to the building of the kingdom.

19. **Exemplifying** a life-style of accountability, integrity, and purity in every level of leadership and throughout every area of church life.

20. **Supporting** and **encouraging** the spiritual leaders that the Lord raises up among us.

21. **Edifying** one another daily through encouragement and speaking the truth in love.

22. **Celebrating** Jesus as we come together in various locations to worship together, pray together, and receive the Word of God together.

23. **Partnering** with believers within the DOVE Christian Fellowship International family of churches and ministries who are meeting from house to house and city to city to reach the world together.

24. **Receiving** the filling of the Holy Spirit to minister Jesus to our generation through the demonstration of His supernatural power and gifts.

25. **Recruiting** disciples to carry the gospel to new regions of the earth.

26. **Training** mission personnel in cross-cultural communication of the gospel.

27. **Placing** seeds of mission into the hearts of each new church plant.

28. **Encouraging** youth revival and awakening, and training teenagers and young adults to go into the harvest fields of the world.

29. **Worshiping** our God and Father through our Lord Jesus Christ.

30. **Spiritually fathering and mothering** within every sphere of kingdom life as the Lord turns the hearts of the fathers to the children and the hearts of the children to their fathers in our day.

Our Values

1. Knowing God the Father through His Son Jesus Christ and living by His Word is the foundation of life.

We believe that the basis of the Christian faith is to know God through repentance for sin, receiving Jesus Christ as Lord, building an intimate relationship with Him, and being conformed into His image. God has declared us righteous through faith in Jesus Christ (John 1:12, John 17:3, Rom. 8:29, II Cor. 5:21).

All values and guiding principles for the DOVE Christian Fellowship International family must be rooted in the scriptures (II Tim. 3:16-17, II Tim. 2:15).

DOVE is an acronym: **D**eclaring **O**ur **V**ictory **E**mmanuel (God with us).

2. It is essential for every believer to be baptized with the Holy Spirit and be completely dependent on Him.

We recognize that we desperately need the person and power of the Holy Spirit to minister effectively to our generation. Changed lives are not the product of men's wisdom, but in the demonstration of the power of the Holy Spirit as modeled in the New Testament church (I Cor. 2:2-5, John 15:5). We believe it is essential for every believer to be baptized with the Holy Spirit and to pursue spiritual gifts (II Cor. 13:14, John 4:23-24).

All decisions need to be made by listening to the Holy Spirit as we make prayer a priority and learn to be worshipers. Worship helps us focus on the Lord and allows us to more clearly hear His voice.

We recognize that we do not wrestle against flesh and blood, but against demonic forces. Jesus Christ is our Lord, our Savior, our Healer and our Deliverer (Eph. 6:12, I John 3:8).

3. The Great Commission will be completed through prayer, evangelism, discipleship, and church planting.

We are committed to helping fulfill the Great Commission through prayer and fasting, evangelism, discipleship, and church planting locally, nationally, and internationally reaching both Jew and Gentile (Matt. 28:19-20, Matt. 6:5-18, Acts 1:8).

We are called to support others who are called as co-laborers, as churches are planted throughout the world. The Great Commission is fulfilled through tearing down spiritual strongholds of darkness and church planting (I Cor. 3:6-9, Matt. 11:12, II Cor. 10:3-4, Acts 14:21-23).

We are also called to proclaim the gospel through the arts, publications, and the media and will continue to believe God to raise up other resources and ministries to assist us in building the church (I Cor. 9:19-22).

4. We deeply value the sacred covenant of marriage and the importance of training our children to know Christ.

It is our belief that marriage and family are instituted by God, and healthy, stable families are essential for the church to be effective in fulfilling its mission. Parents are called by God to walk in the character of Christ and to train their children in the nurture and loving discipline of the Lord Christ (Mark 10:6-8, Eph. 5:22-6:4).

The Lord is calling His people to walk in the fear of the Lord and in a biblical standard of holiness and purity. Marriage covenants are ordained by God and need to be honored and kept (Prov. 16:6, Mark 10:9, I Thess. 4:3-8, I Cor. 6:18-20).

5. We are committed to spiritual families, spiritual parenting and intergenerational connections.

Believing that our God is turning the hearts of the fathers and mothers to the sons and daughters in our day, we are committed to spiritual parenting on every level of church and ministry life (Mal. 4:5-6, I Cor. 4:15-17).

Participation in a cell group is a fundamental commitment to the DCFI family. The cell group is a small group of believers and/or families who are committed to one another and to reaching others for Christ. We believe the Lord desires to raise up spiritual families in many levels including cells, congregations, apostolic movements and the kingdom of God (I Cor. 12:18, Eph. 4:16).

We believe each spiritual family needs to share common values, vision, goals, and a commitment to build together, with the need to receive ongoing training in these areas (Ps. 133, II Pet. 1:12,13, II Tim. 2:2).

We are committed to reaching, training and releasing young people as co-laborers for the harvest, as the young and the old labor together (Acts 2:17, Jer. 31:13).

6. Spiritual multiplication and reproduction must extend to every sphere of kingdom life and ministry.

Multiplication is expected and encouraged in every sphere of church life. Cell groups should multiply into new cells and churches should multiply into new churches. Church planting must be a long term goal of every congregation (Acts 9:31, Mark 4:20).

The DCFI family of churches will be made up of many new regional families of churches as apostolic fathers and mothers are released in the nations of the world (Acts 11:19-30, Acts 13-15).

7. Relationships are essential in building God's kingdom.

Serving others and building trust and relationships is a desired experience in every area of church life. We believe the best place to begin to serve and experience trust and relationship is in the cell group (Acts 2:42-47, Eph. 4:16, Gal. 5:13).

We are joined together primarily by God-given family relationships, not by organization, hierarchy, or bureaucracy (I Peter 2:5).

8. Every Christian is both a priest and a minister.

According to the scriptures, every Christian is a priest who needs to hear from the Lord personally (Rev. 1:5-6).

Every believer is called of God to minister to others and needs to be equipped for this work with the home as a center for ministry. Fivefold ministers are the Lord's gifts to His church. He uses fivefold persons to help equip each believer to become an effective minister in order to build up the body of Christ (I Pet. 4:9, Eph. 4:11-12).

We need to be constantly handing the work of ministry over to those we are serving so they can fulfill their call from the Lord (Titus 1:5, I Tim 4:12-14).

9. A servant's heart is necessary for every leader to empower others.

We believe every sphere of leadership needs to include a clear servant-leader called by God and a team who is called to walk with him. The leader has the anointing and responsibility to discern the mind of the Lord that is expressed through the leadership team (II Cor. 10:13-16, Num. 27:16, I Peter 5:1-4).

Leaders are called to listen to what the Lord is saying through those whom they serve as they model servant-leadership. They are called to walk in humility, integrity, in the fruit of the Spirit, and in the fear of the Lord (Acts 6:2-6, Acts 15, Matt. 20:26, Gal. 5:22-23).

We believe God raises up both apostolic overseers and partner church elders to direct, protect, correct and discipline the church. These leaders must model the biblical qualifications for leadership (Acts 15, Acts 6:1-4, I Tim. 3, Titus 1).

Those with other spiritual gifts including administrative gifts (ministry of helps) need to be released to fulfill the Lord's vision on each level of church life (I Cor. 12).

In every area of church life we believe we need to submit to those who rule over us in the Lord and esteem them highly in love for their work's sake (Heb. 13:17, I Thess. 5:12-13).

10. Biblical prosperity, generosity and integrity are essential to kingdom expansion.

Biblical prosperity is God's plan to help fulfill the Great Commission. The principle of the tithe is part of God's plan to honor and provide substance for those He has placed over us in spiritual authority. Those who are over us in the Lord are responsible for the proper distribution of the tithe and offerings (III John 2, Matt. 23:23, Heb. 7:4-7, Mal. 3:8-11, Acts 11:29-30).

We believe in generously giving offerings to support ministries, churches, and individuals both inside and outside of the DCFI family, and emphasize giving to people as a priority. We encourage individuals, cells, congregations, and ministries to support fivefold ministers and missionaries in both prayer and finances (II Cor. 8:1-7, Gal. 6:6, Phil. 4:15-17).

We believe that every area of ministry and church life needs to be responsible financially and accountable to those giving them oversight in order to maintain a high standard of integrity. Spiritual leaders receiving a salary from the church are discouraged from setting their own salary level (Gal. 6:5, Rom. 15:14, I Thess. 5:22, II Cor. 8:20-21).

11. The gospel compels us to send missionaries to the unreached and help those least able to meet their own needs.

Jesus instructs us to take the gospel to the ends of the earth to those who have never heard. Our mission is to reach the unreached areas of the world with the gospel of Jesus Christ by sending trained missionaries and through church planting. Together we can join with the body of Christ to reach the unreached (Matt. 24:14, Acts 1:8, Acts 13:1-4, II Cor. 10:15-16).

We are also called to help the poor and needy, those in prison, orphans and widows. This includes our reaching out to the poor locally, nationally and internationally. When we help the poor, both materially and spiritually, we are lending to the Lord (Deut. 14:28, 29; Deut. 26: 10-12, Matt. 25:31-46, James 1:27, Prov. 19:17).

12. We are called to build the kingdom together with the entire body of Christ.

Our focus is on the kingdom of God, recognizing our cell group, our local church, and DCFI is just one small part of God's kingdom. We are called to link together with other groups in the body of Christ and pursue unity in His church as we reach the world together (Matt. 6:33, Eph. 4:1-6, John 17, Ps. 133).

We believe in utilizing and sharing the resources of people and materials the Lord has blessed us with. This includes the fivefold ministry, missions, leadership training, and other resources the Lord has entrusted to us (I Cor. 12, Acts 2:44-45).

Our unifying focus is on Christ, His Word and the Great Commission, and we believe we should not be distracted by minor differences (Romans 14:5).

We subscribe to the Lausanne Covenant as our basic statement of faith and Christian values. The scriptures serve as a light to guide us and the Lausanne Covenant along with these values and guiding principles unite us as partner churches as we walk together in the grace of God (Matt. 28:19-20, Amos 3:3, I Cor. 1:10, I Cor. 15:10).

Scriptural Insights for Church Discipline

Types of discipline mentioned in the scriptures:

Positive discipline: First there is discipline that teaches, instructs and equips us through a positive form of discipline. There is the shaping of our hearts and lives to reflect the person of Christ Jesus our Lord, through correction, warning, reproof, rebuking, teaching, training in righteousness, prayer, personal ministry, deliverance, relational accountability, friendship and discipleship.

Punitive discipline: There is a discipline that teaches, instructs and equips us through a punitive form of discipline. This is the shaping of our lives through direct application of governmental authority and consequence. This often results in punitive measures being taken to assert the authority of Christ Jesus within the hearts and lives of the people of God, His church. This may result in public rebuke, direct actions of a corporate accountability, loss of position, loss of fellowship with the church, etc.

Proper church discipline

It is important to see discipline as an opportunity to reassess what's going on in your family, cell, local church, etc. As is true of parenting, that your children will most often reflect the parents, so is it true of ministries and churches. Proper church discipline should cause us all to seek the face of the Lord for insight into what He is saying to us in and through this circumstance.

No Christian leader rejoices over the need for corrective discipline. It is a duty which must be performed when other, more positive methods to cause growth and maturity have failed. Most leaders would prefer never to need to discipline any church member.

The wise leader enters into a corrective discipline situation with compassion and understanding. But the leader also enters into corrective discipline with firm resolve. While the need for such discipline may be tragic, the outcome is at the heart of every leader's purpose. What leader does not want to see individuals cleansed and restored into a protected, united, healthy church?

Areas that may require discipline of church members:

- Unresolved offenses between members
- Idolatry
- Drunkenness
- Racism
- Moral impurity
- Covetousness
- Railing
- Extortion
- Aggressive divisiveness

Confrontation

We begin with the words of Christ in Matthew 18:15-17: "Moreover, if your brother sins against you, go and tell him his fault between you and him alone. If he hears you, you have gained your brother. But if he will not hear you, take with you one or two more, that by the mouth of two or three witnesses every word may be established. And if he refuses to hear them, tell it to the church. But if he refuses to hear the church, let him be to you like a heathen and a tax collector."

Exclusion from fellowship

Discipline, then, may reach a stage of putting a person out of fellowship with the church. This reached a very strong expression in a case at the church at Corinth in I Corinthians 5:3-5,12-13. See also II Thessalonians 3:14-15.

Sin beyond repentance

It is possible for a Christian to fall beyond repentance. The church cannot recover those who have consigned themselves to hell. "A man that is a heretic after the first and second admonition reject," Paul commands in Titus 3:10. A heretic is a sectarian, one who follows his own preferences in a self-willed way, to undermine the church.

Protecting the church

In very severe cases, then, discipline in the church ceases to be a matter of restoring an individual's soul, and becomes a function of the church defending itself against the attacks of the enemy. As in all areas of church discipline, but especially in this one, church leadership must act in a decisive and timely manner. Discipline may benefit not only the ones disciplined, but the rest of the church as well: "Them that sin rebuke before all, that others also may fear" (I Timothy 5:20).

When a person refuses to recover from sin

The church must protect itself: "Now I urge you, brethren, note those who cause divisions and offenses, contrary to the doctrine which you have learned, and avoid them. For those who are such do not serve our Lord Jesus Christ, but their own belly, and by smooth words and flattering speech deceive the hearts of the simple" (Romans 16:17-18).

Confession and cleansing

The Bible gives us clear guidance on the next step of effective discipline that leads to recovery. In this state, the guilty party is responsible to confess, and God is faithful to cleanse (Leviticus 5:5; Psalm 35:1-5; James 5:16; I John 1:9; I John 1:7; Proverbs 28:13). Confession must be directed toward two parties: to God and to the people who have been injured by a sin (Romans 14:7).

Restoration and reception

In this stage, the church has a responsibility to its fallen and cleansed member. In II Corinthians 2:1-11, the apostle Paul is speaking to the church about restoring a previously disciplined person to the fellowship of the local church. The goal of discipline has been achieved–this person has repented of his sin.

To receive this person back into fellowship, the church is told to:

- **Forgive** (II Corinthians 2:7) To forgive someone is to remove all condemnation and critical attitudes toward a person, to release from your spirit all wrong feelings.
- **Console** Speak encouraging words to the one who has repented and is being restored (II Corinthians 2:7).
- **Love** (II Corinthians 2:8) The church people are to assure the repentant one of their love, to reaffirm their love for him, to restore him to his full place in their affections. This step is critically important! Especially when someone has just been separated, the devil will try to turn that into a permanent division. Church leaders and cell group leaders and cell members must aggressively step forward to integrate the person into the local church.
- **Give Satan no advantage** (II Corinthians 2:11) It's time for a cautious double-checking now. The church must make certain that it has definitely and effectively performed the first three steps above, and that no wrong spirits have crept into the process anywhere along the line, among any of the people involved in the process. "We don't want Satan to win any victory here!" is the J.B. Philips translation of part of this verse. The church is forewarned to not be overcome by evil, but to overcome evil with good.

Guidelines for the process of discipline

Step One: Discovery

- **You become aware of the issue(s)** potentially needing disciplinary attention.
- **Begin to seek the face of the Lord** for His wisdom and His discernment, praying also for a full disclosure of the truth concerning all that is going on.
- **You also begin written documentation** of all that has and continues to occur throughout this whole process, from beginning to end.
- **Keep lines of communication open** with all parties concerned at all times.
- **On the cell level,** there must be a commitment to openness, honesty, transparency, and genuine vulnerability by the oversight team (church eldership) leading this process.
- **On the church eldership level,** there should be a commitment to openness, honesty, transparency, and genuine vulnerability by the oversight team (Apostolic Council or individual(s) designated to lead this process).

Step Two: Assessment

- **Engage the process discovering the truth** concerning the issue. Remember: you are not only looking at the truth of specific actions and behavior but a clear discernment of the heart conditions of those involved. This will be important to your judgment process. This is the information and fact finding process.
- **Look for the truth and accurate facts, not senses or suspicions,** or emotions and accusations. This is where you speak to all those involved in the process, if need be.

Step Three: Judgment

- **Make a judgment based upon all that has been weighed and assessed.** This includes the heart issues as well as the specific nature of the events involved.
- **Seek outside counsel** concerning these issues as to your legal options.
- **Consider resources available** to you to deal with these issues redemptively as you prepare for the discipline process.
- **Render a clear decision** at this point. If your decision is such that discipline must essentially follow, then move to the next step.
- **Remember, eldership should always lead this process,** not cell group leaders.

Step Four: Consequence

- **Specific person(s) are assigned as a team,** to walk through the disciplinary process with those being disciplined, providing a point of relationship, communication and accountability.
- **The effectiveness of the discipline should be assessed periodically.** All those involved commit to follow through to a Godly conclusion. The discipline must be specific and measurable.
- **Remember: church discipline is a lot of work** and must flow from Christ's heart.
- **There must be a commitment to seeing God's redemptive purposes fulfilled** in each other.
- **Implementation of discipline actually begins.**

Step Five: Reconciliation with full restoration

- **After following through with the disciplinary process successfully,** there needs to be as much heartfelt commitment and prayer to the restoration process as there was to the disciplinary process. Closure doesn't happen without restoration and healing having taken place.

Additional guidelines

- **Warning:** If at any time in the process of church discipline, a member resigns and leaves the church, all church disciplinary action must be considered ended. (Right to Privacy Law)
- **Soaking this process with prayer.** When considering how to handle a given issue, be sure that you are soaking this process with prayer, and receiving outside Godly counsel from wise men and women of God. It is important to fast and pray to hear clearly from the Lord.
- **Accurate discernment of the heart conditions of those you are working with is critical** to a Godly and just strategy of church discipline and restoration. All church discipline strategies must be truly redemptive in focus and objective with a strong biblical foundation and with a New Testament focus upon Christ Jesus and not on the Law. This is why prayer and fasting are so important, so we keep our focus on Christ.
- **There also must be absolute agreement to the discipline process by all the leadership involved.**

Further resources. The subject of membership, discipline and restoration and basic policies regarding accountability and authority for church leadership are dealt with in more detail in the *DCFI Leadership Handbook*, available from the DCFI Office.

Fivefold Ministry Survey

Identify your fivefold motivations by circling the number that represent the desires that you have.

Apostle, apostolic   AUTHORITY
1) Fatherly authority
2) Mobilizes gifts and resources for outreach
3) Keeps us founded on Christ
4) Keeps a vision for God's purposes before us
5) Imparts callings, gifts
6) Deep concern for unity in body of Christ
7) Lay foundations for new congregations
8) Help to set things in order, in existing churches

Prophet, prophetic   REVELATION
1) Thrust us forward in our vision
2) Activates our spiritual gifts
3) Calls us to holiness and righteousness
4) Keeps us alert to the manifest presence of Christ
5) Imparts a spirit of prayer and intercession
6) Speaks words with creative power to change lives
7) Heart to edify, comfort, exhort
8) Lays foundations in individuals, ministries upon Christ
9) Imparts power and gifts for ministry

Teacher, teaching   TRUTH
1) Maintains accuracy in handling God's Word
2) Enables us to understand God's truth
3) Sets free from deception and error
4) Unfolding practical life-style that fits with sound doctrine
5) Helps people to live by principles, not circumstances

Pastor, pastoral   NURTURE
1) Speaks in a way that brings security and acceptance
2) Draws people together in Christ, gathering into body
3) Breaks bondages of independence, isolation, insecurity
4) Supernatural drawing to oneself for counsel and love
5) Feels with people; concerned from their point of view
6) Becomes intimately involved with his congregation, small group, class
7) Feeds and leads one's people what is good for growth

Evangelist, evangelistic   RESPONSE

1) Helps people to understand and respond to basic biblical message of salvation, cleansing, baptism, filling of Spirit, gifts of Spirit
2) Cause non-believers to find salvation and forgiveness
3) Motivate believers to share the gospel with others
4) Stir people to action, respond to God
5) Breaks bondages of excuses, inactivity, indecisiveness, laziness
6) Brings conviction of sins
7) Helps people to receive Christ and become established in local congregation

To what extent are these anointings evident in me?

Tally the number of circles you have in each category.

	Strong	Some	Little	None
Apostolic	5	3	1	0
Prophetic	5	3	1	0
Teaching	5	3	1	0
Pastoral	5	3	1	0
Evangelistic	5	3	1	0

Name_____Date_____

Christ in you (all), the hope of glory!

Several concepts used in developing this survey were derived from *the book Complete Wineskin*, by Harold Eberle

Used by permission of Teaching The Word Ministries, © February 1993
Email: mail@ttwm.org, Web site: www.ttwm.org
One Mayfield Drive • Leola, PA 17540

Appendix E

Cell-Based Church Planting Tools

A special supplement for church planters

Church Planting Tools

Developing a Vision Statement

Vision

What kind of church do you want to plant? Why would someone be interested in coming to this church? What are the things you value? What is the purpose of this church? What is the mission of this church? To answer the above questions, it is sometimes helpful to start from the desired end product and work backwards (Isaiah 46:10). Picture what the church will look like in five years. Make a list of 30 reasons why someone would want to be involved in this church. Keep trying until you can list 30. Use the "Vision Statement" on the next page.
Note: You should complete your demographic research before you develop your vision statement.

Values

Review the Twelve Scriptural Values for the Cell Group Church (Module I:A). Are these your values for the church? If so, write them out in complete sentences using your own words. Use the "Values Statement" to list fifteen scriptural values for the church plant.

Mission statement

What is the divine purpose of this church? Who is it going to reach? What is going to be done to reach them? How is it going to be done? The mission statement answers all of the previous questions. Go ahead and write a first draft of your mission statement. Remember it must answer the three questions...who? what? how? Now, have a few peers read it and give their input.
Compare it with other mission statements. Read the DCFI mission statement. Review the 30 reasons why someone would want to be involved in this church. Is your mission statement in line with the 30 reasons you gave for someone being involved as you were picturing the church in five years?
Modify your mission statement to fit in one paragraph. Be sure this mission statement is what is on your heart. It will be challenged. People may question it. The enemy will oppose it. You have to be committed to it.

Vision statement

Now you want to boil that mission statement down to just one sentence that is concise, easy to say and motivational. Your vision statement should be able to fit on a banner but yet make sense on a bulletin cover. This is the toughest step of the process and may take the longest time to complete.
Pray, pray, and fast and pray...this is very important. Complete the vision statement, get some input from peers or team members, and revise if needed. Be sure this statement communicates what is in your heart.

Helping You Build Cell Churches

Vision Statement

Why would someone want to be involved in this church?

1. _____
2. _____
3. _____
4. _____
5. _____
6. _____
7. _____
8. _____
9. _____
10. _____
11. _____
12. _____
13. _____
14. _____
15. _____
16. _____
17. _____
18. _____
19. _____
20. _____
21. _____
22. _____
23. _____
24. _____
25. _____
26. _____
27. _____
28. _____
29. _____
30. _____

Church Planting Tools

Church Planting Tools

Values Statement

List 15 scriptural values for the church plant.

1. _____
   _____

2. _____
   _____

3. _____
   _____

4. _____
   _____

5. _____
   _____

6. _____
   _____

7. _____
   _____

8. _____
   _____

9. _____
   _____

10. _____
    _____

11. _____
    _____

12. _____
    _____

13. _____
    _____

14. _____
    _____

15. _____
    _____

Helping You Build Cell Churches

Demographics

A Webster's dictionary definition of demographics is *the statistical characteristics of human populations (as age and income) used especially to identify markets*. Who are they? How do they live? What is the community like? Demographics is very similar to what Moses sent the spies into the promised land to do (Numbers 13:1,17).

Church Planting Tools

There are two approaches you can take to demographics. One is to do your own research. The other option is to purchase information gathered by professionals.

To do your own research is beneficial because it helps you to get to know the community where you are going to be planting the church. There are a number of options to consider. Prayer walks and drives are a great way to find out who lives where and how people spend their time. Check out parks, malls and public places where people congregate to do your research. What kind of cars are people driving? Sit outside the local high school and observe the youth of the community. It can also be very helpful to put together a questionnaire. Your team can take it into your targeted areas to meet people and find out what they feel the needs of the community are. This is a great way to meet people and let them know there is a new church starting in their community. Use the Demographic Research Worksheets as a guide.

Information gathered by professionals can be obtained from U.S. Census data—found at the local library (check out the town history while you are there), city or county planning commissions, school administration offices, university libraries (ask for help), public utilities, real estate firms, banks, Chamber of Commerce, radio stations, newspapers and the internet.

To purchase information compiled by professionals is very convenient. You can get every imaginable population cross section. Information is available in 1, 5, or 10 mile detailed population reports from the intersection of any streets. Surf the internet for information! The following is one option:

Marketing Mapping Software on the internet:
www.scanus.com

Church Planting Tools

Demographic Research

Worksheet A

Selected community/geographic area _____

Median household income _____

Common occupations
1._____
2._____
3._____
4._____
5._____
6._____
7._____

Common hobbies/Leisure activities
1._____
2._____
3._____
4._____
5._____
6._____
7._____

Age distribution
_____% 0-10
_____% 11-20
_____% 21-30
_____% 31-40
_____% 41-50
_____% 51-60
_____% 60

Marital status
_____ % Married
_____ % Single
_____ %Divorced/separated

Housing
_____ % Own
_____ % Rent

Ethnic groups
_____ %
_____ %
_____ %
_____ %

Median number of children_____
Percent of spouses who work_____

Population patterns
10 years ago _____
Today _____
10 years projected _____

Demographic Research

Church Planting Tools

Worksheet B

Description of community _____

_____

_____

_____

_____

_____

Number and type of churches _____

_____

_____

_____

_____

_____

_____

Obvious community challenges _____

_____

_____

_____

_____

_____

Insights from prayer walking/driving through the selected area _____

_____

_____

_____

_____

_____

_____

Insights from conversations with people in the community _____

_____

_____

_____

_____

_____

_____

Concerns of community members _____

_____

_____

_____

_____

_____

Church Planting Tools

General Information

Incorporation/Association

Incorporation laws vary in different states, provinces and nations. Our recommendation is to hire a lawyer to file the incorporation papers. You only need the name of your corporation (church), an initial business address (which can be your home), a statement of purpose, and the initial officers.

Music Rights

For a few dollars a year, you can keep a good conscience with all the overheads and music you use. There is an annual fee that depends on the size of the church. Call CCLI at 800.234.2446 for an application. Their address is:

CCLI
17201 NE Sacramento St.
Portland, OR 97230-5941

General Administration

Check the internet for Church Administration "how to" manuals or books to answer all your general administrative questions.

Cell-Based Church Bylaws

Church Planting Tools

ARTICLE I: NAME

The name of the organization shall be _____ (herein after spoken of as the church) a partner church of DOVE Christian Fellowship, International. Its duration is to be perpetual.

ARTICLE II : PURPOSE

The purpose of the church shall be to provide spiritual oversight for the membership and to meet spiritual, emotional and physical needs of people through faith in Jesus Christ and by resourcing and networking with the Body of Christ in fulfilling the Great Commission.

ARTICLE III : OFFICES

The business office of the church shall be located at _____

ARTICLE IV: GOVERNMENT PRIVILEGES

The church shall have self-governing privileges in harmony with the authority and vision of the Apostolic Council of DOVE Christian Fellowship International (DCFI). Local authority in vision, direction and doctrine shall be vested in the Eldership Team. The Eldership Team may appoint others under them as required to assist in spiritual oversight of geographic areas or ministries. This church is a Partner Church with DCFI as evidenced by a Partnership Agreement entered into between the church and DCFI. Within the Partnership Agreement, the Eldership Team members acknowledge that they have read DCFI's Constitution, Bylaws and Handbook and that they are in agreement with the statements therein and agreed to be bound by the statements contained in these documents.

GOVERNING DOCUMENTS

4-2A. The governing documents of (the church) are the Articles of Incorporation and Bylaws. The Articles of Incorporation take precedence over the Bylaws.

4-2B. No amendments or repeal shall be made to the Articles of Incorporation as adopted except by a 2/3 majority vote of the Eldership Team and affirmation by the Senior Elder. Amendments shall be within the guiding principles set forth in the DCFI handbook, Constitution and Bylaws.

4-2C. The Bylaws of (the church) or any portions thereof, may be amended or repealed by a 2/3 majority of the Eldership Team and affirmation by the Senior Elder. Amendments shall be within the guiding principles set forth in the DCFI handbook, Constitution and Bylaws.

ARTICLE V: DOCTRINE STATEMENT OF FAITH

WE BELIEVE the Bible to be the inspired, infallible, and authoritative Word of God. The Holy Spirit moved upon the writers of the Old and New Testament and inspired them as they wrote the Words of God. God's revelation in Christ and in scripture is unchangeable. Through it the Holy Spirit still speaks today. (II Tim. 3:13-17; Heb. 4:12; Psalm 119:89, 105; I Pet. 1:23-25; Gal. 1:8, 9; Matt. 5:18; Isa. 40:8)

WE BELIEVE that there is One God, eternally existent in three personalities: Father, Son, and Holy Spirit. God the Father—Creator of all things. By His Word all things were created and through the power of His Word all things are held together. He sent His Son Jesus to redeem mankind unto Himself. A relationship with God only comes through Jesus Christ. Jesus Christ—is the only begotten Son of God, conceived by the Holy Spirit, and born of a virgin. He lived a sinless life, and performed many miracles. He redeemed us by His atoning death through His shed blood, He ascended to the right hand of the Father, and He will personally return in power and glory. There is no other name given under heaven by which man must be saved. Holy Spirit—inspired the writers of the Bible, convicts the world of sin, teaches us all things, and brings to our remembrance the Word of God. (Deut. 6:4; Isa. 44:6-8; Isa. 43:10; Matt. 3:16, 17; Matt. 28:19; I Cor. 12:4-6; John 14:23, 25; I Tim. 6:15, 16; I John 5:7)

WE BELIEVE that mankind is perishing because of sin, which separates him from God. But God loves all mankind, not wishing that any should perish, but that all should repent. Mankind can only be saved through a complete commitment to Jesus Christ as Lord and Savior, being regenerated by the Holy Spirit. (Gen. 1:26, 31; Psalm 8:4-8; Gen. 3:1-7; Rom. 5:1, 12-21; Eph. 2:8, 9; Acts 3:19-21; I Cor. 15:21, 22; Gal. 6:14, 15; II Cor. 5:17)

WE BELIEVE in the present infilling of the Holy Spirit to all believers who desire it. The Holy Spirit's ministry to the body of Jesus Christ gives power to live, witness, proclaim the gospel and to make disciples. The Holy Spirit gives us power to cultivate a Christ-like character through the Fruit of the Spirit and to build up and mature the church through the miraculous gifts and ministries in this present day. (John 15:8-10; I Cor. 12:13; John 3:5, 6; Acts 1:4-8; Acts 2:1-4; Acts 2:38, 39; Luke 11:9-13; Joel 2:28, 29; I Cor. 12-14; Heb. 2:4)

WE BELIEVE that the local church is a body of believers brought together by the Holy Spirit as a visible part of the body of Christ and His church universal. The church is responsible to faithfully proclaim the whole Word of God in fulfilling the Great Commission, properly administer the sacraments, and humbly submit themselves to discipline, all for the glory of God. (Matt. 28:19, 20; Rom. 12:4, 5; I Cor. 12:27; Eph. 2:22; I Pet. 2:5, 9, 10; Titus 2:14)

WE BELIEVE that all mankind shall give an account of their deeds in this earthly life before the judgment seat of Christ. Those with their names written in the Lamb's Book of Life will be eternally with God in His glory, those without their names written will be eternally separated from God and tormented. (I Thess. 5:13-17; Rev. 1:7; Acts 1:11; Rev. 20:10-15; II Cor. 5:10; II Thess. 1:7-10; Rev. 21:1-4)

ARTICLE VI: BOARD OF DIRECTORS
FUNCTIONS AND MEETINGS

6-1A. The Eldership Team shall serve as the board of directors. They shall be responsible for the overall vision, direction, focus and shall fully control, govern and operate the business affairs of the church. As a Partner Church of DCFI, we submit to the vision, mission, basic values, and guiding principles of DCFI's Apostolic Council.

6-1B. The Eldership Team shall be given leadership to by the Senior Elder. The Senior Elder shall be the president of the board of directors

6-1C. The Eldership Team shall meet annually for an official meeting in the month of January. The Eldership Team shall record the minutes of the annual meeting including the election of officers; vice-chairman, secretary, treasurer. The Eldership Team will meet regularly as determined by the Senior Elder.

APPOINTMENT

6-2A. The Senior Elder shall be called by God, qualified (I Tim. 3:1-7 and Titus 1:5-9) and willing to fulfill this leadership responsibility. The Senior Elder shall be recognized and recommended by both the Eldership Team and DCFI's Apostolic Council. The Senior Elder shall be appointed by a member of the Apostolic Council or an appointed designate. The Senior Elder shall not be appointed unless there is unanimous agreement with the Eldership Team, recommendation by DCFI's Apostolic Council and general affirmation of the Partner Church's cell group leaders.

6-2B. The Eldership Team members shall be called by God, qualified by scripture (I Timothy 3:1-7 and Titus 1:5-9) and willing to fulfill this leadership responsibility.

6-2C. The Eldership Team members are discerned through fasting and prayer, then nominated by the Senior Elder and the existing Eldership Team. General affirmation of the cell group leaders of the Church and the recommendation

of DCFI's Apostolic Council is required for an individual to serve on the Eldership Team.

6-2D. An Apostolic Council member (or an appointed designate) and the Senior Elder shall install new members as set forth in 6-2B and 6-2C at the annual meeting or as deemed necessary by the Eldership Team.

6-2E. The Eldership Team shall consist of at least two members which includes the Senior Elder.

6-2F. The Senior Elder and each member of the Eldership Team shall be active members of a cell group and involved in the life of the church.

SPECIFIC DUTIES

6-3A. Appoint and commission Deacons and cell leaders.

6-3B. Appoint persons to serve on an Administrative Committee if the Eldership deems an Administrative Committee is needed.

6-3C. Appoint and oversee specific committees or directors, e.g. Missions Council Representative, Worship, Children, Youth, Singles, as required to resource the spiritual needs of the Partner Church.

6-3D. Recognize, appoint, oversee, protect spiritually and provide accountability to the Fivefold Ministers who serve within the local Partner Church.

6-3E. Train and nurture leaders.

6-3F. Provide oversight and spiritual protection to members.

6-3G. Provide assistance during times of crisis for members in cell group or committees.

6-3H. Approve annual and all modified Partner Church Budgets.

6-3I. Recommend a representative to serve on the DCFI Stewardship Group to be appointed by the DCFI Apostolic Council.

TERMS - VACANCIES

6-4A. Eldership Team members, including the Senior Elder, shall be willing to serve long term with an annual evaluation.

6-4B. This annual evaluation will first have the Senior Elder and each Eldership Team member mutually discern the call of God on their own life to serve another year.

6-4C. Annual evaluations shall be conducted by the Senior Elder in cooperation with the Apostolic Council, an evaluation team or a combination of both. A written report shall be given to the Senior Elder and the person being evaluated.

6-4D. Evaluations are for the purpose of growth. In the event of a report that one's service is unsatisfactory or that one is no longer suited for the position, the Eldership Team and Senior Elder shall review the specified deficiencies with the member. The Eldership Team and the Senior Elder shall determine whether it would be best for the member to relinquish their position or continue as a member and work to improve the specified deficiencies.

6-4E. In addition to the evaluations, at any time the Senior Elder and other Eldership Team members may vote to suspend or remove the member if deemed to be in the best interests of the organization. DCFI's Apostolic Council shall be included in the process of suspension or removal. Discipline shall be invoked in accordance with the written Policy of Discipline and Restoration outlined in the DCFI Handbook.

6-4F. The Senior Elder shall be evaluated by members of the Apostolic Council or appointed designates, an evaluation team or a combination of both. A full report shall be given

Helping You Build Cell Churches

to the Senior Elder and the Apostolic Council and a summary report given to the Eldership Team.

6-4G. In the event of the necessity of termination of the responsibility of the Senior Elder due to failure morally, irreconcilable conflicts, disorderly conduct or apostasy, the Apostolic Council shall give leadership to this process along with the Eldership members. The Apostolic Council, with counsel from the Eldership Team, shall suspend the Senior Elder pending a thorough review and application of the written policy for discipline and restoration. The DCFI Apostolic Council, with counsel from the Eldership Team will appoint an Acting Elder immediately, who will serve until restoration or a replacement is discerned.

6-4H. In the event that the number of persons on the Eldership Team drops below the required two for ninety days, then the longest serving cell group leader of the Partner Church shall immediately begin serving. If more than one replacement is required, then the next most cell leader shall be selected until all vacancies are filled. This is a temporary position with full authority until either the person is confirmed or another person is appointed.

Officers

6-5A. At the annual meeting, the Eldership Team shall appoint a vice-chairman, secretary and a treasurer as officers of the Eldership Team. The Senior Elder as the president of the Eldership Team shall oversee the appointment process. Members of the Eldership Team may hold up to two offices. The president shall not serve in the capacity of secretary or treasurer.

6-5B. The designation of officers, except president, shall be by unanimous decision of the Eldership Team. Such appointed officers shall serve in their capacities until such time as the Eldership Team should appoint otherwise.

6-5C. It shall be the duty of the Secretary to keep an accurate record of the proceedings of the meetings of the Board and of Congregational meetings of business, and all such other duties as pertain to this office as may be prescribed by the Board.

6-5D. The Treasurer shall have the care and custody of all funds and securities of the Church and shall deposit the same in the name of the Church in such Bank or Banks as the Board of Directors may select.

ARTICLE VII: COMMITTEES

The eldership team may appoint such additional committees to assist it in the discharge of its duties as it may deem advisable.

ARTICLE VIII: MEMBERSHIP VOTING

The church has a no voting membership. Spiritual decisions affecting the life of the local body of the church are under the care of its Elders.

QUALIFICATIONS

The membership of the church shall consist of those persons who meet the following qualifications:

1. They are in agreement with the statements as set forth in Article V.
2. They shall be a member in good standing of a cell group.
3. They shall be involved in the life of the church.
4. They shall recognize and submit to the elders leadership of the church.

5. They shall express commitment to the church with the understanding that biblical church discipline will be used if necessary.

ACTIVE CELL GROUP LISTING

The Eldership Team will semiannually update the active cell group listing in accordance with its qualifications for members.

ARTICLE IX: DISSOLUTION
SECTION 1 - DISSOLUTION BY ELDERSHIP TEAM

9-1A. In the event that this organization shall be dissolved and liquidated, after paying or making provision for the payment of all liabilities of this organization, the Eldership Team shall distribute or dispose of any remaining property and assets to such organization or organizations established and operated exclusively for religious purposes as, in its judgement, have purposes which are most closely allied to those of this organization; it being provided, however, that each transferee organization, at the time of such transfer, shall:

1. be a tax-exempt, religious Christian organization within the meaning and intent of Section 501 (C) (3) and Section 170 (b) (1) (A) of the Internal Revenue Code of 1954 or the corresponding sections of any successor Internal Revenue Law of the United States of America;

2. have been in existence for a continuous period of at least sixty (60) months;

3. be an organization to which contributions are deductible under Section 170, Section 2055 and Section 2522 of the Internal Revenue Code of 1954 or the corresponding sections of any successor Internal Revenue Law of the United States of America.

9-1B. DOVE Christian Fellowship International (DCFI) shall be given first consideration in this dissolution of assets.

SECTION 2 - DISSOLUTION BY COURT

Any of this organization's property and assets not disposed of in accordance with ARTICLE IX, Section 1, shall be disposed of by the court having jurisdiction of the dissolution and liquidation of a nonprofit corporation organized and existing under and in accordance with the laws of the Commonwealth of Pennsylvania and having jurisdiction in the county of this organization's registered office exclusively to such religious organization or organizations, each of which is established and operated exclusively for such purposes as are most closely allied to those of this organization and each of which, at the time of such disposal, is a qualified, tax-exempt organization as aforesaid, as said court shall determine.

ARTICLE X: LIABILITY

10-1A. No member of the Eldership Team and/or committee shall be personally liable, as such, for monetary damages for any action taken unless:

1. the member has breached or failed to perform the duties of office in good faith, in a manner reasonably believed to be in the best interest of the corporation, and with such care, including reasonable inquiry, skill and diligence, as a person of ordinary prudence would use under similar circumstances; and

2. the breach or failure to perform constitutes self-dealing, willful misconduct or recklessness.

10-1B. This provision cannot by law release a member from liability under criminal laws or for proper payment of taxes.

House to House Cell–Based Church Planting & Leadership
Video Correspondence School

Here it is...practical tools and training for cell-based ministry. The best of DOVE Christian Fellowship International's six month in-house training school packaged into a video school. You can learn the same dynamic cell-based church building principles in your own home or church. Revised and updated! Now available on DVD.

Satellite School Many churches have purchased the modules and set up an in-house satellite school. Homework and tests are reviewed by the local satellite school leadership. Each module is $795. If you buy 2 modules at full price, you get the third module free. This comes to an incredible $550/module!

Correspondence School An individual views the videos, completes the homework and test, and returns the videos to DCFI. There is a onetime application fee of $65. The tuition is $295 per module. You will have four months to complete the course.

Your Instructors This training school contains a wealth of knowledge from experienced Christian leaders.

Three Modules The school has been divided into three self-contained modules, each to be completed before advancing to the next module.

How do I start the Correspondence School? After completing your application and returning it to us with your application fee and Module I tuition, you will receive video tapes or DVDs of 45 classes, a student notebook, four Biblical Foundation books, a final test and other resource materials needed.

Module I
Module I is designed to train leaders for dynamic cell-based ministry in mega, community and house churches. Starting, leading and multiplying cells and churches are covered in detail. Also, an understanding of the biblical basis for relational cell ministry and spiritual parenting will keep cells from becoming another program at your church. You will learn the mistakes others have made. A well rounded equipping for cell ministry is presented including tips for effective leadership, ministering to children and youth.

Module II
Module II emphasizes New Testament leadership for the cell-based church. It focuses on the fivefold ministry and especially the foundation of apostles and prophets and governmental leadership. Teaching is given on understanding gifts and how to release them, building teams for ministry, networking with the body of Christ and building Godly character for a lifetime of ministry. This module covers the basic values DCFI has learned and developed over 20 years of planting cells and churches.

Module III
Module III emphasizes training for practical ministry. Learn how to be spirit led and experience the power of God. The process of developing, casting and birthing vision is covered. Teaching is included on how to interpret the scriptures, sermon preparation, proofs of Christianity and an insightful prophetic overview of church history. Missions, some keys to cross-cultural ministry and many useful leadership skills round out Module III. It will be especially helpful for those who have had no formal training for ministry and want to see the kingdom of God expand into all areas of society.

**For a complete list of topics check
www.dcfi.org**

For information visit: www.dcfi.org
Call 800.848.5892   Email info@dcfi.org

House to House

How God called a small fellowship to become a house to house movement. DOVE Christian Fellowship Int'l has grown into a family of cell-based churches and house churches networking throughout the world. By Larry Kreider, 206 pages: **$8.95** ISBN: 1-880828-81-2

Biblical Foundation Series

This series by Larry Kreider covers basic Christian doctrine. Practical illustrations accompany the easy-to-understand format. Use for small group teachings (48 in all), a mentoring relationship or daily devotional. Each book has 64 pages: **$4.99** each,
12 Book Set: **$49** ISBN: 1-886973-18-0

Biblical Foundations for Children

Creative learning experiences for ages 4-12, patterned after the Biblical Foundation Series. Takes kids on the first steps in their Christian walk. By Jane Nicholas, 176 pages: **$17.95** ISBN: 1-886973-35-0

Elders for Today's Church

Healthy leadership teams produce healthy churches! New Testament principles for equipping church leadership teams: Why leadership is needed, what their qualifications and responsibilities are, how they should be chosen, how elders function as spiritual fathers and mothers, how they are to make decisions, resolve conflicts, and more. Included are questionnaires for evaluating a team of elders. By Larry Kreider, Ron Myer, Steve Prokopchak, and Brian Sauder 274 pages: **$12.99** ISBN: 1-886973-62-8

Elders DVD Training

Twelve sessions taught by the four authors of the book! The complete set includes a copy of *The Biblical Role of Elders* book, a leader's guide, three DVDs and six student manuals: **$89** ISBN:1-886973-69-5

Foundations For Life Video Series

Twelve dynamic video teachings hosted by Larry Kreider, presenting the basics of the Christian faith, helping us confront life's profound questions. Coordinates with the Biblical Foundation books. Two VHS tapes with 12 lessons, each 15-20 minutes, includes one Study Guide: **$49** ISBN: 1-886973-36-9

Advanced Cell Group Ministry 201 Video Training

Gain strategy to reach a new level in cell group ministry. There are seven sessions—each with a half hour teaching followed by questions for discussion. Training set includes: three DVDs, a copy of the book *House To House*, a group leader's guide and six participant manuals: **$89** ISBN:1-886973-70-9

Advanced Cell Group Ministry 201 Audio Set

Hear Ron Myer share from his many years' experience. Gain strategy to reach a new level in cell group ministry. There are seven sessions. Four tape set: **$23.99** ISBN: 1-886973-71-1

The Cry for Spiritual Fathers & Mothers

Returning to the biblical truth of spiritual parenting so believers are not left fatherless and disconnected. How loving, seasoned spiritual fathers and mothers help spiritual children reach their potential. By Larry Kreider, 186 pages: **$11.95** ISBN: 1-886973-42-3

Spiritual Fathers & Mothers Video Training Set

Much of the same great teaching material from the seminar formatted for your teaching needs. Excellent for small groups and for training small group leaders—use at retreats! The complete set includes a Leader's Manual, six Participant Manuals, three video tapes, and a copy of the book *The Cry for Spiritual Fathers and Mothers*: **$99.00**
Extra Participant Manuals **$6.99**
Ten or more manuals: 20% discount
ISBN: 1-886973-47-4

Spiritual Fathers & Mothers Audio Set

Learn the principles of spiritual parenting right in your own home or car. Audio set of six tapes with author Larry Kreider: **$29.00** ISBN: 1-886973-53-9

For additional resources and to order:
Online: www.dcfi.org   Telephone: 800.848.5892
Email: info@dcfi.org

Evaluation Tools

This notebook of reproducible evaluation tools helps to get feedback to determine strengths, solidify vision and mission, open dialogue and discussion, and to provide goals. Evaluations for elders, ministry leaders and staff team. By Steve Prokopchak, 50 pages. **$19.99** ISBN: 1-886973-61-X

Healthy Leaders

How to develop a clear sense of identity and direction as a leader. This book covers the dynamics of godly leadership including insights to these questions: Do we know how to detach from the conflicts while at the same time fully identifying with other people? How do we respond when people react to our direction? By Keith Yoder, 88 pages. **$8.95** ISBN: 1-886973-31-8

House Church Networks

A new model of church is emerging. Discover how these new house church networks offer community and simplicity, especially as they fit the heart, call and passion of the younger generations. These house church networks will work together with the more traditional community churches and mega-churches to show the transforming power of Christ to our neighborhoods. By Larry Kreider, 118 pages. **$9.99** ISBN: 1-886973-48-2

House Church Networks Audio With Larry Kreider and others involved with house churches from four nations. Two Tape Set. **$9.99** ISBN: 1-886973-60-1

Cell Groups and House Churches: What History Teaches Us

A historical backdrop to much of what is happening in cell groups and house churches today. Explore the writings and practices of the Reformers such as Luther and Bucer, as well as the Pietists, Moravians, Methodists and others. These writings show clearly that when God moves in restoring His church, there is a renewal of small groups to aid discipleship and growth into holiness, often resulting in a greater concern for reaching the lost. By Peter Bunton, 108 pages. **$8.99** ISBN: 1-886973-45-8

Prosperity With a Purpose

Unveils God's plan to finance the Great Commission Is it God's will for Christians to live in the desert with only enough to get by or in the Promised Land of God's more than enough? If we only have enough to meet our needs, how can we meet the needs of others? In this book, Brian Sauder unapologetically provides solid, biblical teaching and sometimes comical testimony of his discovery of the God of more than enough. 96 Pages, by Brian Sauder **$9.99** ISBN: 1-886973-65-2

Youth Cells And Youth Ministry

Learn the values behind youth cells and custom-design cells for your youth. Gives the specifics of implementing youth cell ministry, including a cell leader's job description, creative ideas for cells, and how churches can transition. Compiled by Brian Sauder & Sarah Mohler, 120 pages. **$8.50** ISBN: 1-886973-33-4

Youth Cells and Youth Ministry Audio Set $45 ISBN: 1-886973-55-5

Destination Cell Church

How do you move from a program-based to a cell-based church? This book is the story of how a church transitioned to make cell group ministry its central focus. Learn specific keys to help unlock the doors to walk in faith so your church can implement the needed changes in vision and values. By Paul Gustitus, 80 pages. **$8.95** ISBN: 1-886973-43-1

The Tithe: A Test in Trust

This book answers key questions about tithing based on the scriptures, explaining it as both an Old Testament and a New Testament teaching. Written with a variety of illustrations, this book has been used to help believers understand that the tithe is a test in trust—trust in God and trust in our spiritual leadership. By Larry Kreider. 32 pages: **$2.95** ISBN: 1-886973-17-2

Fivefold Ministry Audio

Designed to release healthy, effective fivefold ministry in the local church. Taught by experienced leaders. Topics: Fivefold Ministry, Role and Function of Apostles and Prophets, Role and Function of Evangelists, Pastors, and Teachers, Qualifications of Fivefold Ministers, Ministry Motivation, Fivefold Fathering, Fields of Ministry, Fivefold and the Church Plant, Financing the Fivefold, Prayer and Fasting. Audio Set of 10 Tapes. **$39** ISBN: 1-886973-52-0

For additional resources and to order:
Online: www.dcfi.org
Telephone: 800.848.5892
Email: info@dcfi.org

Counseling Basics for Small Group Leaders

You can be an effective people helper! This manual is specifically geared to train small group leaders and potential leaders to counsel others. Packed with helpful scriptural references with eighteen essential areas covered. By Steve Prokopchak, 88 pages. **$14.95** ISBN: 1-886973-39-3

Counseling Basics Audio Set

The seminar on tape for your home, car or office. Taught by Steve Prokopchak. Includes a set of six tapes and a *Counseling Basics* book. **$29** ISBN: 1-886973-54-7

Called Together

Pre and Postmarital Workbook This unique workbook, specifically designed for couple-to-couple mentoring use, prepares couples for a successful and God-honoring marriage. *Called Together* supplies down-to-earth Biblical wisdom to help couples get off to a positive start. *Called Together* also includes postmarital checkups at three and nine months. Special sections for remarriage, intercultural marriages and remarriages of senior adults. By Steve and Mary Prokopchak, 250 pages. **$12.99** ISBN: 0-87509-991-2

In Pursuit of Obedience

Have you ever felt overwhelmed by the tremendous self-discipline it takes to do what is outlined in scripture? Does God set limits for us because He desires to control us or because He loves us? God's love for us must be the foundation upon which we build our emotional, physical and spiritual health. Yet, how do we obey God when the limit is uncomfortable for us? Ideal for small group study with its discussion questions and activities. By Steve Prokopchak, 80 pages. **$8.95** ISBN: 1-886973-64-4

Teacher Training Course

This training course with an apprentice-type approach is designed for a teacher - trainer to take four student-trainees through a hands-on course while learning to teah and critique themselves via videotape. This four-hour course will train a leader to help any willing trainee(s) learn basic principles on teaching that will bring life into their cell meeting! Can be used over again to train countless people! **$69.95** ISBN: 1-886973-26-1

Teaching with Confidence

Nearly everyone can be an effective teacher with proper training. This book will help believers gain confidence as they learn twelve keys to effectively teach others from God's Word. This excellent book helps small group leaders teach effectively. By Larry Kreider, 32 pages, **$3.95** ISBN: 1-886973-16-4

Seminars

Spiritual Fathering & Mothering Seminar

Practical preparation for believers who want to have and become spiritual parents. Includes a manual and the book *The Cry For Spiritual Fathers & Mothers*.

Elder's Training Seminar

Based on New Testament leadership principles, this seminar equips leaders to provide protection, direction and correction in the local church. Includes the book *The Biblical Role of Elders in Today's Church* and a manual.

Small Groups 101 Seminar

Basics for healthy cell ministry. Session topics cover the essentials for growing cell group ministry. Each attendee receives a *Helping You Build Manual*.

Small Groups 201 Seminar

Takes you beyond the basics and into an advanced strategy for cell ministry. Each attendee receives a *House To House* book and a seminar manual.

Counseling Basics for Small Group Leaders

This seminar takes you through the basics of counseling, specifically in small group ministry. Includes a comprehensive manual.

Marriage Mentoring Training Seminar

Trains church leaders and mature believers to help prepare engaged couples for a strong marriage foundation by using the mentoring format of *Called Together*. Includes a *Called Together Manual*.

Youth Cell Ministry Seminar

Learn the values behind youth cells so cell ministry does not become just another program at your church. For adult and teen leaders!

Church Planting Clinic

Designed to help you formulate a successful strategy for cell-based church planting. For those involved in church planting and those considering it. Includes a *Helping You Build Cell Churches Manual*.

Fivefold Ministry Seminar

A seminar designed to release healthy, effective fivefold ministry in the local church. Includes a *Helping You Build Cell Churches Manual*.

For complete brochures and upcoming dates for seminars:
Online: www.dcfi.org
Telephone: 800.848.5892
Email: info@dcfi.org

Action List

Write down in one or two sentences what the Lord spoke to you after each session.

___ A.

___ B.

___ C.

___ D.

___ E.

___ F.

___ G.

___ H.

___ I.

___ J.

Prayerfully prioritize these areas so you'll know what to focus on.